The Crucial Challenge for International Aid:

Making the Donor-Recipient Relationship Work to Prevent Catastrophe

Mirek Karasek

and

Jennifer P. Tanabe

Copyright © 2014 by Mirek Karasek

All rights reserved. This book or any portion thereof may not be reproduced or used in any manner whatsoever without the express written permission of the publisher except for the use of brief quotations in a book review or scholarly journal.

First Printing: 2014

ISBN 978-1-304-86397-3

Preface

This volume maps, analyzes and presents possible solutions to a very serious problem the world is facing today, namely how to resolve and reduce the risk of conflict between the so-called "developed" and "developing" countries. In particular, the conditions leading to success or failure of international aid from donor to recipient countries are studied in detail. The results offer valuable insight into the dangers the world faces if these efforts fail, and lead to a paradigm that promises success.

The basis of the study lies in ranking societies along a number of characteristics which are economic, political and cultural in nature. It is proposed that the most important factor is not the absolute value of any of these measures, but rather the level of similarity or difference, both within each society and between societies engaged in the donor-recipient relationship. These cultural, political and economic differences—we call them "heterogeneities" in the text—stem from vastly different foundations of cultural, ethical, cognitive and religious histories experienced by the different societies.

Our study, based on academic research as well as direct experience by the first author and including simple algebraic formulations and statistical analyses, leads us to two very important conclusions. The data show that high levels of inter-societal homogeneity between donor and recipient provide the basis for successful aid transactions. On the other hand, recipient societies with high levels of intra-societal heterogeneity pose a significant problem, the most serious occurring when an impoverished country is under the control of militant ethnic or religious zealots who are less interested in receiving aid that will enhance the quality of life of other members of their society than in maintaining and even expanding their own power and control.

These findings warn us that: (1) throwing billions of US dollars into developing countries which the donor countries have little in common with and equally little understanding of their cultural, political and cultural structures, is not just a waste of money but adds fuel to the fires of discontent; (2) Doing nothing is even more dangerous, as an increasing number of countries slide precipitously toward political and economic chaos, resulting in violence that will spread throughout the world.

Fortunately, this "Doomsday Scenario" is not inevitable. Our study provides a paradigm which offers hope, provided it is taken seriously and acted upon before it is too late. This book suggests a way to analyze, assess and understand the inner workings of the developing and/or the world poorest societies' ruling classes. In reality, however, it is up to the governments and NGOs to make sure that donor-recipient aid transactions are carried out successfully and in a timely manner. The paradigm developed here offers a possible solution to the difficulties and dangers encountered in the past, and also a way of avoiding future disasters.

Mirek Karasek and Jennifer P. Tanabe

November, 2014.

Contents

Chapter 1: The Problem 7

Chapter 2: Definitions 11
   2/1   Society, Country, Nation, State 11
       2/1/1   Society 11
       2/1/2   Country 12
       2/1/3   Nation 12
       2/1/4   State 12
   2/2   Generic Society, Homogeneity, Heterogeneity 13
       2/2/1   Generic Society 13
       2/2/2   Intra-Societal Homogeneity and Heterogeneity 13
       2/2/3   Inter-Societal Homogeneity and Heterogeneity 15
   2/3   Political Systems 16
       2/3/1   Developing Country 16
       2/3/2   Legitimate Democracy 16
       2/3/3   Oligarchy 18
       2/3/4   Protectorate 19
   2/4   Risk and Conflict 21
       2/4/1   Risk in Conflicting Socio-political Environment 21
       2/4/2   Societal Conflict 26
   2/5   Group Psychology 28
       2/5/1   Collective Behavior 28
       2/5/2   Crowd 28
       2/5/3   Social Movement 29
   2/6   Decision-Making 30
       2/6/1   Scenario 30
       2/6/2   Conversion Table 31
       2/6/3   Proxy 32
       2/6/4   Criterion of Tolerable Error Limit 33
       2/6/5   Information Technology 34

Chapter 3: Development of Society-Comparison Methodology 37
   3/1   Introductory Remarks 37
   3/2   Theoretical Premises 40
       3/2/1   Free Market Society Conjectures (FMSC) 40
       3/2/2   Mapping Societies' Scenarios of Self-preservation 43
       3/2/3   Socio-Economic Propositions 49

3/3	Conclusions from the Model of Free Market Society	52
3/4	Statistical Interpretation of Real-Life Data	59
3/4/1	Introduction	59
3/4/2	Discussion of Methodology	60
3/4/3	Discussion of Results	61

Chapter 4: Tools for Mapping the D-Curve 63
- 4/1 Introduction 63
- 4/2 Choice of Societies 66
- 4/3 Estimation of "Legitimacy" and "Power" Rankings 67
  - 4/3/1 Feasibility of Converse Rankings between "Legitimacy" and "Power" and their Use 67
  - 4/3/2 Second Step: The Use of Conversion Tables 70
  - 4/3/3 The D-Curve as a Tool for Efficient Estimation of Risk-of-Conflict Disutility 74
  - 4/3/4 Testing the D-Curve Mapping Against Real-Life Socio-Economic Losses 78
- 4/4 Further Results following from the D-Curve Mapping 80
  - 4/4/1 Other Negative Reflections 82
  - 4/4/2 Light-at-the-End-of-the-Tunnel Hypothesis 86

Chapter 5: Risk Assessment of Conflicts 89
- 5/1 Introducing the New Paradigm 89
  - 5/1/1 Statement of the Problem 89
  - 5/1/2 Decision-Making Methodology among Risk-Laden Alternatives 93
  - 5/1/3 Quantitative Assessment of the Risk Factor 95
- 5/2 Conversion Tables for Risk in Conflicting (Exogenous vs. Indigenous) Socio-Political Environments 98
  - 5/2/1 Introductory Remarks and Discussion 98
  - 5/2/2 Tools for Minimizing the Risk Factor 104
  - 5/2/3 Construction of the Risk-of-Crisis Conversion Table 116
- 5/3 Final Remarks 127

Chapter 6: Practical Use of the Paradigm 133
- 6/1 Policy Decision-Making in Risk-Assessment 133
- 6/2 Basics of Political Decision-Making 134
  - 6/2/1 Goal and Alternatives in Decision Processes 134
  - 6/2/2 Factor Tree 135
  - 6/2/3 Assessment of Factors' Utilities 136

6/3 Analysis of an Alternative 137
    6/3/1 General Methodology 137
    6/3/2 Description and Discussion of "Standard" Alternatives 141
    6/3/3 Errors in Analyzing the Alternatives 150
    6/3/4 Concluding Remarks on Methodology and Results 152
6/4 Discussion of the Risk Assessment Methodology Cast into the Systems Analysis Framework 156

Chapter 7: Macro-Economic and Micro-Economic Implications of the Paradigm 163

7/1 Macro-Economic Issues in the New Paradigm 163
    7/1/1 Intra-Societal and Inter-Societal Heterogeneity 163
    7/1/2 Heterogeneous Societies and Escalation of Poverty 165
    7/1/3 Modeling the Societies' Socio-Political Environments 169
    7/1/4 Several Issues Concerning the "Solution" 171
7/2 Micro-Economic Effects of the Paradigm on the Society's Homogeneity 176
    7/2/1 Visibly Increasing Intra-Heterogeneities in Developed Societies 176
    7/2/2 Major Macro-economic Effect: Sub-prime Mortgage Crisis in the US 2007–2008 185
    7/2/3 Analysis of the Sub-Prime Mortgage Crisis 187
7/3 The "Doomsday Scenario" Represents a Serious Threat to Successful *Donor-Recipient* Co-operation 192
7/4 Wrapping up Chapter 7 197

Chapter 8: How to Avoid the Possible "End-of-Civilization" Scare in the "Doomsday Scenario" 201

8/1 Introduction to the Problem 201
8/2 **NORTH**'s Last-Line of Defense against the Religiously Intolerant and Belligerent **SOUTH** 206
8/3 A Feasible "**SOUTH**-to-**SOUTH**" Solution 207
8/4 Concluding Observations 210

APPENDIX 213

A/1 Criterion of Tolerable Error Limits (CTER) 213
    A/1/1 Prerequisites and Problem Formulation 213
    A/1/2 Interval Estimates of Behavioral "RISK" Factors 214
A/2 Basic Formulas, Theorems, and Axioms Used for Conversion Tables 216
A/3 Scheme of Calibrating the Factor Scales 219

    A/3/1   Maximum Utility Principle 220
    A/3/2   Assessing the Given Factor's USF 220
    A/3/3   Lexicographical Ordering Scheme 222
  A/4   An Alternative in the Decision Process 223
  A/5   Supporting Data to "Power of Oligarchy" Scale 224
    A/5/1   Supporting Surveys 224
    A/5/2   Supporting Data for "The Generic Societies" Hypothesis ... 226
  A/6   Conversion Table of the Indexes of Corruption in Individual Countries 228
  A/7   Ranking Methods of Non-Parametric Statistics 229
  A/8   The Gini Index 232

Notes 235

Chapter 1: The Problem

> *MOTTO: "An organization is a collection of choices looking for problems, issues and feelings looking for decision situation in which they might be aired, solutions looking for issues to which they might be the answer, and decision-makers looking for work."*
> (M.D. Cohen, J.G. March, and J.P. Olsen [158])

Here we present a sketch of the problem of concern in this volume, namely, the failures between donors and recipients of international aid, together with an outline of the approach taken to develop a paradigm designed to facilitate successful solutions.

Let us begin by assuming that a developed country, that we shall henceforth call a ***donor***, tries to carry out a transaction giving "bilateral aid" to some other country that we shall call a ***recipient***. The ***donor*** country activities may be carried out by any of its business, banking, government or non-governmental organization (NGO) entities. This "transaction" is, therefore, shorthand for economic aid, business expansion, banking loans or similar activities of NGOs.

Let us also make clear that we shall be using both governmental organizations (GO) and NGO terms and categories. Thus we shall be investigating not only macroeconomic and microeconomic, social and political trends in an individual society, but, above all, the social well-being brought by the transactions of all the GO and NGO entities. It has been observed that, dollar for dollar, NGOs are much more effective in directing aid designed to accomplish a goal where the real need is on the international scene, such as: "improving the economic, social and, perhaps, political wellbeing in recipient countries." The difference is that governments simply hand over a wad of cash whereas NGOs typically have people working onsite at the grassroots level, building schools, training farmers, sewing up war victims and the like [177; p.A14].

The strictly business part of the transaction consists of activities such as: WTO-like bilateral foreign trade agreements (theoretically highly beneficial to both parties), joint ventures in banking and foreign exchange trade, co-operation in macroeconomic management, planning and economic consulting, setting up multinational corporations (perhaps with "farming" out the production to developing countries) together with appropriate transfer of technology (inclusive of professional personnel). The strictly humanitarian (albeit sometimes politically motivated) part includes: emergency loans, aids or grants, and socio-economic humanitarian aid together with "loaned" non-indigenous experts, administrators, managers, and political and military observers and peace-keepers etc. It is important, at this stage, to note that we will not differentiate between the ways the aid or business transactions are carried out.

What matters, in our view, is the reaction to this "bilateral aid or other transaction" in the *recipient* country and society.

The term "country" is, at this stage, interchangeable with the term "society," since it is, after all, the country's society at large that benefits from (or loses because of) the trend in the economic wealth of the country, the ruling classes and/or the government notwithstanding. In the next chapter we make clear distinctions between the following labels: "society," "nation," "nation-state" and "country."

Politically motivated (albeit under the "humanitarian label") capital-infusion transactions to many a developing *recipient* country have assumed that its society remains poor because they are too poor to afford enough capital for development investment. Following the Marshall Plan model, capital was transferred to developing countries in the form of grants and loans. This was found not to work very well because—in the opinion of experts—the recipients, unlike the European countries after WWII, did not have the technical know-how to make use of the capital. This is obviously only partially true and in no way even touches on the key reason, which was not a lack of "know-how" anyway.

If we take into account the amount of foreign capital deposited in Western banks and invested in Western countries by wealthy citizens of developing *recipient* societies, as well as their properties overseas, the assumption of capital shortage due to recipient poverty becomes questionable. Moreover, the success with which this capital has been transferred and invested overseas presupposes a good deal of technical know-how on the part of the recipients' political and economic elite. Had these elite used such knowledge for the public good, development could have occurred much more rapidly.

Let's not mince words here: The Western (or **NORTH**) *donors* have been, for a long time now, losing their grip on an efficient transfer of economic aid, to wit: know-how or technology transfer, while they never had a grip on monetary transfers to **SOUTH** *recipients*; money having mostly ended up in the **SOUTH** ruling oligarchies' Swiss bank accounts.

There is an explanatory argument being aired by some experts. They claim that successful transactions (application of the Western, i.e. *donor's*, know-how and skills) requires the existence of complementary and supporting knowledge and systems that do not exist in the *recipient* environment. Also, Western techniques and processes are culture bound and cannot be applied successfully without changes in attitudes, values and behavior of the *recipient* society. There is some truth to this argument, but not enough to make it convincing.

Thus, the problem we are facing is about the interrelation and evolution of the socio-economic and socio-political divergences, or gaps, between the *donors'* and *recipients'* societies. It is also about the virtual globalization of almost all aspects of life in their societies, and the effect this globalization has and will have on such vastly differing countries. These heterogeneous and homogeneous socio-economic and socio-political phenomena affect the outcome of mutually prosperous existence among the world societies or entities in a variety of ways.

Given such complexities, we must clarify the overall goal of this opus. This goal can be stated as follows:

- Analyze, model and map the societies' social, economic and political environments' differences and their most probable trends. The interacting societies (and/or entities) we shall be investigating are historically different, with different customs, habits, traditions, cultures and evolutionary socio-political trends that together form a quite specific socio-economic and political social-value loss to the intended transactions or policies.

- Then, based on this analysis, make reasonably accurate assessment and mapping of all possible risks-of-conflict—and, above all, their overall and total monetary. While harming the *recipient* societies or entities most, it should be noted that the spin-offs are felt sometimes drastically, as, for instance, in the events of 9/11, in *donor* entities as well. With that in mind, the issue of "early warning against probable serious risk-of-conflict consequences"—as the risk is defined and assessed through the functional relation between the differences in **NORTH** *donor* and **SOUTH** *recipient* societies' general behavior and particular level of behavioral, cultural, cognitive, social and socio-economic gaps—is important and represents a sort of safeguard. It is supposed to tell us in no uncertain terms that the suggested transaction would lead to a serious conflict between the **NORTH** *donor* and **SOUTH** *recipient* entities. Therefore, it would be better to drop the plan before the damage is done.

- Also, as the societies we shall be investigating are historically different, "conflicts" are considered to be the causes of the comprehensive ill effects—in all spheres of political, economic and social mosaic of the society—the resulting **SOUTH → SOUTH** paradigm of this study, that is prevailing now, should make sure that the **NORTH** *donors* (GOs and NGOs) understand the incredible waste of money spent on ideologically "not friendly" oligarchies—especially in these trying economic-recession times—and, hence, should completely re-think their development policies vis-à-vis the **SOUTH** *recipients* accordingly.

- One of the options might be—and in the final chapter of this study this will be backed up by some proofs following from algebraic mapping of the problems—to channel the aid to a given *recipient* through a specifically selected third party that happens to be a **SOUTH** *donor*, more developed, friendly to the *recipient*, ready to help and, above all, one with big clout over given *recipient* that would otherwise be hostile to any **NORTH** *donor(s)*.

Chapter 2: Definitions

Now it is time to define the basic elements of this study. When we say "basic elements" we have in mind phenomena from the political, social, socio-economic, sociological and economic spheres. The definitions presented in this chapter are ordered based on their content and their relationship to each other, and are consequently not simply in an alphabetical (or other externally classified) order.

This chapter covers definitions of terms related to social groups and phenomena as well as elements involved in the decision-making paradigm. It concludes with a new definition of the term "protectorate," developed specifically for the present treatise. Because of the multi-disciplinary domain of our paradigm, the terms society, country, nation and state are defined first.

2/1 Society, Country, Nation, State

There are many working definitions of "society." They depend on the domain of the particular sociological study using the term. For instance, in global studies, "society" might mean the population of the world; when the tribes and similar categories are investigated, "society" could mean just a tribe. Politically, the society is in a certain sense tantamount to a "state." To be more precise, political organizations of societies have usually evolved into the formation of individual states.

There is always the danger of equating the term "society" with "country" (as is common in Europe). It is time to make sure that the terms of reference of basic categories concerning society, country and state are explained, although these categories might have different meanings in different disciplines. Therefore, we shall use cross-section categories from several social, sociological and economic disciplines and have them labeled such that each individual subject or category used in the study will have its specific definition pertinent only to the logic of this study.

2/1/1 Society

A society is a set or association of persons possessing any degree of common interest, usually but not necessarily with a common (i.e. the same, similar or historically relevant) language. They live in a certain—again historically delineated and determined by international law—territory, or state, and entertain the same or similar historically, educationally and even religiously enhanced traits, customs, habits and traditions. They have also undergone the same historical as well as current socio-economic and socio-political trends and aspirations.

2/1/2 Country

Since this treatise investigates political and socio-economic differences among individual states, our definition of "society" would be that of a "country." Most technical literature on the subject [16; pp.32, 103]; [58; p. 87] uses the term "country" in this sense. However, this holds true only as long as the country means the territory of a nation that we mean to be representing a state. In other words, "country" will be used for politically and territorially sovereign entities and "society" for the people and their political organization within the country-state.

2/1/3 Nation

A nation is a similar set of people bound by their similarities in language, cultural and historical trends as in a society. Here, however, "genetic inheritance" plays a much stronger role than in the definition of a society. Genetic transmission goes from earlier, usually very far distant, generations to the more recent ones. Thus, if we go far back in the history of nations then we might better understand the sociological cohesion and importance of supranational entities. These are bound together not by statehood but by societies of blood-related tribes that used to roam together long ago in geographically and culturally distant locations. In our treatise we shall be using the term "nation" in a rather more narrow sense, closer to a tribe, with the appropriately strong culturally-religious and historical common thread, typical of societies of the developing world.

2/1/4 State

Thus, despite common or similar language and the same or similar historical and cultural trends, a **nation is not necessarily tantamount to a state**. In fact most contemporary states are multinational (or multi-tribal and eventually multi-ethnic). However, for the sake of brevity, in this study we shall be considering sovereign nation-states with polities, understood to mean the political or governmental organizations of these nation-states [16; p.20].

2/2 Generic Society, Homogeneity, Heterogeneity

2/2/1 Generic Society

In this text we shall be using the term "generic society," which represents the similarity principle on the societal level. A generic society is a hypothetical society that serves as a common denominator and a standard for a group of societies with the same or similar moral foundation, law abiding behavior, quality of legal framework and law enforcement capability, respect for human rights and credibility of the legal institutions in particular, and of the government in general.

Societies may exhibit homogeneity and heterogeneity with regard to socio-economic and socio-political categories, both within a particular society and in relation to other societies. We define these homogeneous and heterogeneous natures as follows.

2/2/2 Intra-Societal Homogeneity and Heterogeneity

Suppose we have a society where there is obviously social stratification, but, on the other hand, there is also a strong moral foundation, law abiding citizens, general functioning legal framework with strong law enforcement capability, respect for human rights and credibility of the public institutions.

We say this type of society exhibits **intra-societal homogeneity** and suggest that within it the **risk-of-conflict in transactions** does not exist in our terms of reference; the risk category there contains only the standard business risk or, in other words, the risk associated with the theory of games and economic behavior (see e.g. [73]). Such "business risk" is therefore associated with the economic category only, while social and political spin-off effects hardly ever enter the picture.

Nevertheless, this does not prevent economic entities in homogeneous societies from making transactional mistakes. In 2000, a U.S. semiconductor maker decided to launch their product into the "European market." It had minimal success. The first thing the company learned is that you cannot consider Europe a single market, despite significant societal homogeneity. Each country still has its own culture and civilization, socio-political history and traditions, and some sort of "national MO" and in-built cognitive system allowing them to do things "their way."

On the other side, **intra-societal heterogeneity** remains a very significant problem in *recipient* countries today. It has been claimed [98; pp.1,6] that whenever socio-economic stress grips a *recipient* country, the tribal (ethnic) parts of the society—historically with vastly differing trends and levels of economic well-being, social care, political access to state governance, religion and cultural identity—are the weakest link and usually give way first. This has grave economic, social and political consequences. In such a case we say that intra-societal heterogeneity has reached a dangerous level. One has only to reflect on the fate of the former Republic of Yugoslavia which still has open wounds in Bosnia and even greater ones in Kosovo [94; p.B5], and the free-for-all among the ethnic tribes in Central Africa, Sudan, Somalia, Chechnya and, last but not least, in Iraq.

Apart from these examples, the problem has a rather impressive historical background. Intra-societal homogeneity has been the goal of all successful rulers throughout the history of humankind. Benevolent medieval monarchs started large public projects to employ and to pay the poor (Charles IV of the Roman Empire is the classic example in the 15th century) and also introduced unifying religion, such as the Viking rulers of medieval Russia. Generally speaking, and we might consider this axiomatic: **It is not that the society has ever minded historical class distinction as long as the *status quo* of the standard of living was upheld**. Even the rise of new classes (or new religions, for that matter) has been tolerated when the over-all living standard of the society increased. For example, the USSR and other COMECON states were, up until their economic collapse, politically very homogeneous and stable.

Another example of this axiom is provided by the industrial revolution. Subsequent appearances of new classes did not cause societal problems (until the birth of Marxian ideology which was bent on destruction of the "capitalist" states). On the other hand, **all societies have resisted the rise of a new idle class of oligarchs, ideological (or religious) zealots and *nouveau riche* that, to satisfy their ever-increasing needs, lowered the society's standard of living**. The examples transcend centuries, from the decline of ancient Mogul and Chinese civilization up to a close call on South-East Asian societies in the second half of the 1990s. We can therefore conclude that an **increase of intra-societal heterogeneity**, even only a perceived one, is one sure-fire way to bring about the eventual **demise of the society.**

One more comment on the "perceived" threat to a homogeneous society: European Jewry had been living in their respective countries for centuries. It took Nazi philosophy to make "dangers-to-society" and thus "must-be-annihilated" outcasts out of them. The same could be said of the genocides managed by Stalin, Mao, Pol-Pot and others.

2/2/3 Inter-Societal Homogeneity and Heterogeneity

If among several (two or more) societies or countries there exists a social, political and socio-economic environment in which sound moral foundation, law abiding behavior, quality of the legal framework and law enforcement capability, respect for human rights, freedom of religion, and credibility of the legal institutions in particular, and of the government in general, prevail then we call these societies socio-politically homogeneous and use the term **inter-societal homogeneity**. This holds irrespective of social and, sometimes, even political stratification. If this necessary and sufficient condition does not exist, then, logically, we talk about inter-societal heterogeneity.

To define this phenomenon we say that whenever a society significantly differs from some other investigated society in terms of socio-economic and socio-political categories, then there exists an **inter-societal heterogeneity** between the two societies. The two differing environments consist of economic, social, political, cultural, historical and cognitive categories. The heterogeneity is brought in, among other factors, by historical differences in cognitively, educationally and even religiously-enhanced traits, customs, habits and traditions.

As an example of this inter-societal heterogeneity, we can see a classic—and very important for our further analyses—case of a single-nation with two distinctly heterogeneous societies within it. This is Germany more than two decades after re-unification (in 1989). The 40-years of division, after the Second World War, left the former East German (Deutsche Demokratische Republik, DDR) society with behavioral scars from communist-induced "law and order" and a perception of playing social roles in a communist society. In short, two decades after unification of the legal framework and law enforcement capability—that should have yielded respect for human rights, freedom of religion and credibility of the legal institutions—in the former Eastern part we saw substandard infrastructure, 18% unemployment and the flight of young job-seekers to the west [170; p.A18]. We also saw quite harsh epithets, bordering almost on "hatred," used by the former West German (Bundesrepublik Deutschland, BRD) society to describe the "easterners."

2/3 Political Systems

2/3/1 Developing Country

A developing country (also known as a "third world country") **is a country whose society and its socio-economic, socio-political and cultural-historical development has not—for historical, geographical and other reasons—followed the mainstream of traditional European, North American or some of the Far-East nation-states.** These "developed countries" embarked upon laissez-faire economies early on in the late eighteenth and early nineteenth centuries. We find, by contrast, that developing countries are, by and large, former colonies or countries that have always been geographically located on the fringes of the "historical industrialized world." They include countries such as those located in the Far East (meaning east of the Ural Mountains), in Africa and the Arabian Peninsula.

As a result of their positions relatively far from the mainstream, some of these third-world (or developing) countries were not forced to abolish their sometimes outright feudal political systems. Therefore, the indigenous ruling classes and oligarchies were in no rush to grant any rights to their peoples other than those absolutely necessary for keeping the society politically sedated. As Revel [167; p.58] says: *"It is because **economics is subordinated to politics** that the rulers do not have to pay for their mistakes."* This eventually became the basis of growing intra-societal heterogeneity and a base for future political unrest in those countries.

Post-World-War-II history added another element to the "fringe of the civilized world" definitional criterion. We may therefore offer the following opinion: We say that developing (and transitional) societies are those in which the basic democratic codex of rights, together with a generally laissez faire economic attitude, have not been exercised in consistent fashion in the period following the middle of the twentieth century.

Thus, among the developing countries (societies) we can include former third- and fourth-world command-and-control societies of Asia; also, transitional countries that have emerged from former Communist countries (USSR and all the COMECON countries, Vietnam, China, Yugoslavia etc.); and those of the former monarchies or dictatorships of South America.

2/3/2 Legitimate Democracy

In coming to the definition of a legitimate democracy, various sources, such as [51], claim that democracy literally means rule of the people that could be seen as a technology of collective choice and also as a type of social behavior or community organization. In one source, [16; p.110], we read:

> Government by law but not by people is one of the most basic features of the Western model of democracy ... the law, that instrument with which individuals and groups achieve societal goals, is closely related to the legitimacy and power of public institutions.

We also read, in [51]:

> The propensity to view democracy from a long-term perspective can hardly be claimed as altogether new. ... Alexis de Tocqueville announced more than a century and a half ago that "a great democratic revolution ... is taking place in our midst" and added that some saw it as "irresistible" because it is "the most continuous, the most ancient, and the most permanent tendency known to history." This revolution, if we are to credit the de Tocqueville term, is still in progress and its precise shape remains to be determined."

Legitimate democracies, in this treatise, are the complement of developing countries. They are the traditionally and historically civilized societies or states of U.S.A.; Western Europe (inclusive of Scandinavia); and some societies of the former British Empire: United Kingdom, Australia, New Zealand and Canada; and, last but not least, Japan.

It would be, however, a grave mistake to assume that all the classical democracies, plus the neo-democratic societies (some of them in "transition") in Europe, could be aggregated under the technical term "homogeneous societies." Quite a worrying consequence of this notion is the plan for enlargement of the European Union. As Valery Giscard d'Estaing and Helmut Schmidt claim [99; p.8]:

> Already, with only 15 member states, EU institutions are not functioning well ... it is obvious that full integration is not a realistic goal for 30 countries that are very different in their political traditions, culture and economic development .... To attempt integration ... can only lead to complete failure ... the realistic option is integration for those countries which have the political will for it and whose economic and social conditions are nearly identical.

This claim has to be seen in two different lights. Firstly, Western Europe has already been reasonably well integrated economically for some decades. The problem today is a new currency and political surrender. As the currency stability problem is one of perception and thus strictly in the behavioral category, it would be very difficult to manage a uniform perception over those 30 countries. Besides—as the general notion in Great Britain and lately in Denmark's and Switzerland's plebiscite show—there is not any great impatience, let alone rush, to join the Euro (or the EU at all in the case of Switzerland) anytime soon.

The second problem with the EU follows the line of the above mentioned axiom from the field of sociology. Societies do mind, and do mind very strongly, the emergence of a new class, the Euro-bureaucrats, who would take money (and therefore the standard of living) from the member states without giving anything back. And it might as well be the case of "the new class" (as Milovan Djilas defined in [167; p.51]) that:

> As the ruling bureaucracy, might be trying to make both the people and the economy to serve ... power under bureaucratic rule is based not on property, as under capitalism, but on holding office.

This, in nutshell, represents the gist of the problem of inter-societal heterogeneity (or homogeneity) vs. different trends of individual intra-societal homogeneities. It clearly points to some real causes of concern in terms of sudden emergence of risk of conflict. Only detailed research, which we will undertake in this text, is able to map out a strategy for optimizing the well-being of the whole ***donor-recipient*** system.

2/3/3 Oligarchy

An oligarchy is the relatively small ruling strata (or even only a clique) of a society. It consists of the historically evolved class of feudal landlords, newly arrived owners of industrial mega-enterprises and mega-banks, together with top political figures—either former feudal rulers or former generals turned dictators and their juntas—whose only interest is to exercise absolute power over the given society.

This term originated from Plato's [167; p.41] doctrine, which claimed that:

> The people are to be led by a minority that alone comprehends the ideal in its entirety.

Thus, members of an oligarchy have become by this very definition corrupt, despotic and above the laws of the country. They invariably consider the country as their private fiefdom. Some typical examples of oligarchies come from South-East Asia, South America, and Arab Peninsula cultures and societies. The following explanation has general validity.

In so far as the saying ***"absolute power corrupts absolutely"*** goes, there is no difference whatsoever between the economic power-junkies and religious or ideological zealots who, in the name of their religion/ideology, acquired the same absolute power. Therefore, the religious and/or ideological rulers—be it in the former USSR, contemporary Iran, Libya, Cuba, Uzbekistan, China or elsewhere—form the same oligarchic clique as in the societies mentioned above. All these ruling ideologues feature three internal factors that reinforce their backwardness: underdeveloped economies, hatred of foreign (economic) domination and lack of experience of democratic pluralism [167; p.30].

Some of the features of oligarchic societies will emerge later on when the definitions of social movement and collective behavior are discussed. Here we should mention a classic example of the worst possible way in which a new oligarchy has usurped the leadership of the "transitional society." The place is Russia; the time is now. We quote [101; p.8]:

> Ministries, department heads, agencies, governorates, and mayoralties have gone into partnership with private businesses, local oligarchs or criminal elements, creating a kind of 21st century Russian feudalism.

In the following source [16; pp.97-98] we read the classic summary of the subject:

> Hierarchy, an ideal feature of Confucianism for establishing societal order, assumes that **super-ordinates possess more rights** but also greater responsibilities **than subordinates** ... Superiors become authoritarian only when they pay more attention to their rights and privileges ... when they send subordinates' children to battle but their own overseas for graduate study ... when they penalize subordinates but not their relatives for criminal behavior (bold M.K.).

According to the earlier definition, "inter-societal heterogeneity" occurs any time a society significantly differs from some other investigated society (or societies) in terms of socio-economic and socio-political categories. The differing environments consist of economic, social, political, cultural, historical and cognitive categories. The heterogeneity is brought in by, among other factors, historical differences in cognitively, educationally and even religiously-enhanced traits, customs, habits and traditions.

2/3/4 Protectorate

Coming to this final, useful definition we have to introduce its concept first. Historically, the **protectorate**, as a socio-political term, had its use in the early days of empire building. As the colonizing countries in the nineteenth century needed their freshly colonized societies of warrior tribes and nations in a reasonably peaceful frame of mind, the protectorate seemed the ideal political vehicle. Thus, there were many protectorates among the warrior societies of Africa and in Arabia under virtually all of the colonial powers of the time.

In such protectorates, limited home-rule (by the tribal dynasties) would be formally acknowledged, while, in fact, the ultimate power was vested in the "governor" or "protector" who would, as a rule, be a high civil servant from the "protecting" country. While the local culture, religion, tradition and historical habits and traits of the indigenous "protected" society were preserved, the protecting country usually took the education, health and, most importantly, judicial and policing systems into their own hands. This was inevitable since calm and the rule of law and order in the society were their main goals. In other words, as these protectorates were supposed to make bilateral economic ties—i.e. ties between the colonial power that protected the socio-economically inferior society and that society or protectorate—much easier, the basic law codes and particularly the substantive law codices were all imported from the protecting country which was also responsible for upholding them.

During World War II Germany adopted this system, forming the Protectorate of Bohemia and Moravia (in today's Czech Republic) to placate the Czech society, and to enable its highly skilled workers and managers to work for the Third Reich's armament and other heavy machinery industry without interruption due to any serious political destabilization of the society. They subsequently made a protectorate out of Denmark as well. The concept worked without a hitch all through WWII. Based on these historical facts we propose a "new" definition of the protectorate useful for our purposes nowadays.

"Protectorate," in this study, is a temporary socio-political concept which leaves the "protected society" (usually a *recipient* one) intact with regards to its culture, historical social institutions and traditional behavior, but the "protectors" (usually a small group of skilled administrators from *donor* societies; UN, UNESCO, etc.) working with supporting staff—teachers, advisers, judiciary apparatus, security, perhaps even police, etc.—also drawn from the *donor* societies, actually run the society while making sure that the "protected" society obeys the standard legal system and that the moral codex, together with the legal one, is strictly enforced.

2/4 Risk and Conflict

Based on the above discussion, in this treatise we shall not talk about "risk" as it is presented in classical economic or monetary texts, because our category of risk is quantitatively different. Instead, we shall be dealing with the category of "risk in conflicting-socio-political environment."

This is not only a multidisciplinary category touching sociology, economics, politics, culture, cognitive level and even history of the investigated societies. It is also one of the least understood and certainly very difficult categories to quantify because of the utter dissimilarity of its domains. Also, and above all, it is the most dangerous element of socio-economic systems and entities today, because it is unpredictable in its overall consequences. That is why it has become the very raison d'être of this study.

2/4/1 Risk in Conflicting Socio-political Environment

"Risk in conflicting socio-political environment" is risk threatening the whole socio-economic and socio-political fabric of a certain *recipient* society (with possible feedback to the *donor*). It simply assumes that following an initial economic shock—stemming from our earlier assertion that in oligarchies both economy and people serve only the "ruling classes"—further and deeper social and political shocks will take place in the *recipient* society. They bring subsequent destabilization and political unrest with a real possibility of an armed uprising, when *force may 'legitimately' be used to compel the majority of the people's obedience* (inverted commas M.K.) [167; p.41]. Implicit is the further threat that the *recipient(s)* may not ever be able to return to normalcy let alone to any semblance of progress. Tidal-wave shock-effects—societal post-crisis behavior, which may mean that normalcy is never completely recovered during the time of the existing generation—may actually produce direct political and even armed confrontation with the *donor*. That is why we shall call it systems (or systemic) risk. One, unfortunately painful, illustration of the "strike-back" syndrome is the terrorist attack on New York and Washington DC on September 11, 2001.

With regards to the functional relationship between inter-societal heterogeneity and expected conflict, we shall just embellish upon a remark made in the preceding chapter. There we said that the overall systems disutility caused by a conflict between the *donor* and the *recipient* society [49] is a function of the incompatibility between two investigated (socio-economic, socio-political and religious ethical) cultures of the given societies. As the notion of "cultures" appears here, we can describe this incompatibility in terms of differing historical trends in social, socio-political, political, legal, law enforcement and governmental environments, ethical, cognitive, law abiding traits and people's expectations and behavioral standards (affected by religion) in the two societies.

We can also postulate that **incompatibility is the most important qualifier of inter-societal heterogeneity and a direct indicator of the size and depth of the conflict**. In other words, the incompatibility "gap" is functionally related to inter-societal heterogeneity, which is a predictor of the depth of the conflict. Therefore, **the greater this gap is, the greater will be the "scissors" of overall systems disutility that will confront both the *donor* society and the *recipient* society**.

However, this disutility is manifested in different ways. While in *donor* societies the risk of disutility stays within the monetary categories—since the homogeneous *donor* society had not known (before September 11, 2001) other perils—the case of the *recipient* society has been vastly different.

In *recipient* societies, financial losses were immediately transformed into lost expectations and a sense of hopelessness of the whole society, which is a political as well as a sociological category. The losses in the financial and business sectors—remember the money "expropriated" by oligarchs—hit the currency exchange level and savings hardest. Through these vehicles a cash drought permeated all markets and eventually most economic enterprises in the country collapsed. Obviously this did not stop with one country, but a domino effect then ravaged the institutions in the region and, in no time, the "world-wide" effect was well under way (see e.g. [79; p.5]). Rapid pauperization of the middle classes (i.e. retailers, shopkeepers, small traders, artisans, professionals etc.) and falling expectations of the society is the first step. Then, the already charged conflict between the society and its governing oligarchy—eventually between the society and the *donor* country, seen as the source of the doom—becomes highly political and inflammatory.

In the milieu of definitions mentioned above, the system of causal chains depicting the connection between economics and politics in such a society can be graphically denoted as follows:

(2.1)   < Economic crisis → < socio-political crisis

where the "<" symbol denotes "increase."

This causal connection refers to the problems of developing societies with reigning oligarchies who "re-route" their societies' wealth into their own

Definitions

accounts. Subsequent impoverishment, deep-seated grievances and hopelessness among the masses obviously follow.

Increase in socio-political crisis has yet another effect, though. It is usually the last warning for the society's intelligentsia (i.e. professionals, scientists, artists, etc.) to emigrate, either because of their political beliefs or in order to protect the wellbeing of their families. Therefore the arrow in the causal chain in (2.1) can eventually run in the opposite direction. If we now add the efforts of monarchs and governments to suppress the emergence of any new social strata—that would cause the ire of society and their striving for economic nivelization—we arrive at another causal chain:

(2.2) > (<) Intra-society heterogeneity → > (<) socio-political crisis
              → > (<) economic crisis

where the ">" symbol stands for "decrease."

The exodus of professionals heightens the economic crisis. Thus, in (2.2) we find the last segment of the **"devil's spiral."**

From (2.1) and (2.2) with the "increase sign," we can clearly see the mechanics of how the "spill-over" effect from *recipient* society → *donor* society comes about. And it is not just economic crises being exported—via the corporate entities—to the *donor* societies.

More dangerous, because these are long-term and very difficult to solve, are the political and religious problems that are imported into the *donor* societies via the refugees from all the *recipients*. This has become painfully apparent in conjunction with the aftermath of the "9/11" terrorists attack on New York and Washington DC.

However, we do not have to use the currently "politically correct" terms of *donor* and *recipient* societies to explain the vicious spiraling-up (or, conversely, the damping or smoothing-out effect) of causalities (2.1) and (2.2). Even in Ancient Rome the emperors knew that the principle behind the policy of *panem et circenses* (bread and circuses) is to keep the indigenous population happy, politically content and contained, and thus the empire in one piece. Similarly, the author (in [108; p.366]) explained Hitler's policy towards his nation:

The German workers, like the Roman proletariat, were provided with circuses by their rulers to divert attention from their miserable state.

Hitler also exploited the spiraling-up effect of these causal chains for his pre-war expansion. He used the huge German ethnic minority in 1930-1937 Czechoslovakia and the German ethnic majority in Austria together with his focused single-party regime (inter-societal heterogeneous to each European government) to whip up internal political crises in both Austria and Czechoslovakia. Then, with the benediction of fearful European governments, he first annexed Austria and then the Munich Agreement gave him "Sudetenland" from Czechoslovakia, long before World War II actually started. To support our pre-WWII Central-European example we quote one of the best British socio-political experts at that place and time, Sir Robert Bruce Lockhart, who wrote [110; p.112]:

> When the economic conditions were unbearable [in Austria], ninety percent of Austrians were for Anschluss (annexation by or federalization with Germany; M.K.) … when they were relatively good, ninety percent were against Anschluss.

Regarding the above notion of "falling expectations" (as the beginning of the socio-political crisis in a society) we, again, read in Lockhart [110; p.144]:

> I have noticed [in Germany] how slowly yet perceptibly the democratic traditions wither under the pressure of falling expectations.

An increase (rapid or not) **of "intra-societal heterogeneity" means an increase in political instability in any *recipient* country; perhaps in the whole region.** Thus, this is **yet another reason why this category should be called a systemic risk, contrary to the textbook definition of the "standard" business risk.**

At this point we can begin to look at the role of multinationals and hence the role of globalization in a *recipient* country. The moment the gap—between the socio-economic, political, cognitive and cultural levels of countries engaged in bilateral, sometimes multifaceted, transactions—signals big problems ahead, the role of multinational corporations in linking these economic zones of prosperity is crucial. The comparative advantage in creating wealth lies in the private sector. Thus, the *donors*' entities (governments as well as NGOs) are well advised to support multinationals in their effort to help increase wealth in *recipient* economies rather than disparaging, shunning and eventually withdrawing from them.

Here we have to pause a little because the notion of globalization is not nearly that straightforward. First of all, there are at least two sides to it. On the one hand, the economic picture is, according to some recent studies, becoming rosier. There is a reported gradual reduction in inequality among countries since the mid 1980s [118; p.C11]. This is where the multinationals can and do dispense most of their positive impact. Their role then is, at least theoretically, to smooth over differences in corporate culture. As the specifics of corporate culture is based on historical trends and, of course, the current state of cultural, social and political well-being, any difference between the two compared socio-economic entities' political and social trends necessarily adds to the potential risk level to the *donor* society. But if the multinational economic colossus, which carries a lot of political clout, plays its cards right, it may eventually prevail over the oligarchs. The *recipient* society will succeed, if it is successfully navigated through international legal systems and institutions to protect the legitimate rights of both sides and thus to foster co-operation beneficial to both parties. This would root out most of the problems that concern us.

The other, and much deeper, side of globalization is in its political and socio-political impact. Samuel Huntington in his book ***The Clash of Civilizations*** warns that:

> The attempt to spread western civilization (or ***donors***; added M.K.) across the world would trigger responses from civilization with different religious and cultural foundations [121; p.E2].

Indeed, globalization is seen in many societies in the world, often due to the spin put on it by a threatened oligarchy or clergy, as a plot by western *donors* to impose their values and institutions on other societies.

Take the Arab world, for example. Many societies in the Middle East have some of the highest population growth-rates in the world, and these societies are severely challenged to provide jobs for the large number of young people, with access to information, entering the labor force each year. This makes the youth quite restless with a deep sense of hopelessness. Director of the CIA, George Tenet, in testimony before the U.S. Senate select committee on intelligence earlier in 2001 warned [121; p.EE2]:

> At the same time Islamic militancy is expanding, and the worldwide pool of potential recruits for terrorist networks is growing ... international terrorists have used the information technology explosion to advance their capability: raise money and find recruits.

But, even if we forget such extreme cases of politically motivated armed uprising and international terrorist threat, as far as the *recipient* society itself is concerned, it is said that:

> The deterioration of all local values and institutions, including those at the grass roots, as a result of contact with the capitalistic (i.e. *donor*; added M.K.) system, which makes people care primarily for

the economic, material aspect of life; and leadership's lack of legitimacy as well as power to avoid or mitigate this deterioration or substitute viable values and institutions [16; p.54].

Two other excerpts concur with this assessment. The first source [78; p.1] cites Michael Camdessus, the managing director of IMF:

> [T]here are also worrying vulnerabilities in other parts of the world ... slow process of corporate and financial restructuring in Asia and ineffective addressing of poverty in Africa ... all of this combined with complacency could lead to delays in finalization of changes to the world's financial architecture ... but even more seriously, this could lead to delays at the country level of principles adopted at global level.

A second source [85; p.9] clearly states that "some countries have stagnated or slid backwards during this era of globalization."

This all can be easily translated as "worsening of socio-economic, political and social climate" and thus the increase of the actual conflict in the recipient societies and its feedback transfer to the *donor* societies just as causal chain systems **(2.1)** and **(2.2)** indicate.

2/4/2 Societal Conflict

Estimates of the magnitude of societal conflicts in the concept of *donor-recipient* systems can be expressed only in combined sociological and socio-economic and socio-political categories. This is because these conflicts change a society's behavioral attributes—moral values, expectations, ethics and so on—too. These categories cannot be mapped by economic and/or monetary terms, such as the way business utility is usually measured [46; pp.200-201].

As societal conflicts unravel and the *recipient* society's behavior profoundly changes, it may never be possible to completely erase the moral and behavioral post-crisis disutility defined in literature as "pain, evil or unhappiness" [46; pp.84-85]. Contributing strongly to this argument is the self-preservation ability of the oligarchies in the *recipient* societies. They draw, and quite rightly, increasing opposition from their society. To confuse the issue, however, they usually paint the *donors* as usurpers trying to impose their values onto the *recipient* by sabotaging its economy. Hence, a deep-seated sense of grievance, hopelessness and frustration combined with poverty further enhances political destabilization. Consequently a full-fledged intra-societal heterogeneity escalates through the roof.

The only reversible element, following from the Law of Diminishing Marginal Utility [46; p.84], takes place in the correspondent *donor* society. There, some spin-off effects may, temporarily, negatively charge the relevant business conditions. These disutilities are strictly business related, temporal and thus reversible. They may change into systems disutilities only when the originally socio-economic conflict in the *recipient* society escalates into an armed one and, eventually, with the help of (historical) ethnic and/or religious enmity, into a full-fledged civil war that requires army personnel (or peace-keepers) from the *donor* country. A typical example is the conflict in Kosovo and elsewhere in former Yugoslavia. However, by far the most extreme and dangerous alternative of armed political conflicts transferred into *donor* societies is worldwide terrorism, which threatens to become more common in the immediate future. There the composite or systems disutility touches virtually all segments of economy and society, as we have witnessed in the aftermath of the 9/11 attacks on the U.S.

To conclude, three important notions should be heeded here:

(2.3) Systems disutility usually starts as an economic (mini-) crisis due to an ordinary big business deal gone sour. Due to interdependence of the economic and political spheres, noted in (2.1), and the domino-like behavior of crises in both spheres, economic problems in a recipient country almost always trigger societal problems. Hence we postulate that the more intra-societally heterogeneous the recipient society is, the greater chance there is for a major societal disaster.

(2.4) This brings us to an interesting assumption which we shall try to elaborate upon in subsequent chapters. We say that only inter-societal homogeneous societies are able to assess and eventually deal with business problems that occur when dealing with each other, because most of these losses are in monetary terms and thus can be quantified. The greater the inter-societal heterogeneity there is, the more the *donor* society is in the dark about what really goes in the *recipient* societies and, more importantly, what might be the systems qualitative (i.e. socio-behavioral and political) consequences of such losses.

(2.5) Hence, when qualitatively described effects of systems' conflicts are to be assessed and compared, we have to quantify them first. This might suggest the use of cardinal numbers, which would assess the magnitude immediately. These are impossible to find or develop, though. However, as we read [24; pp.41-47, 74-78]: "the ordinal values (scales) can be assumed to be monotonic transforms of the actual behavioral factors," we might start thinking about ordinal numbers—their scales, proxies, intervals etc.—instead. We shall find a sketch of this idea below, and the appropriate apparatus discussed in the Appendix.

Here, we shall also introduce some definitions and discussions of elements that will be needed in the decision-making part of the paradigm. Among them would be essential terms such as: scenario, conversion tables (used for conversion of heterogeneous factor scales into a homogeneous "utilities") and their basic principles (details are to be found in the Appendix).

2/5   Group Psychology

First, however, a few definitions and axioms concerning group (societal) psychology and the related phenomena of interaction, unrest and other antisocial behavior will be presented here.

2/5/1   Collective Behavior

Collective behavior [70; p.507] is bordered on three sides by other social processes. Here, the actions of very small groups are not our concern. Among larger or large groups, collective behavior can be distinguished from *unformed aggregates* (large numbers of people in a given location who have no interaction with each other, and engage in no joint activity) and *social institutions* (collective behavior of established groups such as the University of Toronto, Salvation Army and the Communist Party after it became institutionalized).

In the context of this study, of particular interest is the phenomenon of the **crowd** and its behavior. This is because intensified crowd activity often accompanies the rapid restructuring of society and crowds may themselves act as a vehicle of social change [70; p.508].

2/5/2   Crowd

Crowd is a generic term referring to a highly diverse condition of human assemblage: ***audience*** and ***street crowd*** (assembled around a point of common interest), ***mob*** (a tumultuous crowd liable to acts of lawlessness and outrage), ***riot*** (a violent disturbance of the peace by an assembly of persons, and frequently involving the attack of one group upon the other), and ***panic*** (a feeling of alarm and fear, originating in some real or supposed danger) all fall within the definition of crowd. Any subsequent classification of crowd cannot be decided upon in the absence of a theory of crowds, however. There is, for example, a suggestion [70; p.515] that a crowd turns into a *mob* when the common emotion is intense anger, while it is transformed into a *panic* when the common emotion is intense fear.

For social and political unrest (or rebellion), which will be used in our socio-political, socio-economic scenarios in the next chapters of this study, the following characteristics of the crowds are valid:

In the following source [70; p.543] we read:

> Whoever be the individuals that compose it, however like or unlike be their mode of life, their occupation, their character, or their intelligence, the fact that they have been transformed into a crowd puts them in possession of a sort of collective mind which makes them feel, think, and act in a manner quite different from that in which each individual of them would feel, think, and act were he in a state of isolation.

2/5/3 Social Movement

Social Movements (according to [70; p.584]) can be described as "a form of collective behavior which best fit the criterion of aiming at change in the world, and least qualify as amorphous and unorganized" and "represent an effort by a large number of people to solve collectively a problem that they feel they have in common."

Some movements respond to their desire for physical survival or aspiration toward a more decent, dignified existence (inclusive of better societal welfare; added M.K.). Other social movements embody national (or societal; added M.K.) aspirations or the desire for collective identity.

If a social movement fails to "adapt," and continues to stand in contrast and opposition to the society which surrounds it, it incurs considerable risk to its survival. For example, if it gains power or if conditions improve (i.e. the above disparity diminishes; added M.K.), it may become an anachronism. If, on the other hand, conditions do not improve the leaders of conventional society may feel forced to persecute the members of the movement because they offer a temptation to other victims of the system [70; p.596]. This is quite a fitting description of some of the oligarchic regimes in South-East Asia and South America; the totalitarian government of some states in the Arabian Peninsula also fit the bill quite nicely.

Since social movements are groups which operate on the margins of conventional society, they owe their origins to various gaps between human needs and social responses (i.e. response by the society's powers-that-be) to these needs. This leads to **the crucial paradigm of the study:**

(2.6) Every deficit on the ledgers of progress or, as we denote in this study "growing heterogeneity in social, socio-economic, socio-political and ethical (affected by religion) conditions between the *donor* and *recipient* societies," is a problem situation which could provide the impetus for a collective remedial effort [70; p.589].

2/6   Decision-Making

Now we come to a number of definitions that are necessary components of the decision-making process. These are: ***Decision-Making, Scenarios, Utility (or Disutility) Assessment and IT (inclusive of "social media")***.

2/6/1   Scenario

Scenarios, according to Herman Kahn, are "hypothetical sequences of events constructed with the help of a model for the purpose of focusing on decision points" [63]. Scenarios answer two questions:

- Precisely, by step-by-step analysis, how might some hypothetical situation come about?
- What alternatives exist for the decision-maker at each step for facilitating, diverting or preventing the process?

In the systems connotation, a scenario is an assumed specific set of conditions—we call them factors—which, when all of them work in the predetermined manner, make the system behave in a certain, again, predetermined way. This is, however, exactly what we do not need. As we present individual alternatives (scenarios) of the investigated socio-economic system, our goal is to discuss each of them and then decide on the most useful one.

Thus, scenario analysis then changes the importance-weights of factors or their expected function so that the user obtains an idea of how the system will work under different, specifically tailored, conditions. They also help us to see how robust the "best" scenario is. In other words, we can discover how big a margin for error in the major factors assessments can be and still leave the top scenario ranking unchanged. Or at least the top set of scenarios, for it is not as important to find the very best alternative as it is vital to avoid all the mediocre and bad alternatives.

While the scenarios help decision-makers to zero in on a distinctive set of alternatives, we should make a short detour here and discuss "market decisions"—those denoted as "risk less"—in any *donor* society. Although the discussion is, ostensibly, about market decisions it could easily cover all kinds of decision on whatever level.

We read [58; pp.55-57] that:

> Micro theory is not about behavior at all; it is about decisions ... If the deciders are not clearly identified, how do we know whose behavior it is that is determined? And words like 'firm' or 'households' do not clearly identify the decision-makers ... it is important to determine whether the premise that (1) organizations as such are decision-makers or, alternatively, (2) that only individuals (within and on behalf of organizations) are decision-makers ... the second possibility raises an important question which the first appear to ignore. If it is individuals who make decisions then the organizational 'structure' (or other characteristics) is likely to make a difference.

This significant question raises the following issues. It is not only how each individual in an organization (be it a firm, a household, a government) makes the decisions he faces, but how the nature of the organization creates or contributes to the communication and incentive structure which influences the decisions, as well as the activities that result from them. In the above source we read:

> Individuals are members of organizations. Within the organization there is room for a great deal of non-market behavior ... Hence it seems of interest to start with individuals who make choices, some of which are on a non-market basis, and then to aggregate the results of individual behavior into group behavior. Then we should go on to aggregate groups in order to obtain organizational (that is the entity) behavior.

This feature of non-market decision-making is exactly what our paradigm—with expert-defined menus and Delphi-technique (i.e. individual-to-aggregate) definition of scenarios and assessment of decision (and risk) factors—is trying to institute and improve. And with no less a tool than the complete computerization of the algorithms.

2/6/2 Conversion Table

A conversion table is a tool which converts **ordinal** or behavioral factors with qualitative descriptions—usually verbal, like level of importance statements, or numerical but in differently defined scales, like the Dow Jones Index, temperature in degrees of Celsius, size of an apartment in square meters, etc.—into one dimensionless **cardinal** quantitative scale. We sometimes call such dimensionless scales "Universal Score Function (USF)" and "worth" scales. An example is the ladder of "corruption indexes" which is defined on the interval < 0, 10 > and annually published by ***Transparency International*** [117; p.A13]. It is presented, together with detailed discussion, in **EXHIBIT A 10** in the Appendix.

A simple example of such a conversion table is seen below in **EXHIBIT 2.1**.

EXHIBIT 2.1: Conversion Table

Difficult Qualitative Assessment	Verbal Assessment	Quantitative Assessment Score
.....	Excellent	5
.....	Good	4
.....	Fair	3
.....	Poor	2
.....	Bad	1
.....	Worthless	0

2/6/3 Proxy

A proxy (or instrumental variable) for behavioral variables is a very important and useful tool in quantitative analyses of phenomena from the social, political and generally behavioral spheres of societal life. As we routinely discover causality, or the cause-and-effect chain, between people's behavior (mood, expectations etc.) and quantitative effects of their behavioral changes the need for a quantitative description of these changes is self-explanatory.

Take for example the case of tourism research. Tourism professionals on both sides of U.S.-Canada border would dearly love to forecast the numbers of tourists travelling in the future from one side to the other, and even more dearly love to predict their future spending in the country of destination. While the numbers of tourists and their spending are cardinal variables, tourism professionals know very well that there are hedonic and other behavioral phenomena (liking the place of destination, willingness to spend money etc.) that make them come and spend. To quantify this "willingness to come and spend" several basic factors have been identified, such as relative (to the other country) income level, relative cost of travel, and attraction level. These "proxy" factors and their indexes could then be combined and converted into ordinal scales in conversion tables. Subsequently, it was found that these ordinal scales correlated very well with historical time series of percentage changes of absolute values (i.e. numbers of tourists and spending per tourist). Thus, to map and explain the future behavior of tourists we need only forecast the trend of these basic "proxy" factors [72; pp.337-338].

Generally speaking, it is of paramount importance to quantify such behavioral or qualitative factors. On the other hand, to do that, and to do it well, is very difficult. Several methods have been devised to rectify this problem. This subject is touched upon in the Appendix, together with some basic algebraic tools and techniques.

2/6/4 Criterion of Tolerable Error Limit

The criterion of tolerable error limit in modeling social, socio-political and socio-economic phenomena is based on the quality of answers that a model of these phenomena produces rather than on certain absolute or even relative quantitative characteristics that the model features [72; pp.74-78]. The criterion thus reformulates the standard concept of errors in one-to-one mapping of social systems (into algebraic or graphic images) by emphasizing the functional usability or corroborating quality of the model instead.

For the sake of clarity we put it in algebraic terms: Suppose that we have mapped the "real world" RW by a graphical (or algebraic) image RW* and that there is, naturally, an inherent error E involved in the mapping or modeling of the real life phenomenon. We denote this implicit and logically necessary error E presented in the model RW* by [RW*, E].

Then we define the functional usability or credibility through the interval of E, < E_{min}, E_{max} >, and we say that that we do not mind any size of E_{max} as long as for any two states of real world RW1 < RW2 there holds RW*1 < RW*2 for its model. In which case the usability and/or credibility of the model is achieved and we call E_{max} the maximum tolerable error limit.

It is now clear that one possible scheme of estimating and mapping of the magnitude of risk of conflicts should follow the notion of conversion tables defined previously and the scheme of qualitative-to-quantitative-scale-conversion in the Appendix. If we can attach to each interval-model of the monotonically increasing sequence of risk-of-conflict growth an ordinal number, and if we can, furthermore, establish a one-to-one correspondence between these ordinal labels and a real-life sequence of socio-economic and socio-political crises in various generic societies (even if originally only verbally defined) then we have established a firm base on which we can build our paradigm.

2/6/5 Information Technology

Information Technology (IT) consists of basic electronics, computer technologies and high-tech communication technologies (e.g. Internet). These three branches of IT represent one of the main technological driving forces in the world today. Information Technology is a potential source of enormous progress (e.g. computer technology speeds up all mathematics-related functions) and major increase in well-being for the world population as Internet and e-mail enable the instant retrieval and exchange of information among a world-wide audience. These functional qualities of communication technologies offer the greatest contribution toward globalization.

Regarding the globalization trend, former Canadian Prime Minister Lester Pearson prophetically encapsulated the two sides of the trend more than half a century ago, as follows:

> An age when different civilizations will have to learn to live side by side in peaceful interchange, learning from each other, studying each other's history and ideals and art and culture, mutually enriching each other's lives. The alternative, in this crowded little world, is misunderstanding, tension, clash and catastrophe [121].

And sure enough, there are societies where the communication part of IT is not encouraged by the ruling classes. As an illustration, we read in an excerpt from *Newsweek* [82; p.45]:

> Chinese authorities are clamping down on the Internet. Last week they banned e-mail and Internet-chat mentions of vaguely defined "state secrets." Beijing also recently moved to ban "cyber reporters" and ordered all firms to provide details of their encryption software.

Also, the Internet (and any kind of website or e-mail) used to be banned for civilian use in Saudi Arabia together with TV satellite dishes. The reasons behind these rulings were, in both countries, reasonably clear. Population pressures, limited prospects for economic development, along with growing access to information, are making both societies much more restless. Thus, it is access to information which the rulers want to stop or, at least delay, at all costs.

However, with the latest IT technology, there are several different types of social media that can be integrated via social network aggregation (so important in the "Arab Spring" and other fast-organized social gatherings around the globe): collaborative projects (e.g. Wikipedia), blogs and microblogs (e.g. Twitter), content communities (e.g. YouTube), social networking sites (e.g. Facebook) whose technologies include blogs, picture-sharing, wall-postings, e-mail, instant messaging, music-sharing, crowd-sourcing and voice over IP, to name a few.

From Alvin Toffler, the prophet of *The Third Wave* (i.e. high-tech, inclusive of IT) revolution [92; pp.420-421] we hear:

> Circumstances differ from country to country, but what does not differ is the revolutionary challenge posed by the Third Wave to obsolete Second Wave institutions (inclusive of governments; M.K.)—too slow to keep up with the pace of change and too undifferentiated to cope with the new levels of social and political diversity. Designed for a much slower and simpler society, our institutions are ... out of synch ... this challenge ... strikes at the most basic assumption of Second Wave political theory: the concept of representation ... built to the wrong scale, unable to deal with interrelated problems, unable to keep up with the accelerated drive ... with a high level of diversity, the overloaded, obsolete political technology of the industrial age is breaking up under our very eyes.

For all the inherent problems IT presents to *recipients,* there is yet another issue that is a much more serious threat to *donor* societies. This is the strange milieu of computer viruses, and their purveyors, that presents a powerful example of the challenges that law enforcement faces in the era of computer crime. It is one thing that virtually anybody with sufficient skill can inflict multi-billion dollar damage on *donor* societies via the Internet which connects the global communication infrastructure. It is another thing altogether when we realize that this global communication infrastructure opens the door to virtually unlimited cyber-terrorism since the globalization of technology is not matched by "globalization" (or uniformity) of criminal laws, law enforcement, extradition treaties or even the global cooperation of Internet security experts.

As a result, such a cyber attack could be launched from the Third World *recipient* countries which do not have adequate criminal law, let alone computer criminal law. The possibility of such attacks or terrorist acts (with stratospheric damages attached) is getting greater all the time.

As powerful a tool as IT without a doubt may be, there are a lot of unwarranted over-optimistic hopes about this issue. In a recent article [105] we read for instance that:

> Instant and universal access to (the accumulated world knowledge; M.K.) ... will lead us, almost inevitably, into a new Renaissance.

To understand what this could mean let us start with the notion that *renaissance* has to do with intellectual rebirth and/or revival of the heights of the Ancient Greek or Roman cultural environments. Even if we forget the 15th century Renaissance goals, we still have three key words here: **intellect, culture,** and revival (i.e. **increase**). And all three have one common denominator that may be defined for short as *"minds that are able to cross and extend the current frontiers of knowledge and culture"* and we denote it by **M**.

Now, let us see how the ability "to access world knowledge instantly and universally" could help us to acquire this elusive **M**. We begin with Sir Karl Popper's eloquent definition of the (universal) problem-solving scheme [64; p.164]:

(2.7)   Original problem → tentative theory → error elimination
→ new problem.

Now, assuming that the *"original problem"* **comes from within the current knowledge** and culture niveau, then **we need M to formulate and/or formalize the (new)** *"tentative theory."* Unfortunately, Information Technology and the Internet cannot help us at all with this first causal chain simply because these tools need **M** to function; the opposite causality is not known to exist. Mouse clicking can and will help only with the *"error elimination"* part of the scheme. In fact, the faster it can eliminate false alternatives (based on false premises, false information etc.) the better. **But no *"new problem* (which is actually the pure M) will ever come from the scheme without a *"tentative theory"* which is totally independent of IT (inclusive of Internet) as we just said above.**

Chapter 3: Development of Society-Comparison Methodology

3/1 Introductory Remarks

Some two decades ago the socialist-cum-communist systems of (Eastern) Europe crumbled and the transition to democratic and free-market oriented societies began in earnest in those countries. Before that there had been numerous other (former Third World or developing) countries in the former colonies, as well as recent monarchies or oligarchies particularly in the Far East, that had also decided to go the free-market path. Numerous schemes to build functioning free-market systems have been tried. However, problems—in the spheres of economy, social fabric, welfare institutions and politics—have been slowly mounting there instead.

These problems started in the sphere of international finances. International financial activity involves risks of certain sorts that are nonexistent in domestic transactions, as we have briefly discussed in the definition of the inter-societal heterogeneity in the previous chapter. There are no international courts to enforce contracts—particularly not in the strongly intra-society heterogenized *recipient* countries where the rule of law is usually substituted by the law of jungle; which suits the ruling oligarchy just fine—and a bank cannot repossess a nation's collateral, because typically no collateral is pledged. Problem loans to sovereign governments [59; p.207] have received most of the "debt problem" publicity, but it is important to realize that loans to private firms can also become non-performing because of capital controls or exchange rate policies.

A typical example unfolded in China. There [124; p.9]:

> The National Audit Office found that $320 million of bank funds had been diverted ... through unlawful loans ... investigation revealed a pattern of mismanagement ... 'every bank in China has problems like this ... they are product of the system, and unless the system changes ... they won't disappear (said a Chinese banking expert).'

In the following source [124; p.7] we read:

> Why has there been such a monumental global misallocation of capital? ... The opponents of globalization have concentrated .... primarily on trade, labor and environmental issues. The problem (is however; stressed by M.K.) ... of excessive and unstable capital flows ... little has been done since the Asian crisis to address these ... the

capital market forces that brought recent US corporate debt disasters such as Global Crossing and Enron (two huge US corporations that have financially melted away; added by M.K.) are the same ones that earlier provided absurdly easy money both to Asian corporations and to the government of Argentina (which has financially melted away too; M.K.) ... but the easier it is to borrow, the more dangerous the eventual outcome ... in all these cases lending was driven more by the greed of the intermediaries than by the real need of a borrower ... overinvestment is a consequence both of easy access to borrowing and of warped view of globalization.

And so the loans, and hence cases of banks going bad, have multiplied. In the Czech Republic it all started with a spectacular crash of twelve banks in 1997; the same year in which sixteen banks crashed in Bulgaria [2]. Then Czech president Havel's observation about the *"lousy mood and gloom in our society"* [1] was subsequently superseded by the devaluation of the Czech Crown by 30% in summer 1998 [2]. In Russia the financial, economic and political crisis, culminating temporarily by summer 1998 with the devaluation of the Ruble by 34%, aptly summarized in the article "Could it lead to fascism" [3], seems to be just gathering and threatening to wipe out the world-wide banking system in the process.

After two or three years of IMF's frantic effort to plug the holes in the banking system the world over, a report from Ukraine [77] noted:

Amid a deepening economic crisis and allegation of misuse of international aid, Ukraine approached lenders (mostly IMF; added M.K.) here Monday with a proposal for a measure of relief on its crippling foreign debt.

Then there are two "doomsday" reports from the Czech Republic. The first [75] states:

The chairman of Komercni Banka AS (Commercial Bank Inc.; MK) of the Czech Republic has resigned during an investigation into suspected fraud at the ailing state-controlled bank, the largest in Central Europe ... the bank has accumulated some of its bad loans in the last two years ... but a greatest portion of its bad portfolio dates to the early and mid 1990s, when the bank was lending heavily to recently privatized companies and fledgling private businesses.

If this news was bad, the second one is truly frightening. It says [103; p.5] that the third largest bank in the country (IPB) collapsed and government under the threat of the subsequent economic meltdown (*"the deposits represent about one half of the national budget"*) has taken over the full responsibility for the bank's clients.

Enter the much "tigerized" neo-capitalist systems of south-east Asia, thought to be invincible ever since the early 1990s. But, all of the sudden, in the late 1990s all of them began reeling under severe currency crises—the onus of which is being invariably put on the banking sector—that has permeated into a fully fledged economic and eventually social and political crisis. Little wonder that even three years after the crisis in an article from February 14, 2000 [78; p.1], Michael Camdessus, then managing director of the IMF, saw the situation still so depressing as to announce:

> The world economy was showing many symptoms similar to those seen in East Asia before that region's recent economic crisis (in 1997-1998; M.K.), including a failure to take note of the reality of the situation.

The problems have, of course, systemic features and therefore almost constant duration. Alan Friedman writes in 2002 [123; pp.1,4]:

> Japan's huge debt, a dire economic condition, could, if it further deteriorates, trigger global financial instability ... this is the biggest risk to the global economy in 2002 ... there is a Himalaya of debt that is crushing the economy at a time of recession and deflation (put in K. Courtis, vice-chairman of Goldman Sachs) ... with total outstanding debt expected to reach 140% of GDP in fiscal 2000 ... Mr. Courtis also said: 'the level of debt makes Enron look like nothing.'

What is it, in both of these former colonial, lesser-developed, or communist countries, that has been causing the very same socio-economic disintegration in both, seemingly very different, types of societies? [4]

One possible explanation of the Asian problem is given in the following excerpt [5]:

> The command-and-control societies of Asia, designed to foster political stability and security during the cold war, are failing to manage today's fast-paced laissez-faire economies. And so they're being swept away.

Not only is the explanation far from satisfactory, it does not even exactly apply either to the Russian situation, where the government has been in no hurry to liberalize anything, or to the Czech situation where the government has been virtually preoccupied by the drive for laissez-faire economy since 1990.

In the context of these obviously dangerous threats to the world-wide banking system, let us examine the nature of the free-market society which so many diverse societies are unsuccessfully attempting to establish.

3/2 Theoretical Premises

3/2/1 Free Market Society Conjectures (FMSC)

Here, we introduce a collection of axiom-like excerpts from the literature on the free-market society. This collection forms a sort of causal-chain system with inputs, outputs, and necessary conditions for its functioning. We shall call such a system *"Free Market Society Conjectures"* **(FMSC). It will serve as the epistemological criterion on which we shall test our paradigm:**

(3.1) (Co-operative) society, however, cannot subsist among those who are at all times ready to hurt and injure one another [7].

(3.2) Opportunism is not a 'natural' trait of human behavior uniformly shared by individuals; it is a habit which can be reinforced or discouraged by the working of the (social) institutions [8]. Therefore: Corruption is the problem of systems (or societies; added M.K.) and not of individuals [55].

(3.3) Social institutions (are) ... spontaneously evolved interaction patterns, or rules, which by discovering and co-coordinating dispersed knowledge reduce the complexity faced by individuals enable them to co-ordinate their actions. These rules are largely implicit in that they contain the accumulated tacit knowledge of past generations [9], [4].

(3.4) The spontaneous order which the market achieves is a way of life which derives its energies and behavioral incentives from the right ownership, contractual freedom and a government under law [10], [4] ... a complex system of moral codes, rules of fairness, as well as an articulated system of punishment for the violators ... systems under which bad men can do least harm [11].

(3.5) Hence, whether a particular market exists and is stable depends on a learning process ... Unless people are given a chance to learn how to play the social roles of which market relations consist, no market society will be established [12].

(3.6) Exogenous changes (pushed by public decision- and policy-makers; added by M.K.) interfere with the constraints that are voluntarily arrived at when individuals are free to impose restriction upon themselves [13]. The result is a contraction in the social opportunity set [14]. The transition process via exogenous changes could not and did not deliver the goods [15].

Two separate scenarios can be derived from the FMSC:

(3.7) When the key condition **(3.5)**—learning process how to play the social roles of which market relations consist—holds, then a spontaneously evolving loop between **(3.5)** and **(3.3)**—implicit rules containing the accumulated tacit knowledge of past generations—that is a function of time, usually measured in terms of generations, enhances not only the state of **(3.4)**—a complex system of moral codes as well as a system of punishment for violators, a system under which bad men can do least harm—but also the ultimate criterion of success in **(3.1)**—co-operative society.

As this occurs, the spontaneous energies following from conjecture **(3.4)** marginalize opportunists and other elements harmful to the society.

(3.8) When condition **(3.5)**—learning process—is absent, then the social structure defined by interaction among conditions **(3.5)**, **(3.3)** and **(3.4)**—spontaneously achieved system of moral codes—will not work. Negative contents of criterion **(3.1)**—society that cannot subsist among those ready to hurt and injure one another—will then effectively inhibit and, perhaps, even destabilize the society. Then, substitution of **(3.6)**—exogenous changes (pushed by policy-makers) interfere with ... voluntarily arrived at social order—for the above interaction will probably jump-start the self-perpetuating and oligarchy-and-opportunism-strengthening loop between **(3.6)** and **(3.2)** leading to the same decay of the society. For the sake of clarity, we shall sketch the behavior of the two basic scenarios in EXHIBIT 3.1.

Here we must mention the most important element that alone can be responsible for turning a single society from a "democratic" to an "oligarchy-driven" one. Presumably the opposite development is possible too. However there have not been nearly as many cases of oligarchy-driven societies going genuinely democratic all of a sudden, i.e. **(3.8)** → **(3.7)** scenario-wise, as there have been cases of slide-down weak democracy to ruling-class rule. This means, in our notation, from scenario **(3.7)** to scenario **(3.8)**.

EXHIBIT 3.1: Learning Process Scenarios

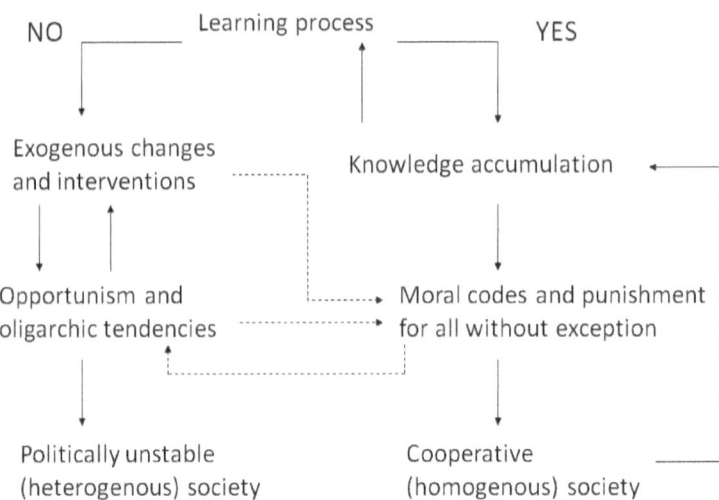

EXHIBIT 3.1 (above) explains it reasonably well: Clearly, if there is no accumulated previous knowledge and experience with democratic institutions, they must be brought in through exogenous intervention (and/or ruled in by the indigenous government). But this only jumpstarts the vicious circle of opportunism by which the oligarchy gets stronger still. The dashed line from "exogenous (power) intervention" → "moral codes and general punishment" and back to → "opportunism" just denotes the theoretical possibility, but real-life futility, of expecting the democracy can be installed by intervention from outside or through an already existing ruling class. Both these alternatives stand and fall on the all important social category **"moral codes, law and order and general punishment for all without exception."** However, the self-preservation ability of a ruling oligarchy would strongly fight any notion of being stripped of its various money-grabbing schemes. After all, in [167; p.26] we read:

> The transition to totalitarian rule is irrevocable, except in the case of some cataclysm like a world war.

Hence, the only alternative (for transitional societies) is to let an indigenous institution—substituting for the "knowledge accumulation"—that is strong, prestigious and morally, ethically and professionally enviable enough throughout the society to be able to install at least the basics of moral codes, ethical behavior and social roles into the society and thus short-circuit the long-time learning process that, under normal condition, contains the accumulated knowledge of past generations.

Thus, the above diagram only reiterates the axiomatic notion that the key and most important element of safekeeping democratic principles in the society is the unconditional adherence to, and enforcement of, the existing legal and judiciary system. In other words: to uphold *contractual freedom and government under law and a complex system of moral codes* partly learned from the past generations and partly enforced by the *system of punishment for all the violators without exception.*

One typical, almost too typical, example is the case of the German Weimar Republic after World War I. In one very influential and scholarly source [108; pp.94-95] we read:

> The failure of the duly elected government to build a new Army that would be faithful to its own democratic spirit and subordinate to the cabinet and the Reichstag was a fatal mistake for the Republic. ... the failure to clean out the judiciary was another ... administrators of the law became one of the centers of the counterrevolution, perverting justice for reactionary political ends.

This very "fatal mistake" triggered the wave of unlawful, not to mention antisocial, behavior that consequently polarized the previously homogenous society. In fact, so much so that Hitler's Nazi party then came to power with a simple program of stopping the drastic increase of intra-societal heterogeneity and installing law and order.

3/2/2 Mapping Societies' Scenarios of Self-preservation

Now, we shall dig a little deeper into individual societies' ideas of self-preservation and longevity.

As we said at the beginning, there are societies with various degrees of political, cultural, ethical, social, and epistemological and cognitive backgrounds and trends. Also, based on those differences, they have different levels of general and particular knowledge of current science and economics, technical know-how and practical modern schooling that is much needed in today's technology-based world. In our parlance stemming from **DEFINITION 2.1** they are all **inter-societal heterogeneous**.

The Crucial Challenge for International Aid

In fact, the following statement by Rubens Ricupero [79; p.5] says it all:

> Countries find themselves at extremely different vantage points as they attempt to achieve coherence or to promote universal aspirations. One should not lose sight of this extraordinary variety of conditions and inequality of assets.

Their differences notwithstanding, they all have **one thing in common: the inherent goal to survive**.

Given this inherent goal of every society to survive, we shall find that at one time or another some societies are supplementing their lack of all-important assets and are spontaneously developing what is described in conjecture **(3.4)** as a **"spontaneously derived ... system of moral codes ... of fairness and punishment for violators under which bad men can do least harm"** by means of increased exogenous controls and central economic policy decision-making.

In other words, we are assuming (with more than a little conviction, given the extensive discussion of two basic sets of socio-political conditions defined in the criterion statements **(3.7)** and **(3.8)**) that every society can be allocated onto the ladder of two clashing socio-political environments: **LEGITIMACY** (of the democratic society) **vs. OLIGARCHY** as defined in the two criteria **(3.7)** and **(3.8)** (see [52]).

Clearly, these ladders of qualitative or, better still, socio-political behavioral phenomena (**OLIGARCHY** and **LEGITIMACY**) have to be mapped or numerically classified and compared. Thus, we invoke conversion-table **DEFINITION 2.9** and qualitative-to-quantitative-scale-conversion scheme **(2.6)**. Also, for the sake of simplicity, we postulate that the levels of these phenomena would be on the interval of ordinal numerals from 1 through 10; i.e. 1, 2, 3, ... 10.

Next, we postulate (in **ASSUMPTION 3.1** below) that the self-preservation goal of every society calls for maximizing of the criterion premise—such that its sum (i.e. value of the given society's Y-axis scale *plus* value of the same society's X-axis scale) would have to come close or equal to 10—we shall deal with societies with **LEGITIMACY** scale equal to 9 and the **OLIGARCHY** scale equaling 1; the same two scales at 8 and 2; 7 and 3; 6 and 4; ... 2 and 8; and finally 1 and 9.

But first, we shall borrow a "polity viability chart" [16], seen in **EXHIBIT 3.2**, as a first step in quantification. It is immediately apparent that the "polity viability chart" provides quite an interesting allocation of societies-countries along the two extreme poles of the political spectrum.

EXHIBIT 3.2: Polity Visibility Chart

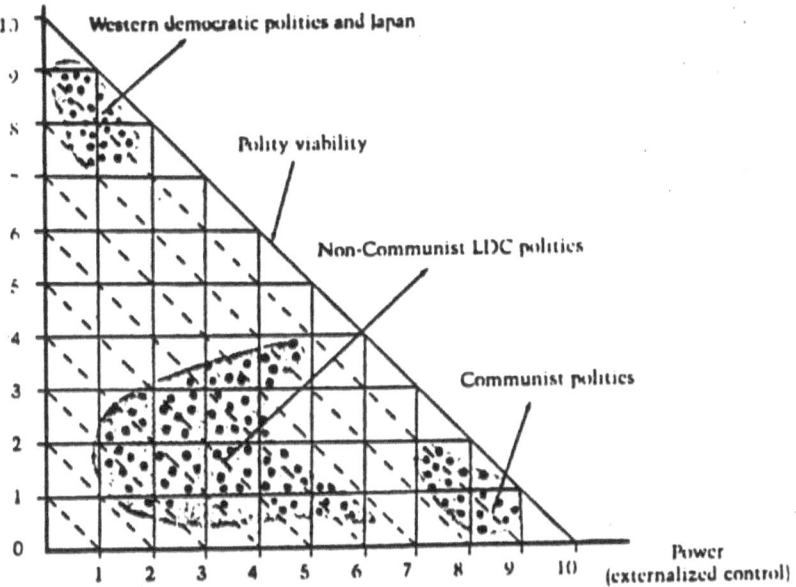

On the one side, we recognize the typical (almost **classical**, relative to the societies in the current world) democracies as we know them in the West. We shall call such political entities "**LEGITIMATE**" (political entities) and they are bunched on the upper end of the vertical ordinal scale which is labeled "**LEGITIMACY**."

On the other side, we recognize the power-hungry dictatorships in the part of the rest of the world where **POWER** (and/or **EXTERNALIZED CONTROL**) is the only thing that matters. Thus, the "hungriest" ones are bunched along the end of the ordinal scale labeled "**POWER**" or "**EXTERNALIZED CONTROL**."

There are two problems with the graph in **EXHIBIT 3.2**. First of all, the graph sees the ideal allocation of individual societies on the straight line intersecting two perpendicular scales only. This may not matter that much, as we know a lot of graphical and numerical methods in economics (e.g. linear programming etc.) that borrow linear functions to map the society. The second problem is, however, more serious. The **POWER** and **LEGITIMACY** rankings of individual countries were originally assigned impressionistically by the author of reference [16] and, even at that, for Cold War societies only.

The main element of the idea of bi-axial ranking is, however, very sound and we shall build on it. It is not only sound, but, because of its obvious attractiveness in capturing the seemingly complicated societal mapping in two-dimensional space, it is also very handy. We shall, therefore, start with the scenarios derived earlier on in the text.

As we have postulated in scenarios **(3.7)** and **(3.8)**, every single society can be ranked according to two basic and, also, contradictory criteria: **"traditional legitimacy of the democratic free-market society"** (as in scenario **(3.7)**) and **"exogenous control of society by a power-wielding group"** (discussed in scenario **(3.8)**).

We shall now adapt the Polity Viability Chart in **EXHIBIT 3.2** for our purpose by adding several assumptions and propositions:

ASSUMPTION 3.1:
Assume that every society, in its quest for survival, inherently strives to maximize its polity viability index which is—for simplicity and to follow the scales in EXHIBIT 3.2—an integer from the interval 1 through 10. The index consists of "legitimacy" L part defined on the Y-axis and of "power (or exogenous control)" P part defined on the X-axis.

To translate **ASSUMPTION 3.1** into simple and easily understood terms, let us assume that integer 10 is the maximum possible numerical level of the overall sum of rankings on the axes **LEGITIMACY** and **POWER**. As we set the integer 10 to be the maximum of the sum on both axes, we have inherently assumed that a certain part (say **LEGITIMACY** on the vertical scale) can be expressed by a positive integer (eventually by a simple fraction) from the interval 0 to 10, and thus the conversion table would be able to make a direct conversion between the ordinal and cardinal variable, explained in [52; Ch.3] and discussed briefly in the Appendix.

As we can see in **EXHIBIT 3.2**, some of the examples of "Communist Polities" feature the level between 0 + 1 on the **LEGITIMACY** scale and around 9 on the **POWER** scale; the sum being very close to 10. (**NOTE:** The conversion tables, their merit and some examples can be seen in the Appendix.)

For example, in the conversion table it is easy to equate 10 percent (i.e. 1 on the scale with maximum integer = 10) of **LEGITIMACY** to *"VERY LOW LEVEL OF LEGITIMACY"* once the proper conversion table is brought forward (as it will be in the next chapters).

Now, we have to tackle this practical and virtually ever-present problem of graphical mapping in **ASSUMPTION 3.1**. The assumption claims that **every society by definition strives to maximize its political viability index.**

The graphical image is quite clear.

The theory of maximized bi-variate space in the linear programming exercise usually calls the straight edge going through the farthest point (from the origin) on the *per-(linear)-parts* the parabolically defined image of the possible solutions.

Thus, the inherent proposition puts all sub-optimal solutions inside the triangle formed by the straight edge and axes X and Y. A typical example can be seen in [43].

In **ASSUMPTION 3.2** we have used this maximized bi-variate solution—that means, the set of straight edges—for every single investigated society and we say:

ASSUMPTION 3.2:
To maximize its polity viability index, every society and its social, political and socio-political environment strives to put its image, a point, on a straight edge intersecting Y and X axes, while any point inside the triangle formed by two axes and a straight edge signals a sub-optimal index. For the same reason, these straight edges then form an envelope for a hyperbolic curve D, seen in EXHIBIT 3.3 and EXHIBIT 3.4, representing an abstract continuum [17].

As **EXHIBIT 3.3** (below) sketches the first important step in the way of mapping of individual societies according to their complex socio-economic, social, socio-political environment, following scenarios **(3.7)** and **(3.8)** and the idea of biaxial ranking of Polity Viability Chart, **we should be able to allocate virtually every single society's political and socio-political conditions on the hyperbolic curve** similar to that in **EXHIBIT 3.3**.

For the sake of convenience we shall present—at this point without accompanying methodology, which will be added later—the D-curve with 9 points on it (the tenth point is on the X-axis) in **EXHIBIT 3.4**. By doing so, we have acquired a reasonably good stepping stone for any possible comparative-analytical method.

EXHIBIT 3.3: Scheme of Constructing a Hyperbolic D-Curve

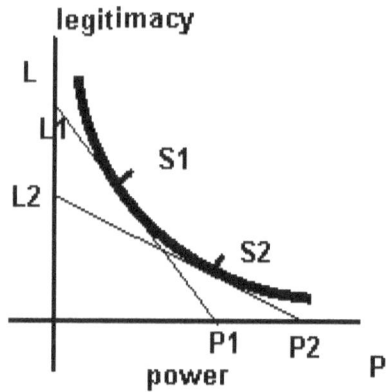

For any such future function, and particularly for the sake of being able to add analyses of economic conditions into the picture, we shall now show **that any society's allocation on curve D is unique.**

EXHIBIT 3.4: Envelope for Hyperbolic Curve D

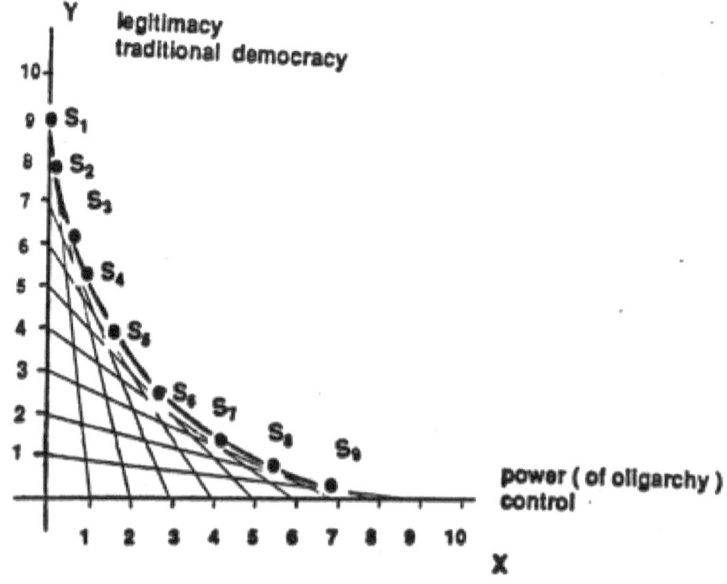

PROPOSITION 3.1:
We claim that the necessary and sufficient condition for a unique definition of social, political, socio-political and socio-economic environment of the i-th (investigated) society is that there exists a point S_i on curve D in which the tangent from the non-zero end points of line segments OL_i, OP_i touch hyperbolic curve D, where OL_i ... is a measure of "legitimacy of traditional democracy" on the scale of Y-axis and OP_i ... is a measure of "power (or exogenous control)" on the scale of X-axis. Thus S_i represents the i-th society and such a representation is unique.

PROOF: The uniqueness follows from **ASSUMPTION 3.1** transforming the basic grid of **EXHIBIT 3.1** in **EXHIBITS 3.2** and **3.3**, where $OL_i + OP_i = 10$. Within the two-dimensional space of axes Y and X, let us assume that there are two sets of measures, $(OL_1 \neq OL_2)$, $(OP_1 \neq OP_2)$, i.e. two different socio-economic environments, that yield one representation, say, S_1. But that would be tantamount to saying that a continuous function $y = f(x)$ can have two different derivatives at one single point. This contradiction furnishes the proof.

LEMMA 3.1:
If, for some reason, we are not able to estimate rank, or access the level of "legitimacy" as the length of segment OL_i, i = 1...m on the Y-axis in EXHIBIT 3.3, we can substitute it by estimating the inverse ranking of the "power" or "oligarchy" segment OP_i on the X-axis.

PROOF: Follows from **PROPOSITION 3.1** and its proof.

3/2/3 Socio-Economic Propositions

PROPOSITION 3.1 and **LEMMA 3.1** have only one goal. They are expected to define the unique social, political and socio-political conditions of an investigated society. Also, each of the investigated societies—which could be taken as a generic model of the group of countries with the same intra-society homogeneity—has been allocated a point on a two-dimensional graph. And since the graph in **EXHIBIT 3.3**, and each point on it, visually represents social, cultural and political aspects of one generic society, we have all of a sudden acquired a criterion (and a measure) by which we can assess and compare real-world societies if and when they interact.

It is now time to introduce socio-economic factors into the mosaic and see how and whether something meaningful can be said about them and their interrelation with the political ones. Also on the agenda is the validity assessment of these preliminary theses and, and at long last, what exactly can be done to support the propositions with hard data.

PROPOSITION 3.2:
Let the external and negative economic pressure be constant for several investigated societies (all represented by points Si, i = 1...m in EXHIBIT 3.4). Then, the ensuing socio-economic and socio-political disruptions—we shall call this, for simplicity, CHAOS—worsen with increasing of intra-societal heterogeneity in these societies (i.e. lessening of the traditional democratic values).

PROOF: Let: 1) the "traditional democratic values" (see e.g. in [4]) be denoted by **DEM**; 2) the "external (negative) economic pressure" be denoted by **PRE**; 3) the "worsening of socio-political environment," tantamount to "increase of opportunism, nepotism and oligarchy" (in [5], [18]), be denoted by **OLI**; and 4) the "worsening of chaos and destabilization in a society" [19]—where one of the most probable cause of the 'worsening' is explained in notion **(2.1)** in Chapter 2—which is tantamount to negative contents of criterion **(3.2)**, be denoted by **CHAOS**. From scenarios **(3.1) - (3.2)** the following functional relations can be formally presented:

(3.9)   OLI = f [(1/ DEM); PRE], where PRE is constant.

(3.10)   CHAOS = f [(OLI, PRE); DEM], where DEM is constant.

Then, from **(3.9)**, **(3.10)** we have:

(3.11)   CHAOS = F [f (PRE/DEM)] and for any constant PRE the proposition clearly holds.

This proposition has been, in its simple practicality, essentially from day one on the mind of every monarch or ruling class in virtually every society in the world. As "democratic principles" could be substituted, in yesteryears, by "avoiding chaos and/or keeping the society in political calm and happiness," all kinds of socio-political tools have been used throughout human history to achieve just this. Ancient Rome's *panem et circenses* ("bread and circuses") and the Third (i.e. Hitler's) Reich's ***Kraft durch Freude*** ("strength through joy") are just two examples of such policies.

PROPOSITION 3.3:
Let two societies be defined by points S_i, $S_{(i+k)}$, k = 1...(m-2), on the D-curve in EXHIBIT 3.3 and assume that both societies are subject to the same-intensity external negative economic pressure (PRE). Then the society whose point is located down and/or to the right of the defining point of the other society on the D-curve will end up with greater socio-economic and socio-political disarray, eventually CHAOS.

PROOF: Let us start with **EXHIBITS 3.2** and **3.3** and assume that point $S_{(i+k)}$, $k = 1\ldots(m-2)$, denotes the society whose socio-economic and socio-political disarray is less than the one featured by the society denoted by S_i, while the external economic pressure is the same on both. From **PROPOSITION 3.1** it follows that the tangent to curve D at $S_{(i+k)}$ intersects "legitimacy" on the Y-axis at some point, say $L_{(i+k)} \neq L_i$, and for the ensuing segments holds

(3.12) $\qquad OL_{(i+k)} > OL_i$,

where L_i is the intersect of the tangent at S_i (on hyperbola D) with Y-axis and O is the origin. But then inequality **(3.12)** contradicts **PROPOSITION 3.2** and the proof then follows from Rasch's conjecture in [20].

There is much more to add to these last two propositions. We can, for example, use the definitional point of a certain i-th investigated society, S_i, as the approximate definitional point of another society, say k-th, about which we are only certain that exogenous shocks or inputs will have caused similar effects in its socio-economic environment. This is a very useful feature of the D-curve and one-point-models of societies on the slide curve. It follows from what we assumed in the previous paragraph, that the **host of "generic" societies (i.e. those with the same or similar intra-societal homogeneity) can be represented by one point on the "slide" curve D**. To formalize this feature we can, perhaps, put forward the following proposition that stems from **DEFINITION 2.13** (in Chapter 2) and is also known as the "criterion of tolerable error limits" in the suspect data-bases of social, political and economic systems.

PROPOSITION 3.4:
Let us assume that we have well researched and thoroughly investigated a one-point-model of a society, S_i, and that its location on the D-curve (in EXHIBIT 3.3) is well-founded and final. Just for this exercise we will distinguish between a real-world society S_i and its model $S_i{}^*$ on the D-curve. Assume now that we have another society S_{i+k}, $k = 1\ldots n$, $n \neq m$, about which we do not know much except that at least two major exogenous shocks (or inputs) of certain magnitude but, generally, different direction have solicited effects, denoted by ' and ", that might be denoted as

(3.13) $\qquad S_{i+k}{}' < S_{i+k} < S_{i+k}{}''$

Now, if the similarly strong or the same strength, shocks (inputs) of the same direction produce similar, or the same, effects in the thoroughly investigated society S_i, we find

(3.14) $\qquad S_i{}' < S_i < S_i{}''$

we say that

(3.15) $S_i^* \cong S_{i+k}^*$

and thus that both societies should occupy the same (or nearly the same) location on the D-curve.

PROOF: Suppose that the two societies react to the same (or similar) inputs the same way, i.e. inequalities **(3.13)**, **(3.14)** hold, but that **(3.16)** $S_i^* \neq S_{i+k}^*$. Since their equality would mean that we cannot "model" (denoted by * in **(3.15)**) the real society in a unique way (i.e. two different "modeling points" can describe two societies that behave the same). But if **(3.13)** and **(3.14)** hold then we can freely interchange and/or substitute society S_{i+k} for society S_i and then contradiction between the free interchange and/or substitution and **(3.16)** yields the proof. (**NOTE:** Detailed proof of the Criterion of Tolerable Error Limit, defining the interval of generic societies on D-curve and subsequent discussion, can be found in [72; pp.77-78]).

3/3   Conclusions from the Model of Free Market Society

First, this preliminary model has brought the analytical theory, epitomized by the different allocation of definitional points-images on the D-curve, close to the real world situation. We are reminded of this by the following excerpt [79; p.5]:

> Countries find themselves at extremely different vantage points … one should not lose sight of this extraordinary variety of conditions and inequality of assets.

It is right here where one feels that the axiomatic laissez-faire of Adam Smith would have to be amended, and perhaps outright suspended, whenever there is a question of any economic-cum-political deal being negotiated between inter-societal heterogeneous societies. Whenever we have two countries functioning under different socio-economic and socio-political scenarios, such as the proverbial "democracy" in **(3.7)** and "oligarchy" in **(3.8)**, conflict is virtually inevitable. The question is only how great it would be, not whether it would come at all.

Because the *recipient* state (represented by the ruling oligarchy) is the sole economic, banking and political entity of the society, while the political interests in *donor* societies may be different from that of its own "financial-economic" entities, we feel that there is every reason to allow the 'visible hand' of the state or, better still, collective hand of *donor* societies, to shield both societies from potential disasters. One of such disasters may be a social political uprising in the *recipient* society, first against its own government which allowed the economic crisis to happen in the first place, and then—in terms of 'finding the culprits'—against the ***donor*** society represented by the donor entity. This sudden appearance of unexpected political crisis may freeze any other planned deals between both countries for a long time.

Therefore, somewhere around this juncture, we should start suggesting what data-bases, quantitative and qualitative variables and factors, techniques of both behavioral and social psychology and management science—such as: technique of rational decision-making or optimization theory, theory of collective behavior, etc.—might also be incorporated into the study. This would permit their technical support to yield feasible and practical techniques that could alleviate the critical problems emerging from interaction of the two inter-societal heterogeneous countries' interactions.

However, at this point we feel that we should recapitulate and discuss the main points of the presented algebraic apparatus in plain language first.

Let us, for the sake of easier comprehension, henceforth use for the D-curve in EXHIBIT 3.4 the following synonyms: SLIDE, slide curve D, or just D.

Also, assume for the moment that uniqueness of allocation of both originally investigated societies or, more generally, socio-economic entities S_i, $S_{(i+1)}$, and, hence, every other investigated society or entity on that slide-like-curve is fixed. From all of the presented assumptions, propositions, lemmas etc. the following axiom follows:

AXIOM 3.1
The higher the given society (i.e. its "point" image) resides on the hyperbolic curve D the more it is indifferent (not to say 'impervious') to negative economic pressures caused by one-off economic disruptions or shocks.

In the already mentioned source [79; p.5] we read:

> We have learned a hard lesson: that development will not necessarily make countries less vulnerable to external shocks ... one of the key challenges is the search for coherence between the external economic environment and domestic policies ... the notion that efficient and honest government, human rights, investment in human resources, and a healthy environment (which are the attributes of countries high-up on the D-curve; M.K.) are all indispensable to a sustainable development strategy (and, again, one visible attribute of high-up D-curve residents; M.K).

From AXIOM 3.1 it also follows that:
If two societies (or entities) reside at two different points on the D curve (e.g. Si, S(i+k)) and both are subject to the same external negative economic pressure—again, caused by unexpected economic shocks, meltdowns, overall

crises etc.—then the society whose defining point on the D curve (in EXHIBIT 3.3) is located down and to the right (i.e. S(i+k)) of the comparable society's point (Si) must end up with greater socio-economic disarray (eventually CHAOS).

However, the above theorems open the door not only to the comparison of two different societies; the reverse is also possible. Once we have established the location of one particular society on the slide-curve D, we can use the location of the point-model as an approximate location of any inter-societal homogeneous society-country. We have said that such a "generic" (used instead of "similar") society has similar historical roots and historical trends and, above all, reacts to shocks and exogenous inputs of the same magnitude and the same direction in the same (or similar) way as the original well-researched and investigated society. This is important. Let us show this feature in a real-life example.

Martin Khor writes [85]:

Some countries gain more than others from liberalization and ... globalization creates losers as well as winners ... some poor countries have stagnated or slid backwards during this era.

Needless to say, the above preliminary theorems provide an ideal base for comparison of two different societies and/or entities. What we need is some conversion table that would translate the graphical differences of two points on the hyperbole-slide D into, first, cardinal-numerical quantity and, eventually, into a risk-of-conflict qualifier pertinent to the resulting difference between the ***donor*** and ***recipient*** societies.

There are several countries in Central (or East-Central) Europe that are in transition to becoming democratic and market-oriented. These are: Czech Republic, Slovak Republic, Poland, Hungary, Romania, Ukraine, Bulgaria, and elements of the former Yugoslavia: Slovenia, Croatia, Serbia, Montenegro and Bosnia and Herzegovina [83]; all former COMECON countries. Suppose our in-depth investigation started with the Czech Republic, about which we have obtained detailed socio-economic, socio-political and social information. The professional conclusion is that virtually all the problems in this country and society stem from "continuity" of the law that had been made and upheld during the communist phase of this society, i.e. until 1989, while no transfer of either law or enforcement capability of the public sector (from some Western model-society) has ever been attempted. Therefore, armed with that knowledge, we can simply check an unknown transitional country in the block, say the Slovak Republic. If we find the same, say economic and political, problems [77;

p."Europe"] then we need only search for one other additional piece of information: What has happened to Slovakia's legal system?

If we find similar "continuation of the pre-transitional (i.e. communist) law system" as in the Czech Republic (and find it, we did [77; p."Europe"]), we know that the point-model of Slovak society must be located in the immediate vicinity of the Czech model-point on the D-curve.

It goes without saying that **if the two societies are intra-societal homogeneous they will be sharing a single (or similar) location on the D-curve "SLIDE."** And all of that holds despite the obvious higher standard of living in Czech Republic; standard of living in itself is not a factor that would keep any society from socio-economic and socio-political, sometimes brutal, slide-down.

After all is said and done we should, perhaps, close this chapter with a real example of scenario **(3.8)** from a transitional society we already mentioned: the Czech Republic. It tells the story of "oligarchic" tendencies and practices—not in some former Third World Country but in a highly-educated society with reasonably long-reaching pre-second-world-war democratic traditions with which the society had, theoretically, embraced the free-market ideology ten years ago—succinctly enough. As the society moved formally from the rank of COMECON countries of Central Europe in 1989 to become a free-market democracy (with all the trappings and trimmings of a sovereign state) **it forgot to novelize the old communist-induced legal system and its transparency, particularly the substantive law**, to go with the private ownership. (**NOTE:** The jury is still out on the cause: whether by reason of mental sloth of the Czech intelligentsia or by design of well entrenched communists in parliament and other high offices).

Consequently, for ten years the oligarchy—former communist bosses, former high-ranked secret police officers and former communist state and district attorneys (i.e. the people with best contacts, monetary reserves and information)—has been using the law of the jungle there to hoard big industrial firms, banks and real estate by cheating and outright theft, all under the watchful eyes of a "too understanding" bill of rights.

Actually, this is nothing other than the causality of **PROPOSITION 3.2** that has already been discussed in the previous chapter and denoted by causal chains **(2.1)** and **(2.2)**. Let us now return to the oligarchy's dealings. Because of the essential importance of the causalities of their combined action, we shall present them here as **(3.17) - (3.18)**, where

(3.17)   < (>) economic crisis → < (>) socio-political crisis

55

and where < denotes "increasing" and > denotes "decreasing."

This refers to the problems of the (third-world) developing societies with reigning oligarchies that "re-route" the societies' wealth into their accounts and the subsequent deep-seated grievances and hopelessness among the masses they were trying to alleviate by various policies. History is full of them.

Various monarchs and governments have dealt with this problem ever since the time of the Pharoahs. Several examples follow. In medieval times Charles IV, the Roman Emperor in the 14th century, initiated large public projects, mostly roads and fortifications where the masses of poorest citizens worked for meager wages and food. In modern history it was the American president Franklin D. Roosevelt whose economic program, called the New Deal, paid for with federal sources was designed to stave off the post-1929 economic crisis in the US. At the same time Adolf Hitler, the newly elected German chancellor, solved mass unemployment in Germany by generating huge national infrastructure projects (mostly modern highways of which most are still in service) and, of course, the armament industry. In [108; p.357] we read:

> Nazi economic policies ... were devoted largely to putting the unemployed back to work by means of greatly expanded public works and the stimulation of private enterprise. Government credit was furnished by the creation of special unemployment bills, and tax relief was generously given to firms which ... increased employment.

The devil's spiral following causality **(3.17)** starts with a simple economic crisis which gets worse to the point of society's revolting (arrow from left to the right hand side). At this point the intelligentsia starts emigrating to more homogeneous, and therefore stable, societies—as discussed in **(2.2)**—making the economic crisis even worse. This is denoted by the second causality in **(3.18)**:

(3.18) > (<) Intra-society heterogeneity → > (<) socio-political crisis →

→ > (<) major economic crisis → civil uprising (riots)

where, again, sign > stands for "decrease." The same, unfortunately, holds for "increase" with the opposite sign in the parentheses (<).

At this point the spill-over effect to the *donors*—consisting of the parts of the *recipient* societies, which are, for all we know, heterogeneous in relation to the *donors'* societies—takes place. As causality **(3.18)** is in effect tantamount to **PROPOSITION 3.2**, and **PROPOSITION 3.3** holds too, the following proposition, examining history, might be very useful for understanding current events.

PROPOSITION 3.5:
Suppose that the above causality (3.18)—in which > (<) intra-society heterogeneity → > (<) socio-political crisis → > (<) economic crisis → > (<) CHAOS, and where the sign > stands for "decrease," the opposite sign in brackets (<) holds for "increase," and → stands for "yields"—generally holds in every society, then the emergence of any new strata (or religion) in the society would destabilize and hence increase the historical level of intra-society heterogeneity and, thus, bring even greater socio-economic disarray and chaos into the society.

PROOF: Follows from **PROPOSITIONS 3.2 - 3.3** and the reversed causality (3.18).

Historical and most recent examples of **LEMMA 3.1** abound. Oliver Cromwell's Puritans vs. Cavaliers in 17th century England; European medieval kings fighting against independent highway robbers-knights and their pillaging bands and, also, against too independent aristocrats; French kings battling (and evicting) Huguenots in 16th-17th century France etc. One of the most recent examples is best summed-up by the caption [159]: *"The jailing of Russia's richest citizen* (Mikhail Khodorovsky by Russian president Vladimir Putin; note by M.K.) *could be a chilling sign that its brief experiment with capitalism has gone awry."* Nothing could be further from the truth here. Mr. Khodorovsky's money was being used for his own political ambitions and—inasmuch as president Putin, relatively successfully, homogenized and "politically tamed" the Russian society—he could not afford to let the Russian Federation slip into another political and, following that, economic chaos, as source [160] explains very clearly.

Unfortunately, all monarchs, oligarchs and governments are not enlightened. Because of their hunger for political and economic power the ruling classes have been stepping up the quest for absolute monopoly in both these areas. This accomplishes two effects: (a) it keeps bringing the country down on the "sliding curve" D, and (b) at the same time, it increases the general discontent and lost expectations in a society which is now on the brink of collapse. The society rebels and the circle is now complete and ready for another round. That the whole poisoned socio-economic and socio-political environment could be credited almost solely to this ruling oligarchy (see [22; p.2], [2; pp.17-19], [15; p.117] and [75; p."Europe"]) is beyond any doubt by now.

There is one other, and by far the most dangerous, by-product of this slide. It starts when the country is in deep socio-economic and socio-political crisis and sliding down. The indigenous oligarchy immediately begins to accuse the ***donor(s)*** of sabotaging the social, economic and cultural (read current political) fabric of the given society. The spin is to show "the plot" by ***donors*** to impose their values and institutions on the society and in the process to destroy the rest of the society's still functioning socio-political environment.

This description of events resembles the scenario [16; p.54] that originally defined a Third-World society (and pretty much fits the problem defined and discussed above in criterion **(3.8)**):

> The deterioration of all local values and institutions, including those at the grass roots, as a result of contact with the developed free-market societies, which makes people care primarily for the economic, material aspect of life; and leadership's lack of ... power to avoid or mitigate this deterioration or substitute viable values and institutions.

A far more serious conclusion can be made about the investigated transitional country and about the validity of the **PROPOSITIONS** presented above. Deep growing poverty (remember the society is sliding down along curve D) and a sense of hopelessness eventually become the breeding ground for international terrorism.

From **PROPOSITIONS 3.2** and **3.3**, we can claim that the society in the said country (where democratic traditions and pretty much a classless society were the norm for twenty years before the World War II) should, sooner or later, start showing signs of increasing alienation between the society at large and the state along the causal chain **(2.1)**. Here the state is shorthand for government, governmental institutions and the 'ruling' class (oligarchy).

Sure enough, in reality a new pattern of social movement has been detected in that society in the last few years. At least two petitions, originating from among the society's intellectual and student environments, calling for the voluntary demise of members of the council of ministers, both chambers of parliament and some other high officials of important governmental institutions, has officially been circulating among the people. The significance is not that these petitions have surfaced at all, it lies in the fact that they have been endorsed and duly signed by hundreds of thousands people in the country's capital and major cities alone.

Such is the predictive quality of **PROPOSITION 3.4**—derived, just as the above mentioned **PROPOSITIONS 3.2** and **3.3**, from the cause-and-effect "sliding feature" of the societies' images on the D-curve—that the very same society's sentiment is reported to emanate from an East Asian country, where socio-political (if not necessarily socio-cultural) conditions are very similar. The country is South Korea and Don Kirk reports from Seoul [81] under the headline "In South Korea, a Quiet Revolution":

> Viewed as the most significant political movement in South Korea in more than a decade, the civic action campaign appears to be an overwhelming success among citizens fed up with entrenched and elitist politicians filling many of the seats in the 299-person Assembly. The citizens' coalition has blacklisted more than 100 politicians, including 67 who hold Assembly seats and more than 40 others regarded as backstage figures that might influence the outcome of the election.

Thus, according to **PROPOSITION 3.4**, the reverse proof has just put South Korea's definitional point S_i on the D-curve in the very near vicinity of (if not exactly on the same spot as) the definitional point of the originally investigated country. The fact that both countries come not only from different parts of the world but also from very different historical backgrounds has no bearing on the current socio-economic and socio-political similarities, a phenomenon we call inter-societal homogeneity.

3/4 Statistical Interpretation of Real-Life Data

3/4/1 Introduction

The first author served with European Commission's TACIS Programmes in Central Asia and knows a great deal about the NIS states too. Therefore for further confirmation of both **PROPOSITIONS 3.2** and **3.4** and causal chain relations **(3.17)** and **(3.18)** we have chosen several Central Asian and Trans-Caucasian countries. We might also add that personal experience and polling of opinion and expectations of many indigenous professionals in all five countries is meshed with the NGO's data-bases and information.

Since exact quantitative assessment of either the strength of oligarchy—alternatively the weakness of democracy (eventually market-oriented economic base)—or the trend of the standard of living in the investigated countries is impossible, we have to use ranking instead. Therefore, non-parametric statistical methodology—in our case, the classic *Pearson Rank-Correlation Statistics*—will substitute for standard parametric treatment.

3/4/2 Discussion of Methodology

For the ranking of independent (centrist tendency of oligarchy) factors and dependent ones—trends of living standards and **life satisfaction in a society relatively free of corruption, nepotism and persecution for one's success**, while the extension of the living standard by the "life satisfaction" (for a long time assumed to be a major behavioral "moving factor" in both developed and developing societies; as seen in [215])—we use information from several published sources ([149], [150], and [155]), personal experience and polls introduced by the author to intellectual elite in each investigated country. The definitions of both variables' ranks are as follows:

Rank 1 denotes the local oligarchy's, quasi-ruler's or ruling clique's absolute power; rank 2 denotes somewhat lesser centrist tendencies; up to rank 6, which denotes the shared rule with several other important parts of the investigated society. Subsequently, we have assigned the following ranks to individual countries: Turkmenistan with rank 1, Uzbekistan and Azerbaijan sharing second place and, hence, they co-rank at 2.5, Kazakhstan 4, and Kyrgyzstan, Tajikistan and Georgia with co-rank of 6.

EXHIBIT 3.5: Individual Countries Ranking

State (Republic)	Living Standard	Oligarchy
Azerbaijan	2.5	2.0
Georgia	6.0	4.5
Kazakhstan	4.0	5.5
Kyrgyzstan*	4.0	5.5
Tajikistan	6.0	5.5
Turkmenistan	1.0	2.0
Uzbekistan	2.5	2.0
	Pearson r_p = 0.83	

NOTE*: In March 2005, Kyrgyzstan exhibited some sort of a "bloodless clannish revolution" augmented by American activists—in reality nothing more than a chance for another "shift" of professional politicians to get to power—in which then president Akayev fled the country. Since the political situation has been clearly a part of the US policy to rob Russia of its traditional influence in Central Asia (see [174], [175]) with no change in the domestic political scene, there is no reason to change the ranking at all.

Tabulation of the above rankings is seen in **EXHIBIT 3.5**, together with the resulting Pearson correlation coefficient **rP** = 0.83 shown in the last row. This causal-chain correlation is quite significant, with P ϵ <0.02, 0.01>. A detailed discussion of rank-correlation methodology is provided in the Appendix and by Maurice Kendall [153].

Improvement (or decrease) of the given country's **living standard and good mood for the society to try its best in workers' productivity** ranked similarly from: 1 (sharp decrease), 2 (somewhat slighter decrease), to ... 5 (most improved). The assessment of this factor leads to the following assignation: Uzbekistan and Turkmenistan co-rank at 1.5, Azerbaijan at 3, Kyrgyzstan and Georgia co-rank at 4.5, and Tajikistan and Kazakhstan co-ranking at 5.5.

3/4/3 Discussion of Results

Now, this, albeit very primitive, statistical analysis of real-life occurrences confirms one basic theorem and validates another that we have presented, algebraically proved and discussed above. In PROPOSITION 3.3 we asserted that when the same economic pressure is applied to two differently positioned societies on the D-curve, the one with greater socio-economic disarray—which is tantamount to tighter centrist regime and, hence, greater intra-societal heterogeneity—ends up with much worse socio-economic disarray and much worse standard of living (and mood of the society) than the society up and to the left on the D. The same statistical result also confirms PROPOSITION 3.4 which is directly derived from PROPOSITION 3.3 and, finally, the result confirms the causal chain in (3.18), asserting that an increase in intra-societal heterogeneity leads to an increase in socio-political disarray and to increase in economic downturn (even crisis) in any given investigated society.

To make a point of showing a real-life example of what we have just asserted in this chapter, let us mention reasonably recent events in Azerbaijan [156]. The author writes:

> In the former Soviet bloc's first dynastic succession (there's another one in the making in Turkmenistan; M.K.), Illham Aliyev, son of the ailing Communist-era holdover Heydar Aliyev, has now become president ... the violence surrounding the election was shocking yet predictable, as the government for years has shut the opposition out of the political process. In the months leading up to the poll, Azerbaijani

authorities blatantly manipulated the electoral process to ensure that Ilham Aliyev would inherit his father's presidency ... the opposition had nowhere to go but the streets.

However, one of the best confirmations (if not proof) of our "behaviorally" derived correlation between the strength of the oligarchic rule in a society and the actual or perceived trend of the living standard comes next. There is a noted indicator of stratification of wealth in sociology called the Gini Index—detailed description of which is in the Appendix—that more or less denotes similar phenomena as our variable "living standard." We have performed the same correlation as in **EXHIBIT 3.4** except that the Gini Index, converted to rank statistics, substitutes for the variable "living standard." The correlation is less significant, but still significant enough to confirm the merit of our methodology (of introducing non-parametric, ranked data into sociological analyses). A comparison of both correlations is in **EXHIBIT A.12** of the Appendix.

Chapter 4: Tools for Mapping the D-Curve

4/1 Introduction

Since this chapter constitutes the collection of elements essential for construction and understanding of the whole paradigm we shall devote a short introduction to it.

We have already established that it would be worthwhile to have a concise hypothesis—which, if proved valid, would constitute a paradigm—that would newly re-assess the risk of conflicts in economic, social-aid, and financial-cum-political deals between the *donor* (i.e. any developed country or NGO) and a *recipient* (i.e. developing or transitional country.) The only necessary and sufficient condition, for the hypothesis or paradigm's practical usefulness, is that both (*donor* and *recipient*) are inter-societal heterogeneous. This means that their societies' socio-economic, social, socio-political, historical culturally-institutional environments leading to legal, behavioral and cognitive traits are dissimilar.

In previous chapters we suggested that the greater inter-societal heterogeneity between the *donor* and a *recipient* society, the greater the risk of conflict, and hence the greater possible combined loss to the *recipient* society. It is important to have in mind that we are talking here about serious conflicts, inclusive of armed uprising, civil war and, last but not least, international terrorism. These notions have, however, been missed by most of the *donors* (and never really cared about by *recipients'* ruling classes) since the onset of the "gold rush" to globalize the Earth "lock-stock and barrel."

There is one good reason for *donors* missing this danger. For typical intra-societal historically homogeneous society it is sometimes difficult to imagine to what lengths of morass the dealing with an outright heterogeneous and in all aspects different, and difficult to imagine, society might lead to. **Especially difficult might be reasoning with the *recipients'* indigenous oligarchies whose motto might be translated perhaps as "we live only once and to hell with the hoi-polloi;"** which also used to be a motto of ruling classes of Czarist Russia up until the revolution in 1917.

As different as the *recipients* societies-countries are, they have several things in common:

1) They are extensively populated; 2) there is a tacit promise of available market for modern consumer products; 3) they need a completely new

infrastructure; and 4) their governments seem to be in favor of the necessary reform drive to unleash the countries' potential so that the ruling oligarchy can be served by both people and economy [167; p.51].

What has happened next, during the "reform drive," is another story. Not long after the money started to pour in, the investors started to pull out almost as quickly as they piled in. What went wrong? The intra-societal heterogeneity—social, ethnic and religious disparity and, particularly, its most visible and dangerous factor, poverty—took over, meshed with a rudimentary banking system, virtually no stock market and virtual lawlessness in society.

But it is not just the poverty *per se* that is the problem. It is the complex historical behavior and cognitive traits of, *de facto*, tribal societies spoon-fed by mixture of xenophobia, cheap populism and political, ethnic and religious "cards" played by the ruling classes (in their strive for self-preservation) that frightened off ***bona-fide*** investors with the exception of ever so naïve NGOs who missed the whole point: **Indigenous ruling oligarchies needed the *donors'* money. But not for their societies; for themselves.**

Hence, much of the blame for the serious drop in foreign investment lies with the ***donors*** themselves; they have chosen and/or managed to overlook the social, political and economic stratification of the ***recipient*** society and the risks tied to it. This is in our "tech-speak" tantamount to forget that **not all countries are intra-societal homogeneous.**

NOTE: We have touched upon this issue when discussing **LEMMA 3.2** in the previous chapter, where the smoothing of intra-society heterogeneity is left to the intentions (and the moral strength) of the individual governments or rulers.

And this is also the 'leitmotif' of this study. We all want to make deals—be it a direct economic or monetary aid, economic co-operation, technology or know-how transfer—to improve the economic level leading to more serious international trade with these countries. **But the tacit assumption has been that the indigenous governments will behave in the way governments generally behave in Western developed countries.**

This is not the case, however. Reforms in these countries have been, if at all, slow and modest. They have often been accompanied by capricious new rules, installed to make corruption easier while inefficiency is systematic and prevalent. As the local governments muddle through, their peoples all seem to be badly off, their banks go bust every so often and with them the trust of the people in their respective governments. Worse than that, despite—or perhaps because of—the major NGOs' (e.g. IMF, The World Bank, UN, Europe Aid, USAID, etc.) life-lines being thrown at them every so often, nothing but sheer despair is the order of the day (as the aid never trickles down to the society at large. At the same time society's minorities, such as: big-time *de facto* gangsters (with connections to ruling classes), oligarchs and, generally speaking, the ruling classes seem to thrive upon these spectacular socio-economic collapses. It is easy to see why; most of these IMF *et al.* handouts usually end up in their offshore bank accounts.

Thus, **one can instantly form a conclusion, though so far only tentative, that the axiomatic laissez-faire of Adam Smith has to be amended if not outright cancelled whenever there is economic cooperation between widely heterogeneous societies on the horizon to allow a 'visible hand' of the state or, better still, a 'collective hand' of several states to shield both societies from potential disasters**, such as: socio-political upheavals and destabilization of the *recipient* societies leading to (armed) upheavals or civil wars with burned "bridges" between the *recipient* and *donor* societies, grievances against *donors* and sense of threat to *recipient* civilizations from the *donors'* side [97; p.6]. Worse still, situations whereby these phenomena are likely to culminate into armed uprisings or terrorist actions aimed against Western (in nowadays terminology: Northern) civilization, spread domino-like over the region and eventually spill-over onto a substantial part of the world *donor* societies.

To understand fully the situation leading two heterogeneous societies to a conflict and, eventually, to the above disaster one would now need a modeling tool representing the investigated societies. One of the feasible and more useful tools is a graphical one. Linear programming and Nomography comes to mind immediately. If we can find a way in which a society can be mapped on a graph—and we have subsequently found that the mapping is possible via special techniques of 'conversion tables' [24; pp.41-43]—then these images can reflect the ranking of individual societies' major socio-economic strengths and weaknesses.

Also, the graph—on which every society can be defined in terms of a single point to promote greater intelligibility and clarity—would form the basis of the two-society graphical comparison to give rise to the possibility of risk-of-conflict assessment. Last but not least, it would also serve as an important criterion of feasibility and credibility of the data and information.

This is why we have introduced the D-curve in the previous chapter on which most of the theoretical, yet provable in real-life, notions and conclusions—elements of the paradigm—can be explained. As the construction of the D-curve was, in the first instance, made theoretically, the time has come to support the theory by the real-life data.

4/2 Choice of Societies

We have investigated several societies for which relevant data, other information and published socio-economic rankings, published comments, discussions and assessments were available. They were: **NATO:** which will henceforth, for the sake of brevity, encompass U.S.A., Canada, U.K., and the six founding EU members (Belgium, France, Germany, Italy, Luxembourg and the Netherlands); Japan; Czech Republic; Russia; Indonesia; Hong Kong; South Korea; Malaysia; Singapore; and Taiwan.

Apart from data availability, there is another good reason why we have chosen these societies-countries. They have all been touched, some less, some more, some even drastically, by the great financial meltdown that started in South East Asia in 1997. This banking and financial crisis has since made its mark virtually all over the developing world and, as it happens, over the banking sectors of the developed world as well. The meltdown eventually developed quickly into socio-political crises in many societies in which civil disturbances, uprisings and even occasional armed conflicts flared here and there.

The choice helps in another matter too. The investigated countries represent a very large spectrum of societies with wide socio-political systems' heterogeneities. From this point, each investigated society is a "generic" one. They embody what the already noted source [79; p.5] calls "extremely different vantage points countries finds themselves at." Therefore, whatever conclusion is made on this sample it may easily be expanded to a much larger representative sample. In fact, it could offer notions and axioms of general validity for development on a global-scale economy.

For the sake of clarity, algebraic and statistical formulas—although we cannot dispose of them entirely—will be kept at minimum. Also, and above all, we shall make sure to translate the major hypotheses and findings into much more intelligible graphs and flow-charts.

In the next paragraph, in which "legitimacy" vs. "power" rankings will be estimated, one major finding from the previous chapter should be useful. There, in **LEMMA 3.1**, we concluded that if we cannot estimate the rank of "legitimacy" we can substitute it by inverse ranking of "power" (or "oligarchy").

4/3 Estimation of "Legitimacy" and "Power" Rankings

4/3/1 Feasibility of Converse Rankings between "Legitimacy" and "Power" and their Use

The gist of the matter here is to make sure that **LEMMA 3.1** holds even under the most adverse conditions, because if it did it would then cover most of the conditions of the real-life world. Although the converse relationship between the **LEGITIMACY** and **POWER** (or **OLIGARCHY**) has, up till now, been intuitively taken for granted—after all the **Polity Viability Chart** in **EXHIBIT 3.1** has, again intuitively, showed just this relationship—we should base this converse functional relation on more than just an intuition. A reliable database and rigorous quantitative analysis of the database—although the investigated one-to-one correspondence would be lingering among verbal definitions, cardinal and ordinal scales—should be the first step on the long journey to the general credibility of the thesis.

As it follows from **ASSUMPTION 3.1** and **PROPOSITIONS 3.1** and **3.3**, to be able to define points S_i on curve D estimates of the length of segments OL_i on the L-scale, or, failing that (according to **LEMMA 3.1**), assessments of the length of segments OP_i on the P-scale are needed. Furthermore, from the tenor of Section 3/2/2 it follows that we can substitute estimates based on ordinal numbers. Thus, at least for the first iteration we have to find the societies' ranking on one or the other axis.

Let us begin with the "legitimacy" L-scale in **EXHIBIT 3.2**. For the first step we use the scale of the chart in **EXHIBIT 3.1** with two provisions: (a) Japan does not belong into the NATO group of "century-old liberal democracies" [4]; we put her somewhere between NATO and the rest of the investigated societies instead [5], and (b) Czech Republic and Russia are not communist societies anymore but the first is "oligarchy in democratic disguise" and the other is, as one source puts it [4], a sort of "illiberal democracy" and according to another source [101; p.8] "a kind of 21st century Russian feudalism." From yet other sources corrected by Russian and Czech data ([21], [2], [3], [22] and [23]) we shall use six rankings of socio-economic and socio-political factors.

For the relative ranking on L-scale, i.e. "Legitimate Democracy," we use the following factors-proxies: (from [24]) "Political Rights Index" (#34) supported by "Civil Rights Index" (#35) with factor "Economic Capability Assessment" (#61) used for distinguishing among the many tied ranks (the theory being that "self-sufficient" nations have had enough time to put themselves firmly into the camp of more democratic societies).

For the ranking on P-scale, i.e. "Power of Oligarchy," (to be used according to LEMMA 3.1) we use the following proxies: (from [24]) "Percentage of GDP Received by Richest 10%," (#50 in [21]) "Percentage of GDP Received by Poorest 20%," (#51 in [21]) "Population in Absolute Poverty," (#52 in [21]) used for distinguishing among the tied ranks. The numerical entries of the investigated societies—with their final ranks calculated from the above sources for the two scales—are seen in EXHIBIT 4.1.

EXHIBIT 4.1: Data Base that Supports Finding of LEMMA 3.1

Country	"Legitimacy" Ranking	"Oligarchy" Ranking
Japan	10	2
Malaysia	1	11
South Korea	7	4
Indonesia	4	9
Singapore	5	5
Thailand	3	10
Taiwan	2	8
Hong Kong	6	6
Czech Republic	9	1
Russia	8	7

There are many more proxies that can, up to this point, implicitly describe the power of oligarchy or failings of the free-market notion. In a table used as supporting material to **EXHIBIT 4.1** there are tabulated, by consensus agreed upon and thus partially quantified, statements such as:

> "It is better to have a good friend than a good product," "It is extremely difficult to 'break into' ethnic or kinship-oriented oligarchic informal network" or "Maintaining smooth and regular contacts with government is an essential part of doing business."

All of these are summarized and discussed in the Appendix. Some specific discussion on the merit of, and indeed the reason for, proxies is seen in **DEFINITION 2.13** in Chapter 2.

NOTE: Assessments of ranks of factors #34, #35 are, for obvious reasons, correlated [$R^2 = 0.7$, $F = 16.3$, $t = 4$, P-value= 0.007]. The same goes for factors #50 and #51 [$R^2 = 0.9$, $F = 29$, $t = 5.4$ and P-value = 0.001].

Since the non-parametric statistics' characteristic, called Spearman r_s (discussed in the Appendix), has a **t** statistic with $t_{0.001,11} < |-6.18|$, we can claim that **LEMMA 3.1** holds for real-life situations. The result is important for what will transpire next.

Before anything transpires, however, we should make clear what the table in **EXHIBIT 4.1** has told us. Also, we have to show the reader—who may not be exceedingly well versed in non-parametric statistics, let alone in using various proxies for investigated variables and other elements of applied statistics—that our explanation and use of the particular techniques is sound. Although the details are to be found either in the above mentioned literature or in the Appendix, a few plain words should be said here. There are basically two issues: The first is theoretical and the second is practical, verging on empirical and almost axiomatic, knowledge.

We shall take the theoretical issue first. Assume that we try to make the D-curve as close as possible to the existing world. That means putting the reference points S_i on it. Hence, we simply must be confident, as much as possible, about the locating of those points-images, each of which represents the cluster of intra-societal homogeneous societies. In other words, societies with similar socio-economic, socio-political and eventually historical and cultural trends and expectations.

Statistically speaking, there must exist reasonably narrow (probabilistic) confidence or credibility intervals within which each cluster of societies, also known as the **"generic" society**, fits. This is what we have been doing. We have employed small-sample statistics only. Large samples from a hundred or so countries would be great but such data and information unfortunately do not exist, and anyway, we have shown that the statistical characteristics of correlation—or, in our case, a functional relation between two sets of **numerically expressed social behaviors** within the domain of investigated societies—agree very well with the *ex ante* formulated hypotheses about these behavioral relations.

As far as the practical issues go, there is no database in the world that would list characteristics such as "oligarchy" (not to mention its qualitative assessment) for any one country. This is a "politically incorrect" characteristic to circulate. And for a simple reason: Not a single country in the world is keen to advertise what must be the single most damaging factor-image. To be a little more specific: corruption as a society's norm [55] would not only effectively close the doors to various *donor* countries and thus would stem the flow of international emergency, investment, or other funds which the oligarchy needs for its own purposes, but international repercussions on the diplomatic or international law front might damage such self-advertised oligarchies even more.

Therefore, other characteristics available in various UN, UNESCO and similar publications, causally correlated to the definition of "oligarchy," have to be used instead. Such characteristics are called **proxies** [24; pp.55-57]. In this way it is possible to substitute one proxy or, even better, a combination of several proxies for one such behavioral phenomenon we need to quantify, but about which no information can be obtained from official sources.

Having this in mind, we have investigated the data source documenting '**Asia Pacific Difference.**' It is a survey of European managers dealing with Pacific Rim countries and with their experience of doing business there [50]. Out of eleven societies listed in **EXHIBIT 4.1**, this source deals in detail with eight Far and South East Asian societies. From many tabulated rankings we have put together two proxy characteristics for **DEMOCRACIES** ("Business relationship based on trust are essential for success" and "One has to demonstrate to partner a long term interest in a business venture") and three proxy characteristics for **OLIGARCHY** ("Government influence in business," "There is a high level of government influence in business" and "The government grants preferential advantages to local firms").

Despite the completely different source of the data—not to mention the different purpose for which it was made (see [50])—the compiled proxies showed Spearman characteristic with a t statistic $t_{0.01,8}$ smaller than - |5.06|, which again more than supports **LEMMA 3.1**. Tabulated data from that source are seen in the Appendix. Now we can move on to the next step.

4/3/2 Second Step: The Use of Conversion Tables

Judging from the labels of the two scales (on axes Y and X) it appears that any further, meaning more detailed, information that could be used for more precise ranking of societies would be available for the P-scale only. This is because media and professional publications prefer negative, more "newsworthy" reporting—such as financial and market-economic crises in many countries, for example [2], [3], [22], [25], [26], [27], [28], and [29]—over positive ones. Thus, after compiling these data, we use the technique of "conversion tables" [23] to come up with a more general and therefore handier and more useful P (i.e. oligarchy) ranking-scale than the one based on the characteristics mentioned above (#50, #51, #52 from [21]). Although the more detailed explanation of this concept has been (and will be) found in **DEFINITION 2.19** and in the Appendix, a few words at this time might dispel some misunderstanding.

Generally speaking, conversion tables are used when some behavioral ordinal-scale variables or factors, such as preferences, importance weights, categorical assessments of obedience, lawlessness etc. have to be considered and analyzed together with numerical, for instance cardinal, scales. As we have these behavioral levels expressed verbally (and/or in the literature [168; p.252]), it is imperative to be able to attach quantitative labels to these phenomena so that we can use various quantitative methods for mapping and analyzing them. There is virtually no chance that we can ever assess the cardinal or absolute values of these qualitative factors. However, well-constructed ordinal values, sufficient to recognize that a higher numerical characteristic defines higher, more intense, of better quality or a more important factor, would suffice and, in fact, would be all we can ask for. For the sake of convenience we call some of these universally recognizable scales—discussed in the Appendix—**Universal Score Functions (USF)**.

USF are most useful in the situation in which we have to combine several qualitative factors (of various levels) with the aim of attaching to every special combination one single numerical characteristic. This is our case.

Although the example of a multi-factor conversion table presented in **EXHIBIT 4.2**—transforming "qualitative verbal assessments" into a USF: "oligarchy-P-scale ranking" for points $S_1 ... S_9$ on hyperbolic curve D—looks just like an ordinary illustration without any meaning other than to illustrate the point, it has a very substantial, if not crucial, role in the paradigm.

Its role stems from the fact that it is derived from actual data and information from the above sources, many others, listed in the Appendix and/or references of literary sources, and from discussions with indigenous experts in these societies. However, it is the other feature of this conversion table that makes it so important. It makes graphically apparent the major hypothesis of the paradigm derived from **PROPOSITIONS 3.1 - 3.4** and **AXIOM 3.1**, to wit: **The overall intra-societal heterogeneity increases as we move lower and to the right (LR) along the D-curve.**

So, here we have the conversion table—our main sociological tool and a stepping stone for further analyses—whose goal is two-fold.

First, it converts the verbal assessment of the quality of socio-economic, socio-political, and social environment in each of the generic societies into quantitative ordinal scales that can be assumed to be monotonic transforms (see (A4) in the Appendix or [104]) of the actual behavioral multi-factor variables. An actual example of a similar conversion table is the ladder of "corruption index" in individual countries of the world which, on a scale of <10, ... 0>, is annually published by *Transparency International*. We can see the table-ladder for the year 2001 in the Appendix.

Second, it attaches this quantitative ordinal value to certain, though generic, verbally defined levels of intra-societal heterogeneity and by doing so, it in effect **provides the first causal link between intra-societal and inter-societal heterogeneity**.

From the conversion table in **EXHIBIT 4.2** thus follow two important items: **(a)** how does the intra-societal heterogeneity allocate the society-defining points S_i on the D-curve, and **(b)** how, in turn, does the physical distance between the two specific points S_i and S_k, $i \neq k$, define the inter-societal heterogeneity between the two societies.

NOTE: It is fair to remember that this conversion table is by no means the only one imaginable. Anybody can come up with slightly similar, a bit (or a lot) different, even a very different list of scenarios. The only criterion here is that the scenarios should list and rank the major non-negotiable qualities: power of oligarchy and democracy either in ascending or descending order using the principles of lexicographical ordering (see Appendix and [24; pp.47-50]). The detailed contents of the scenarios may, therefore, vary from case to case.

EXHIBIT 4.2: Conversion Table for Scenario-Defining Points S

Key Verbal Assessment	Point S_i
Liberal democracies with sanctity of basic liberties, private property and contracts, and the rule of transparent law accepted by the whole free-market oriented society; rules of society are implicit, the oligarchic tendencies are checked; political adjustments possible but economic instability leading to political polarization is unthinkable [NOTE: S_1 usually represents USA, Canada, UK and the original EU "SIX"]	S_1
Liberal democracies with sanctity of basic liberties, private property and contracts, and the rule of transparent law; free-market conditions where rules of society are, on the whole, implicit; some traces of growing oligarchy; political changes frequent but economic instability leading to political polarization is highly improbable [NOTE: Point S_2 can represent all NATO societies]	S_2

Tools for Mapping the D-Curve

Fledgling democracies with basic proclaimed liberties, private property and contracts, and the rule of law; free-market conditions and strong but inept bureaucracy give rise to growth of oligarchy; political adjustments frequent with occasional unrest but not dangerous enough for political or economic destabilization of society [NOTE: **Point S_3 may represent South Korea and Japan**]	S_3
Fledgling and/or illiberal democracies with relatively highly exogenous regulations; free-market conditions but not very transparent law; rigid bureaucracy conceive interlocking conglomerates; inept authoritarian oligarchy cannot cope with fast-changing economic environment, particularly in the banking industry; political polarization probable but outright political destabilization of society improbable [NOTE: **Point S4 represents Czech Republic, Slovak Republic and Slovenia**]	S_4
Illiberal democracies with high exogenous regulation; elections but opaque law leads to few liberties and individual rights; institutional and legislative paralysis gives rise to powerful opportunistic oligarchy; this new ruling class uses banks to obtain stronghold on economy via widespread frauds; political polarization possible but outright political unrest and destabilization of society less likely [NOTE: **Point S_5 represents all new EU South-East Europe members**]	S_5
Illiberal democracies with opportunistic oligarchies and quasi-democratic institutions work against any notion of individual rights and liberties; ruling inept oligarchies, intertwining politics and business, using banks for cheap lending to other cronies; all of this leading society into periodic economic downturns and ensuing political polarization; serious political unrest possible with armed conflict not improbable [NOTE: **Point S_6 can represent Turkey and Ukraine**]	S_6
Corrupt ruling opportunistic oligarchy, intertwining politics and business, together with their cronies in quasi-democratic institutions, such as government, have managed to acquire most of the companies but is unable to run them; this new ruling class is not accountable to the rest of the society; political big-wigs are ready to make concessions to popular demand only when strongly pushed; serious economic situation renders serious political unrest probable; armed conflict far from impossible [NOTE: **Point S_7 may represent Thailand and Uzbekistan**]	S_7
Corrupt ruling oligarchy take a country for a private fiefdom, particularly its banking sector, where fraud prevails; this inept and thoroughly opportunistic oligarchy is not accountable to the rest of the society; parts of society are pushing for some inroads into political and economic monopoly of out-of-touch establishments' "dinosaurs"; economic crises are likely to provoke serious political (possibly armed) unrest [NOTE: **Point S_8 can represent Kyrgyzstan and Zimbabwe**]	S_8
Ruling oligarchy is also the country's religious (or political "apex"), nothing works because political and/or religious zealotry makes the Communist era societies of the '60s or '70s supremely efficient by comparison; rampant mismanagement, while cronyism and opportunism is the rule; inept oligarchy is not accountable to the rest of the society which is effectively shut out of any decision and governing processes whatsoever; economic meltdown gives rise to serious polarization of society and serious political (including armed) export excesses highly probable [NOTE: **Point S_9 may well represent North Korea**]	S_9

The Crucial Challenge for International Aid

Generally speaking, the conversion table in **EXHIBIT 4.2** will provide the next and practical step from the solely theoretical images of the P-scales on the **SLIDE** in **EXHIBIT 3.3**—while **LEMMA 3.1** will improve understanding the merit of L-scales—and will finalize the first iteration in our striving for more precise mapping of points S_i on **slide curve D**. The graphical image of this phase, yielding points S_i, i = 1 ... 9, on the D, is seen in **EXHIBIT 4.3**.

EXHIBIT 4.3: Mapping of Society-Defining Points on D-Curve

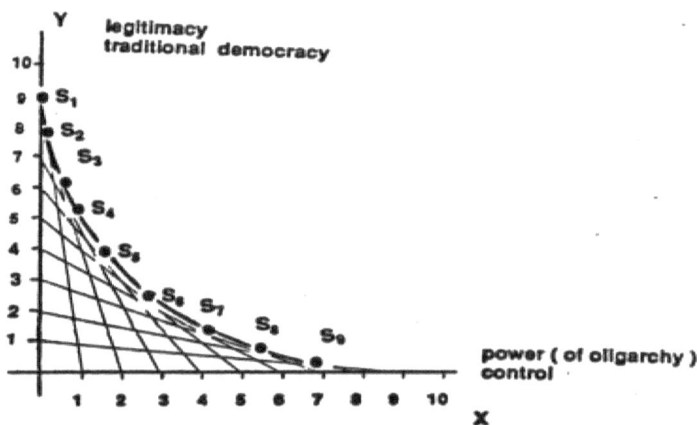

At the same time, however, it is important to remember that the sliding D-curve, seen here as **EXHIBIT 4.3**, is just the same hyperbolic curve of bi-axial graphical rendition of "legitimacy" vs. "power" of two or more intra-societal **heterogeneous** societies-countries S_i and $S_{(i+1)}$ which we have suggested in **EXHIBITS 3.2** and **3.3**. The procedure of step-by-step building of the conversion table only allocated the appropriated "generic" societies onto the hyperbola.

4/3/3 The D-Curve as a Tool for Efficient Estimation of Risk-of-Conflict Disutility

Once we have obtained the **D-curve** in **EXHIBIT 4.3**—one that maps the current state of combined socio-political environments of various (generic) societies in two-dimensional space—we are ready for the next step. There, we shall have to show that it is feasible to extend the previously suggested correlation of **PROPOSITION 3.2** and causal chains in **(3.17) - (3.19)** that could be simplified into one simple causal chain (holding its causality for both increase and decrease):

Economic crises → socio-political chaos and/or political unrest

This covers the relationship between the socio-political and economic factors, particularly when economic stresses, shocks and the like take place. In fact, we shall devote the next paragraph to this end. But before we do so, it might be prudent to go back a little and stress the importance of several issues that we have already discussed in previous chapters.

Suppose that we are a *donor* entity and suppose also that we are about to initiate the process of negotiating a business or a social aid deal with a certain *recipient* country. Now, in the classical business texts:

(a) The standard business or financial assessment of any deal in which risk-taking is sometimes the norm can be done only when both societies uphold the same or similar business law norms and have the same or similar business ethics and standard of behavior. In this case both societies are inter-societal homogeneous and the realized loss stays in the financial category. While in Chapter 2 it has been suggested that we shall not be concerned with this case at all. Instead:

(b) We are trying to map and analyze the risk-taking between two (or more) **inter-societal heterogeneous societies**, which belongs to a vastly different category altogether in which economic crises give rise to socio-political effects. These effects then usually lead to serious polarization and unrest in the society, eventually to a complete social and political meltdown. And this is exactly our case.

Here we are talking about two inter-societal heterogeneous partners in the economic transaction whose allocation on the hyperbola D differs, perhaps by a lot. Therefore we say that the risk to the *donor* society (usually situated on the upper-left-part of the D-curve) is not only a financial or an economic one. The overall socio-economic and, hence, the socio-political conflicts in the *recipient* society, due to the financial and economic collapse of the deal, will more than likely spill over to the *donor* society with substantial combined and lingering disutility as a final effect.

In such a case, we are in a situation in which **we must carefully assess the *recipient* society's level of heterogeneity: gauge the incompatibility in cultural, ethical and religious, social, political socio-economic and general behavioral trends between the *donor*, and the *recipient* society**. This might be a tedious and complicated procedure under some circumstances.

However, it does not have to be that complicated, much less tedious. Some basic sociologic axioms have to be taken into consideration. As the sliding-curve graph in **EXHIBIT 4.3** has already put both investigated societies (i.e.

the *donor* and the *recipient*) into one picture, the only other thing we need to do is to derive some sort of conversion between the physical distance of both societies on the slide-curve and the measure of potential risk of conflict to the "*donor-recipient*" system.

One, previously discussed, feature and practical use of the D-curve graph can help us here. **PROPOSITION 3.4** allows us to equate one society, of which we know only sketchy information, to one that we have investigated and analyzed at great length. The criterion of similarity tells us that both societies react the same way to the same impulses (economic shocks, etc.). Our real-life application of this feature involves the Czech Republic about which a lot of factual data and inside information is known (see, for example, [1], [2], [22], [23], [54], [68], and [84]) with the relatively sketchy information on Poland [77; p. "Europe"].

The principle works as follows: We only have to be sure that one or two major socio-economic trends in both or more societies (countries or, generally, entities) are similar or the same. If this is so and the society with sketchy information behaves in the same way as the thoroughly analyzed one, we say that single-point models of both (usually *recipient*) societies are located within the immediate vicinity of each other, if not at the same location on the curve D. This is how we were able to place several societies at or around one point-model S_i in the conversion table in **EXHIBIT 4.2**. We have also said that **the society represented by point-model S_i is a generic one**.

One of the recent surveys [106; p.4], having been debated at a seminar in Brussels some years ago, shows extraordinary support for the notion of a generic point-model. It lists the answers to the survey questions in four countries: Czech Republic, Poland, Hungary and Lithuania.

The agreements of the parts of societies (in %) to the questions are listed in two tables. The first in **EXHIBIT 4.4** reflects the *"degree of democracy as it seems to the society at large."* In **EXHIBIT 4.5** the same societies, or their factions, list *"how do they assess their economic conditions."*

First we have tested the "generic quality" of the four-country survey results in both tables. The Paired Two-Sample t-test showed—with t = 1, where t = 2.1 would have been significant and a lesser t value more significant—that the elements in the two tables are coming from the same "generic" sample. Additional testing of the tightness of the correlation between the corresponding cells in each table, which should support the "democracy failure → economic disutility" hypothesis, yielded an R-square of 0.7 with F = 8.6 and t statistic at 2.0. Again, we find a very tight fit that could be read as definite support for the hypothesis. Details of the two testing methodologies can be seen in the Appendix.

EXHIBIT 4.4: Assessment of Democracy

Agreement in %	Czechs	Poles	Hungarians	Lithuanians
"satisfaction with the functioning of democracy"	36	30	27	23
"government acts in the interest of the whole society"	25	13	24	8
"we can influence the political environment better after 1989"	20	41	30	4

EXHIBIT 4.5: Assessment of Economy

Agreement in %	Czechs	Poles	Hungarians	Lithuanians
"living conditions are good"	27	22	8	8
"the economy of the country is sound"	4	12	6	1
"changes after 1989 have brought bigger profits (generally)"	23	24	15	7

The above two tables clearly show that similarly structured and developed societies have the same socio-economic problems, at least in the eyes of their own population. The similarity among the four investigated societies then lies in the fact that all of them had been under communist rule up until 1989 and all of them have been attempting to transition to the full-fledged democratic and open market block of countries ever since.

There is yet one part of this discussion still unanswered. This is the comparison of socio-economic, social and political environments with the economic ones via some meaningful statistical technique. So, our next goal is to demonstrate the correlation between the socio-political conditions and the economic conditions and, perhaps, to derive some meaningful conclusion for real-life problems.

4/3/4 Testing the D-Curve Mapping Against Real-Life Socio-Economic Losses

Let us first present some economic facts. As we mentioned above, the "sloppy banking practices"—that enable the oligarchy to siphon money into their bank accounts and leave the society deprived of much needed fiscal base—in emerging "capitalist" societies of East Asia are largely dependent on the degree of democratic tradition of these societies and less on the proficiency level of the banking professionals (as seen in **PROPOSITION 3.2**). Here are some useful statistics.

In one of the sources [30] we find *"Non-performing loans as % of total loans, estimates, latest"*: USA (as a proxy for NATO): 2%, Singapore: 4.5%, Malaysia: 16%, South Korea: 17%, Indonesia: 18%, Thailand: 19%. The most recent numbers for this characteristic will probably show the same trend, on a different level perhaps, while the real figures will probably never be known.

In another source [31] we find *"Principal stock-indexes % change year-to-date"*: Tokyo (Japan): -18.21%, Seoul (South Korea): -20.82%, Singapore: -24.61, Hong Kong: -24.88%, Jakarta (Indonesia): - 26.88%, Bangkok (Thailand): -40.71%, Kuala Lumpur (Malaysia): -42.85%, while source [32] lists the following *"Stock market declines (November 1996 - November 1997)"*: Japan: 25%, Singapore: 25%, Hong Kong: 27%, South Korea: 59%, Indonesia: 60% (in the first half of January [33] the figure is 75%), Malaysia: 68%, Thailand: 75%, with Czech Republic [23] : 50% - 60%.

NOTE: Russia's RTS index fell by 60% in August 1998 alone [39].

Finally, in source [34], we note *"Devaluation of currencies against the dollar; November 1997"*: Singapore dollar -9%, South Korean won -11%, Taiwan dollar -14%, Malaysian ringgit -28%, Indonesian Rupiah -33% (in the first half of January [33] the figure is ... minus 50% and sliding), Thai baht -35%, while Czech Republic's devaluation [23] has come to -25%.

NOTE: Russia's currency lost 66% of its value in the August 1998 alone [40].

Some **corrections** to previous [34]-based figures provide more recent data. According to [41], *"Percent change in the value of currency against the U.S. dollar since June 30, 1997"* reads as follows: Russian ruble -194.2%, Japan yen -15.2%, Malaysia ringgit -50.5%, and Thailand baht -64.6%.

To conclude the testing of the premise **"less democracy → more economic problems"**—which we have attempted in tables in **EXHIBITS 4.4** and **4.5**—we are going to test the hypothesis that **"oligarchy ranking is very closely correlated with the ranking of socio-economic disutility."**

EXHIBIT 4.6: Database Supporting PROPOSITIONS 3.2-3.4 & AXIOM 3.1

Country	Economic "Disutility"	"Oligarchy" Ranking
Japan	2	2
Malaysia	11	11
South Korea	7	4
Indonesia	9	9
Singapore	3	5
Thailand	4	10
Taiwan	4	8
Hong Kong	6	6
Czech Republic	5	3
"NATO"	1	1
Russia	8	7

If successful, the test will provide strong numerical support for **PROPOSITIONS 3.2** and **3.3**. The table with rankings is seen in **EXHIBIT 4.6** (which is a reprint of the table in **EXHIBIT 4.1**, used for a slightly different purpose).

The database for the first column of table in **EXHIBIT 4.6** includes several sources presented in this paragraph plus a MSCI graph of "Estimated Value of the Stock Markets in Billions of Dollars" in IHT, November 15-16, 1997 and other sources: [80], [101], [98], [26], [90], [84], [81], and [75]. The correlation tightness is seen immediately. Its coefficients and indicators are:

$R^2 = 0.9$, $t = 6.75$, $F = 45.2$ with $P = 0.0001$ respectively. On the whole, the test shows convincingly that the philosophy behind the mapping of individual societies on D-curve, and some basic postulates following from the graph, have quite a firm support in real-life data.

NOTE: We performed similar statistical tests with different data sets in Chapter 3. There we installed in place of the "Economic Disutility" factor called "Change in Living Standard" and let the intelligentsia in the six investigated Central Asian countries assess their own perception of positive or negative change of Living Standard in their respective countries. The only difference from the theoretical assumptions of the tests in **EXHIBIT 4.6** was that all six countries investigated in Chapter 3 had more or less the same economic "starting blocks" when the USSR disappeared and subsequent, again pretty much the same, economic shocks rocked all the investigated societies. There the results—increase or decrease of Living Standard—correlated very closely (Pearson $r = 0.85$ → P ϵ < 0.02, 0.01 >) with socio-political improvement or the greater disarray in socio-political environments.

4/4   Further Results following from the D-Curve Mapping

The **EXHIBIT 4.3** D-curve has a set of society-defining points S_i, $i = 1 \ldots 9$ mapping the nine generic types of investigated societies. These seem to fit, both verbally and numerically, reasonably well with the real-world situation. There might be, even at the point of writing, let alone in future, some changes in the rankings. Most of the Middle East countries are slipping down fast and recently Serbia (see [89; p.1], [33]) has been dropping significantly, with Russia (see [39] and [40]) not far behind.

These and other changes will, however, be confined within the societies defined by the same or similar verbal definitions in conversion table in **EXHIBIT 4.2**. Here, we might be tempted to rejoin the well-known adage [55] noted in statement **(3.2)**: *"Corruption is the problem of systems* (and societies; added by M.K) *not of the individuals."*

In our case, it means that within the lowest ranked societies anything is possible. The fast slide downwards is practically an axiom. However, the general principle can be detected cross the board. And so we put forth the following.

PROPOSITION 4.1:
For each society, defined by a point Si, i = 1...m, on the D-curve, holds that its socio-economic and socio-political environment tend to deteriorate with time

(albeit slowly and, perhaps, imperceptibly) such that the society-defining point Si has a natural tendency to slip down on curve D.

PROOF: We offer a two-pronged sketch of the proof. First we deal with the "democratic" societies. The classic democracy scenario **(3.7)** is based on conjecture **(3.3)**: *"social institutions ... are interaction of ... rules ... coordinating actions ... of individuals."* This is an action to battle the Law of Entropy. The ensuing elite however tends to overreact. The elite then: **(1)** Creates very inclusive societies in which a peaceful conflict, but conflict still, between the "democracy-creating-and-controlling elite" and the masses could start [96, p.B7] and **(2)** *"becomes oriented more towards maintaining their power* (and with it the "positive sanctions" [37] in terms of money or influence) *than promoting the interest of rank and file."* Thus, a new political process: democracy → oligarchy suddenly appears in scenario **(3.7)**. Although, admittedly, the process is slowed down considerably by democratic societies' "checks and balances," it is still theoretically plausible. The "inevitability albeit imperceptibility of the society's decay" also follows from the following quotation: *"in spite of their democratic ideology, the actual structure of* (every; added M.K.) *democratic organization tends to be transformed to an oligarchic form"* [38]. Further application of a loop between **(1)**, **(2)** then proves **PROPOSITION 4.1**.

For other societies, we start with the organizational processes described by Michels [35] and [36] as the "**iron law of oligarchy**."

The elite "has become oriented more towards maintaining their power (and with it "positive sanctions" (3.7); i.e. money or influence) than promoting the interest of rank and file (i.e. masses)."

From the **Free Market Society Conjectures** and from scenario **(3.8)** the growth of the self-perpetuating, negative loop between conjectures **(3.6) and (3.2)**—which, in the absence of self-correcting social institutions self-perpetuates and reinforces oligarchy thanks to oligarchy's nonsensical exogenous changes pushed on the society—**is** assured. Thus, because of the faster pace of the society's decay, conditions for success of the conflict interest groups ([35]) brighten.

But this is an extreme step of society's decay or, at the very worst, destruction. In fact, the deterioration of the society and its all local values and institutions—just because the people (and above all the ruling oligarchy) have taken the material aspect of life for the only criterion of success—has been discussed previously.

LEMMA 4.1:
Such a slip-down, described by PROPOSITION 4.1, comes more naturally and with a much stronger effect for the societies modeled by the points at the lower-right end of the SLIDE.

SCHEME of PROOF: Let us start with the claim of **PROPOSITION 3.2** and **AXIOM 3.1**, that : "if two societies defined on two different points on the D-curve are subject to the same external economic pressure, then the society located down and to the right of the compared to society ends up with greater socio-economic and socio-political disarray." Then, from the proof of **PROPOSITIONS 3.2 - 3.3**, societies on the far lower-right of curve D have to use a lot of exogenous pressure (as in statement **(3.6)**) because they haven't got traditional democracies' "checks-and-balances" built in the system. But then, the vicious circle, embodied by criterion **(3.7)**, will cause the fulfillment of **LEMMA 4.1**.

4/4/1 Other Negative Reflections

Thus, we have just realized the inherent strength of the principle that furnishes command-and-control societies—such as those of Asia [5]—with strong, corrupt and opportunistic oligarchies. The ensuing vicious circle, described in scenario **(3.8)**, in various literary sources e.g. [16; p.54], and in one part of the proof of **PROPOSITION 4.1**, can worsen the societies' socio-economic and socio-political situation dramatically in very short time.

All of that notwithstanding, there is another great feature implicitly imbedded in the D-curve graph in **EXHIBIT 4.3**. It may not be immediately apparent and we have probably skipped over this quality a bit. But because the graph maps, above all, the socio-political environment—which is known to be fairly constant (at least relatively to the economic infrastructure)—the distribution of the society-mapping points along the D-curve should be fairly constant too.

This constancy is important in that it provides a base for long-term strategic planning and scenario-building in the policy-making institutions of the *donor* societies. There are many examples of how useful this "constancy" feature really is. Take for instance some of the Far South-East Asian societies, in which economic turmoil in 1997 almost caused civil war. Now, decades later, when the problems with wholesale bank and business crashes is long over and new—this time, if not democratic at least populist—governments are in power, the society is still "at war" against "new" corrupt oligarchy and against itself (e.g. Indonesia, Philippines) and in some instances ethnic minorities (fomented by exogenous interests, as in the Philippines) are more troublesome than ever before.

In China, in the meantime, the student-led protests in and around Tiananmen Square in 1989 are largely forgotten. However, a new 'player' appeared on the Chinese society horizon: the Buddhist-like sect Falun Gong. And the sect is, again, trying to satisfy society's need for belief, social interaction, security and righteousness; just like the students before and, undoubtedly (after the crackdown on Falun Gong) some other social movements in the future. In other words, if there are problems in the society, these problems will not go away overnight; sometimes, it takes generations to change basic societal attitudes and norms. You may keep interchanging the spots on the lower-right part of the D-curve, especially within a short interval of group of reasonable similar societies, quite easily and within a short time period. You may even do it on the upper-left-part of the D-curve. But that's just it; because here we touch on the other important conclusion following from this chapter.

As **LEMMA 4.1** suggests, it is very easy to slide down quite a bit, given the right anti-social incentives. In view of **LEMMA 4.1**, though, it is very difficult, if not outright impossible, for any society to improve its position in a substantial way.

So now we have the 'down-and-out' societies that are on the one hand getting approached with increasing frequency by 'do-gooders' and politicians-cum-economists trying to pour money into them, cost what it may, and on the other hand the illiberal rule of corrupt oligarchy tightening the screws on money markets and on any semblance of at least basic political life.

As we have suggested in previous chapters, the greater inter-societal heterogeneity between the *donor* and *recipient* societies, the greater the risk of conflict. Also, from **LEMMA 4.1** we learned that any socio-economic and social-political slip-down comes much more naturally for the societies at the lower-right end of D-curve. These are the ones in which the intra-societal heterogeneity (i.e. tribalism, ethnic nationalism and social-political stratification) is highest. The noted columnist William Pfaff writes in [112]:

> Nationalism and ethnic nationalism in particular, was the most powerfully political force of the 19th century, and arguably it will be that of the 21st century, as well.

Ethnic nationalism notwithstanding, there is a much more powerful and formidable political force to deal with nowadays: Islamic fundamentalism.

Islamic fundamentalism or radical Islamism perverts traditional religious ideas and sentiment into new political ideologies; it derives its energy from the resentment of those who feel economically or culturally dispossessed; it employs the most modern techniques in the service of essentially primitive concepts; and it sanctions unrestrained violence and ruthlessness in pursuit of totalitarian power—exactly as Nazism and Communism did in all these respects. As Osama bin Laden demonstrated quite forcefully on September 11, 2001, the spill-over of armed politico-religious conflict can now reach even the capitals of democratic superpowers.

Therefore we have to conclude that conflicts in the world, triggered by these huge wholesale crises in the systems of these societies, should be expected to be more frequent, dangerous and even critical from now on. To frame this notion into a system of formal behavioral axiomatic we propose the following statement.

PROPOSITION 4.2:
Suppose we have a society mapped by point Si, i = 1...m, on the D-curve and also suppose that Si represents a generic society that has been denoted by a verbal definition of socio-economic and socio-political conditions via a certain conversion table. Then when we detect a politically strong radical fundamentalist ideology—pertinent to a certain ethnic or religious strata—in a certain investigated society, we shall have to reassess the point's position Si+k, k = 1 ... m-2, way lower and way to the right on the D-curve from the original spot (found for the generic society) and such that resulting Si+k will feature k ≥ 2.

PROOF: From **PROPOSITIONS 3.2** and, particularly **3.5**, it is clear that an **infusion of any new strata into intra-heterogeneous society will increase the intra-society heterogeneity**. Let us assume that a minimum such increase would simply put the society to the point S_{i+k}, where **k = 1**. But, the infusion of strong radical fundamentalist ideology into the already existing conflict then refutes any standard socio-political solution and, according to reverse reasoning of **PROPOSITION 3.3**, the slip would have to be at least by 2 points on the D-curve (and probably by more).

DISCUSSION: Assume that in the recent history of the world (inclusive of the present time) there have been three major fundamentalist ideologies: Nazism, Communism and radical Islam. We know that: **(1)** all three sanction unrestrained violence and ruthlessness in pursuit of totalitarian power, and **(2)** all three ideologies are what Burke called "armed doctrines" [122; p.A16]. Let us now assume any verbal definition of socio-political and social environment in a generic society which does feature social and political upheavals and complete decay of political and social structures. However, the **combination of (1) and (2) immediately brings an armed conflict into the previously pure political and/or ideological one.** Hence the **society's decay assumes an automatically unsolvable proportion and a steep downhill trend which has to be mapped by reassessing the society's definitional point down and to the right from the original "generic" society mapping.**

EXHIBIT 4.7: Reassessment of Conversion Table in View of New Political Realities

Fledgling and/or quasi-liberal democracies with relatively highly exogenous regulations; free-market conditions but not very transparent law; rigid bureaucracy conceive interlocking conglomerates; inept authoritarian oligarchy cannot cope with fast-changing economic environment, particularly in banking industry; strong religious-political radical (fundamentalist) movement detected in part of society, political polarization highly probable following with outright political destabilization of society [NOTE: Point S_4 can represent Romania, Turkey while point S_6 maps, perhaps, Egypt or Pakistan]	$S_4 \rightarrow S_6$
Illiberal democracies with high exogenous regulation; plenty of elections but few actual liberties and individual rights following from opaque law; institutional and legislative paralysis gives rise to powerful opportunistic oligarchy; this new ruling class uses banks to obtain stronghold on economy via widespread frauds; strong armed religious-political radical (fundamentalist) movement became very active in the society ; political polarization, unrest and destabilization society highly probable with outright armed political upheavals and destabilization of society likely [NOTE: Point S_5 represents e.g. Uzbekistan or Kyrgyzstan while point S_9 apart from Sudan might represent Central African Republic]	$S_5 \rightarrow S_9$

Following the message of PROPOSITION 4.2 we see that any such change in socio-political niveau of the country we want to map via the conversion table will have to bring also a change in the transformation algorithm "qualitative verbal assessment" → "oligarchy-P-scale ranking." Let us, for example, assume that in the two newly analyzed societies, represented in **EXHIBIT 4.2** by society-mapping points S_4 and S_5, we have detected a strong, armed, religious-political minority whose leaning has recently become more and more radical. In **EXHIBIT 4.7**, where the changes or additions are underlined, we show how we might reassess the ranks vis-à-vis these new realities.

This is just one example of how we have to continuously keep abreast of new developments in the political and social scene of the investigated societies. It is also a reminder that any serious underestimating of the socio-political (and socio-religious) niveau might bring a very seriously underestimated mapping-of-the-society score S_i and might thus result in yet another "unexpected" dire occurrence in the ***donors***' societies.

4/4/2 Light-at-the-End-of-the-Tunnel Hypothesis

Despite the well-documented worsening of the socio-political situation—and hence the faster shift towards societal polarization and subsequent militancy—in the lesser developed and/or developing countries, globalization might bring about a ray of hope. We are saying "might" for a good reason. It is not hundred percent certain that what we think might happen, or ever will, but in the following we shall explain the ray of hope.

Although the promotion of global culture through multinational corporations and the so-called information revolution has some politicians railing against "cultural pollution," they usually make no mention of the fact that many foreign companies have "gone native" and, consequently, have brought many opportunities for smart young people. *"They now have options because of the multinationals"* says Erla Zwingle [151]. Among the denouncers of Western cultural influences there are also many Westerners. James Watson, a Harvard anthropologist, isn't one of them [151]:

> The lives of Chinese villagers I know are infinitely better now than they were 30 years ago. ... China has become more open partly because of the demands of ordinary people. They want to become part of the world—I would say globalism is the major force for democracy in China. People want refrigerators, stereos, CD players. I feel it's a moral obligation not to say "Those people out there should continue to live in a museum while we have showers that work."

NOTE: More about China in Chapter 7, where professionals, having toured China extensively and recently, are not exactly of Professor Watson's opinion.

While this notion is obviously valid enough, it is still only one part of our hypothesis. Another assumption concerns the generations of teenagers. This author showed—in [152]—that the youngest generation in the Eastern European communist orbit in the 1950s and 1960s had been completely won over by the West through the emerging rock-n-roll culture—we should term it "cultural revolution"—broadcast into Czechoslovakia, Poland, Hungary and Eastern Germany via the ultra-strong US army transmitters in West Germany. The final effect was that, although the ostensibly "communist" regimes of Eastern Europe did not officially fall until the end of the 1980s, in the last 15 years of their existence not even the leading "apparatchiks" (coming from that "beat generation") had any illusions about, let alone beliefs in, the system's longevity. Since the USSR had been outside of the impossible-to-jam zone, the Russian young generation lost about 15 to 20 years to the "globalization" of teenage culture. Hence, this generation became much more vulnerable to the domestic political tussles of Gorbachev and Yeltsin era and, to a certain extent, gullible to oligarchs disguised as society "saviors."

Yet rock-n-roll played exactly the opposite effect in the West in the early 1970s. As the *Daily Mail* put in its July 24, 2002 commentary [157]:

> Social historians in the future may be able to draw the ironic conclusion that Mick Jigger and his friends (i.e. the Rolling Stones and similarly "revolutionary" oriented bands, such as The Who; note by the authors) were **the ultimate weapons in the hands of the Establishment**—high priests of a new religion which, this time, really was the **opium of the masses**.

Next we note the assertion in [151] about the current sociologic development. It claims that:

> The critical mass of teenagers—800 million in the world, the most there have ever been—with time and money to spend is one of the powerful engines of merging global cultures.

Further quantification of this phenomenon comes from Quebec (the perennially "secessionist-sounding" French enclave in Canada) where the French language and culture has been firmly, even brutally upheld by authorities for centuries. Now, a survey by a former school commissioner finds that 90% of the films watched by the school children were from the United States and the author concludes the study by stating ([161; p.6]) that:

> The risk of seeing the French language and Quebec culture disappear within 50 years is very real.

As this author spent almost 22 years in the Middle East and (in other Moslem societies) in Central Asia, his personal experience from these countries allows that a viable **light-at-the-end-of-the-tunnel hypothesis** be formulated from all of the above elements.

There are two problems with the hypothesis. First is its inherent "generation gap." The "generation gap" defines the time (let's say, about 15 to 25 years) before these new—much more global culture minded—leaders take over in their societies. Within this gap, everything is possible. Secondly, when they become the ruling classes of their (tribal) societies they might revert to their fathers' self-preservation-driven tricks and they might feel that further fomenting of xenophobia, cheap populism and political (read: "anti-Northern"), ethnic and ultra-religious mood in their societies will buy them more time for their extravagant lifestyle of pleasure.

After all, by repeating the adage from [55] that notes in statement **(3.2)**: *Corruption is the problem of systems (and societies;* **added by the authors***) not of the individuals*.

Chapter 5: Risk Assessment of Conflicts

5/1 Introducing the New Paradigm

5/1/1 Statement of the Problem

As we formalized the ranking of "generic" societies—those with similar socio-economic, socio-political and usually also similar cultural and cognitive environments—of Asia, Europe and North America vis-à-vis their reaction to certain financial and economic pressures, several conclusions have been made.

First of all, it became clear that the free market concept alone is not nearly that magical condition for a successful socio-economic system (see [22]) as has been preached. Not even the freely elected government and successfully rejuvenated political niveau can pretend to be one. Both of these elements are just two of several necessary conditions of such a system (and not even the main ones at that.)

As a rule, whenever the same economic drought, depression or downturn hits two societies with different intra-society heterogeneity, the one with greater intra-society heterogeneity ends up in (much) worse shape and its socio-economic disutility is deeper and longer and (in *recipient* societies) this is usually combined with a sharp increase in political instability.

This conclusion has been also established by **PROPOSITION 4.2** dealing with the different allocation of the graphical images of generic societies on D-curve. There, the physical distance between the assessments of the two investigated societies' image-points S_i, S_{i+k} signals that two different disutility functions are taking place. This has, as we have asserted, direct impact on the magnitude of whatever potential conflict's final damage—aftermath of the deals-gone-sour between the ***donor*** and ***recipient***—we might expect.

Now we start the second round discussion of the risk-of-conflict within and between societies. As we said in previous chapters, the categories of standard business risk and risk-of-conflict (between heterogeneous entities) might just have a similar initial appearance—of business failure in the ***recipient*** society—as seen in the following excerpt from [44]:

> At the ideal (risk) market competition there exists a trend towards certain price equilibrium ... problems with (strategic) prognostication and business forecasts make this structure highly suspect: we are

getting equilibrium that is volatile all the time ... **uncertain world necessarily involves the risk and somebody has to bear this risk.**

The idea here is to touch base with the category: **risk in the standard business transaction**, even though such category is not our *raison d'être* at all. We mention it because it makes a **clear distinction between risk-of-conflict in a private business** loss due to direct and indirect risk—whether forecast and/or managed is immaterial. If the worst comes to the worst, the company loses money and/or the loss is catastrophic and the company folds and workers lose their jobs (the bigger the business the more people are going to lose jobs)—**and risk-of-conflict based on heterogeneity between macro-socio-economic entities.**

NOTE: Speaking of business risk within one society going haywire, a few rogue risk takers were responsible for the indigenous US financial and fiscal crisis in 2008-2010, to wit: Fannie Mae and Freddie Mac started a microeconomic "business-risk" event. As so many people were affected, the crisis eventually became a macroeconomic issue spreading all over the world. It may eventually lead to socio-political catastrophe in the EU, inclusive of possibly civil unrests leading to local civil wars on the European continent. We shall discuss these items further in Chapter 7.

In the case of the risk-of-conflict based on heterogeneity between macro-socio-economic entities nothing had ever been forecast, let alone managed. This was caused partly by an unlimited "do-gooding" attitude by the *donors* and partly by the completely erroneous assumption about the *recipient's* behavioral and moral "sameness" with the *donor's* own society.

The *donors* might mean well but, at the very most, they probably know only **the Process of Comparative Advantage** which is an oblique way to say that different levels of productivity can be a source of profit [46; pp.399-400], and perhaps a reason for economic aid itself. Knowing the intra-society homogeneity and behavioral environment in their own country they assume the same in the *recipient* society.

However, this assumption would be true if and only if the *donor* and the *recipient* societies' definitional points Si (*donor*) and Si (*recipient*) were virtually interchangeable.

Then, of course, we would call both societies "**intra-societal homogeneous**" and, hence, also "**inter-societal homogeneous**."

Also, "different levels of productivity" and "being intra-societal heterogeneous (and thus, perhaps, vastly different) from the *donors*" are terms from two completely different categories and as such must not be mixed, let alone equated. The first is strictly an economic phenomenon while the other is the subject of sociology and political science.

As it is, the scheme of the debacle is clear. Starting as the standard business risk in the better (i.e. upper-left) part of the D-curve, the conflict's overall propensity to crisis—**fuelled by the distance between both players on the SLIDE**—kicks in. A product of socio-economic and socio-political heterogeneities (the distance on the slide curve D), it features spectacularly different result than expected. Growing social, socio-political and socio-economic discontent has, eventually, been substituted by a lingering and all-encompassing economic and political crisis in the whole *recipient* society.

As we quoted from one source [86; p.65] earlier:

> Much of the blame for the collapse in foreign direct investment lies with the investors themselves, who **chose to overlook the political and economic** realities of the place (**i.e.** *recipient* society; M.K.).

It is not that the push for monetary gains is any weaker in the *recipient* societies than in the *donor* ones. It is the intra-societal heterogeneity of *recipients* that makes the singularity of their alien cultural, political and social traditions, behavior and conducts so difficult to understand to *donors* that have never been exposed to a life in such societies (and most did not even read about it beforehand).

To put it in other words, the problem does not lie only in the *recipient* country's markets or economy. The **crux of the problem lies in the recipient country's society**, which is *terra incognita* for the *donors*. This is what notion **(2.6)** says about it:

> Every deficit on the ledgers of progress or, as we denote in this study, 'growing disparity in the social, socio-economic, and socio-political conditions between the donor and recipient societies,' is a problem situation which could provide the impetus for a collective remedial effort [70; p.589].

This is simply nothing other than a dire warning that political actions may and probably will follow from the unchecked growth of the inter-society heterogeneity.

Here, a disclaimer of sorts should be put forward. It would be wrong to insinuate that risk analysis has not been known and systematically applied any time commercial banks co-operate with a developing country on business loans or other international business deals. In fact, country risk analysis has become an important part of international business [59; pp.207-

214]. It is—similar to elements of our methodology—determining the degree of risk associated with a particular country while considering both qualitative factors, such as political stability, and financial factors, like evaluation of a country's ability to repay its debts. Country risk analysts examine factors such as external debt, international reserve holding, exports, economic growth, etc. and look for the list of "country credit ratings" [59; pp.210-213]. There, similar to our D-curve in **EXHIBIT 4.3**, societies-countries that are listed at the bottom would find new commercial bank lending practically impossible to obtain.

The problem with this type of risk analysis is, however, twofold. **First**, it is based on a short-run and equally short-sighted **view that a business transaction between the two inter-societal heterogeneous countries** [58; pp.12-13] **is solely a market-economic endeavor**. Consequently, any problem with the societies' interaction would stay frozen in the economic sphere only. Therefore, **to look beyond the solely economic impact** into the over-all impact the problem may have on the whole *donor-recipient* system **is deemed superfluous**; and, sometimes, outright impossible too.

The **second** problem is this. In the compartmentalized systems of most *donor* entities there are top decision-maker(s) and then there are individual "experts cells" who always skew, garble, or disregard (due to ignorance) the information. Consider furthermore, that even for a decision about a trifling matter, one needs information from several compartmentalized sources. **The more important the subject of a decision, the more loops there are to be scrutinized, sometimes with bewildering contradictory contents which makes a perfect set-up for the Peter Principle**, to wit: *"everybody rises to his own level of incompetence,"* combined with Parkinson's Law [60; p.35] type of activities.

Even the most believable process of decision-making that involves pooling the knowledge of a group of independent experts (as in the Delphi Technique) is not ideal. There, we end up with a set of independent but entirely subjective opinions which hardly ever can be traced to an objective data or information on the subject at question. The expert status, however high it might be, simply cannot substitute for a structured, systemic, and quantitative decision-making algorithm looking at the matter holistically. Thus, the important question here still is:

> How can the nature of the *donor*'s organization or entity create or contribute to the communication and incentive structure which influences decisions? [58; p.56].

5/1/2 Decision-Making Methodology among Risk-Laden Alternatives

Let us now try to suggest how the proposed decision-making methodology should be structured so that it would address the **problems of risk in conflicting socio-political environments**. We outline the methodology in a sequence of steps:

STEP 1: Ideally, we should be able to quantitatively assess the possible overall systems disutility—i.e. the monetary sum of all losses, abortive measures and failures in economy and social and political environment—directly from the length of distance between the investigated societies. The real incidents historical databases—some of which we presented in previous chapters—in which all such recorded disutilities would have been transformed into a single monetary losses should help us here.

DISCUSSION: **Conflicts within the *recipient* society are the function of intra-societal heterogeneity**, particularly that of socio-economic and socio-political stratification and sketchy social welfare in that society. **These factors drive the "in-between-society" or, as we say, "inter-societal" characteristic, further away from the *donor* society → that is the physical distance between the investigated societies on the D-curve.**

Methodologically and graphically speaking, we have to allocate the definitional point **Si** of the *recipient* society on the D-curve first. This is the measure of intra-society heterogeneity. Assuming the *donor*'s point is known (if not, we have to allocate this point as well) **the magnitude of inter-society heterogeneity is then mapped by the physical distance between the two.** As we should strive for a modern, computer-enhanced decision-making process, programming this stage, with allowance for frequent real-life numerical updates, is not very difficult to achieve.

STEP 2: Once we have the physical distance between the points S_i and $S_{(i+1)}$ measured, and thus the magnitude of the "risk-in-conflicting-socio-political-environment" assessed, we shall immediately use it as one of the major input-factors in the decision-making technique which is presented in detail and discussed in the next chapter.

DISCUSSION: At the moment a sufficient thing to say is that the technique is based on the "factor-and-importance-weight trees"—explained in greater details in the Appendix—that will investigate various, quantitatively enumerated scenarios before settling on the optimal one.

STEP 3: As the decision-maker will have had all the basic data, their infrastructure and causal-chain effects in one simple graphical model, with just a few definitional tables of individual, quantitatively defined scenarios and alternatives, it would be relatively easy, and virtually foolproof to instantly assess the short-term, medium-term and long-term overall disutility effects stemming from the *donor's* decision on one or the other policy alternative.

DISCUSSION: First of all, only simple computer software is needed here. **The most important** thing would be to make sure that all the scenarios—inclusive of all the quantitatively defined **conversion tables**—are being constantly upgraded and updated by independent experts.

However, first things first. **In order to make the "risk in conflicting socio-political environments" characteristic the centerpiece of this study we have to algebraically formalize the notions presented in this and previous chapters.** Therefore, we invoke the last two propositions in Chapter 4, particularly **LEMMA 4.1**. This claims that the **slip down along the slide curve D comes more naturally and is much deeper** (or longer if the distance in the curve D is considered) **for a society positioned on the lower-right-hand end of the SLIDE** than for one allocated on the upper-left-hand (or on the middle part) of the curve. Therefore the allocation of societies, particularly those on the lower-right end of the slide, adds, according to notion **(2.6)**, an extra danger of risk to the overall picture and we say:

ASSUMPTION 5.1:
Assume that, according to DEFINITION 2.7 and PROPOSITIONS 3.2–3.4, the magnitude of risk of conflict in business transactions (and/or in simple economic aid) between the two incompatible socio-political environments S1 and S2 allocated on the D-curve can be mapped and measured by the physical distance between the points-models of a DONOR and a RECIPIENT society along the arc—which we denote as S1 $\cap$ S2—on the slide curve D.

This assumption presents a good theoretical basis for graphical mapping of the risk factor for the *donor* country and one that can be transformed into an ordinal numerical characteristic. Also, through the ordinal numbers, we can reasonably precisely formulate the relative magnitudes of risk for any two pairs of investigated societies, or for one *donor* and several different *recipients*.

Still, the question stands: **Can we interpret and quantify the upcoming crisis associated with the risk factor appearance on the D-curve in real monetary terms?** Because only in these terms will the decision-making scheme make any sense at all. The answer is: **Yes**. The way to quantify the risk factor is to start with the numerical difference between the ordinals S_i.

5/1/3 Quantitative Assessment of the Risk Factor

Assume two societies: A *donor* at the 2nd point from the "top of the D-curve" and a *recipient* at the 7th point on the hyperbola, well down and to the right from the first point. Then we say that the risk magnitude equals the difference of 5 points on the graph. The same *donor* and another *recipient* at 4th point have only 2 points difference and we say the risk of conflict attached to the second pair's interaction is "smaller." That agrees with the notion **(2.5)**—and of scheme **(A.4)** in the Appendix—which says that qualitative behavioral phenomena can be mapped by interval estimates of instruments [91] into the ordinal sphere of characteristics. It means that the monotonic transforms of the difference of the ordinal values or, specifically, one-to-one correspondence of the "smaller risk" to the real-life numerical datum or numerical information should be the final product of the algorithm. Thus, the elaborate conversion table in **EXHIBIT 4.2**—which is not at all about risk—shows just the first part: verbal definition-to-ordinal scale. **The actual quantification of the label "smaller" or "greater" (for that matter) is left to a one-to-one correspondence between the verbal definitions and the actual quantitative data to be supplied by real-life database.**

Therefore, we should treat the problem of increasing or decreasing ordinal values of ranks of points S_i, i = 1....m—that under the circumstances spelled out in **ASSUMPTION 5.1**—as mapping of increasing or decreasing heterogeneities of complex socio-political environments.

PROPOSITION 5.1:
Suppose we have a *donor* society, allocated as point Si and a *recipient* one Si+k, both of which, according to ASSUMPTION 5.1, have a specific (or near specific) allocation on the curve D. We say that the more "generic" score-points, Sk, k = 1 ... (m-2), in EXHIBIT 4.3 there are between these two societies on the sliding curve D, or (in the graphical sense) the greater the arc Si ∩ Si+k, the greater risk and thus the greater expected overall (i.e. economic and even political) systems disutility there exists for the *donor* society, which finds itself in conflict over the goal of the original deal initiated with the politically and/or religiously incompatible *recipient* society.

PROOF: Let us start with **PROPOSITION 3.3** and its claim that a society whose point $S_{(i+k)}$ is located behind (i.e. down and to the right of) another society's characteristic S_i, i =1 ... m, ends up with greater socio-economic and socio-political disarray given the same negative economic shock, impetus, down-pressure etc. Logically then, society S_{i2} ends up worse off than S_{i1}, with society S_{i3} worse off still etc. **ASSUMPTION 5.1**, which is in fact only **DEFINITION 2.7** expressed graphically, and the following approximation

$$S_i S_{i+1} + S_{i+1} S_{i+2} + \ldots + S_{i+(k-1)} S_{i+k} \cong S_i \cap S_{i+k}$$

where k = 1 ... (m-2) then completes the proof.

Practical acknowledgment of this proposition can be drawn from the following excerpt from the merit of the list of "creditworthy" countries [59; p. 213], which to certain extent simulates the D-curve in **EXHIBIT 4.3**:

> Still, all of the countries at the top of the list are good risks to which banks readily extend new credit ... those countries at the bottom would find new commercial bank lending practically impossible to attract.

Obviously, this relates to the responsible big financial institutions that have developed some sort of self-protective risk-aversion policy. Unfortunately, for each such individual "responsible *donor*" there exists several risk-taking individuals for which big risk equals big profit and/or the presumed big increase in the *recipient* society's well-being.

Next, we shall leave the things as they stand now and, instead, we split the definitional scale of societies on the D-curve in **EXHIBIT 4.3** into three distinct groups or intervals:

In the first group we have the so called NATO societies represented by **points S_1 and S_2**. For almost a century in the West (in our case denoted as "NATO" although NATO itself exists only half that period and, moreover, some important Western countries such as France are not NATO members), democracy has meant liberal democracy—not just free and fair elections, but also the sanctity of basic liberties, like free speech and assembly, private property and contracts, and the rule of law [15] as it is also delineated in scenario **(3.7)**.

For the second group—in our case group defined by $S_3 \ldots S_6$, among which the members belong to the Gulf states (Bahrain, Kuwait, U.A.E.), also Singapore, Taiwan, South Korea, Mexico, Pakistan and all the so-called transitional (i.e. former COMECON and other single-party-rule) countries—the situation and future is not so clear. We see, at best, illiberal democracies (also known as "pseudo-democracies" with plenty of elections but few individual rights [4]), where a powerful oligarchy is always ready to bypass the parliaments. In the cases of Gulf States' monarchies, there is not even any pretence insofar as "democratic" institutions are concerned.

With no checks-and-balances built in, these societies' socio-political trends may sway wildly from simple democratic-cum-oligarchic symbiosis, to authoritarian-oligarchic rule by decrees and even to general anarchy, in which only crooks prosper, in any one country within a few years time. Examples abound: Mexico in the early 1990s (and two decades after), Zimbabwe within the last two decades, Azerbaijan's, Turkmenistan's and Uzbekistan's recent slide into the third group, Iran's slow descent into a political and socio-economic abyss, etc. The crucial criterion, the one we presented in **PROPOSITION 4.2** and discussed thereafter, is the presence of armed fanatical-ideological or fanatical fundamental-religious groups in those societies. They are capable of inciting terrorist actions in whatever country they choose—preferably though in the major *donor* ones—and thus immediately plant huge potential disutility back into the *donors*.

And then there is **the third group**, $S_7 ... S_9$. These are typical, old-fashioned and corrupt, ruling-class-led regimes with economies taken for their private fiefdoms: North Korea, Zimbabwe and a few Central African countries where genocide is still a prevailing method of social policy. These countries do not, in effect, differ much from the old communist systems. Oligarchy-assumed and used centrist rigidity, in which the conditions of scenario **(3.8)** flourish with entirely negative impact, are providing a real-life illustration of **LEMMA 4.1**. Malaysia, Indonesia (and perhaps Thailand) are obviously prime candidates for membership in this group, but the jury is still out on whether counties (and societies) such as Saudi Arabia should not belong there too.

The most troublesome finding is that **in the case of serious economic pressure the only relatively safe societies are those in the first group,** which immediately poses the big question for current and future global political, monetary and economic decision-makers:

Q1: How, in the term of **PROPOSITION 5.1**, can we minimize the risk-of-conflict while interacting with societies without long, historical, democratic and laissez-faire economic traditions; in other words: with societies that lie somewhere way down and at the right-end of the slide curve D (in **EXHIBIT 4.3**) from the *donor* society?

This question can be even extended to cover more general conditions when we use the graphically expressed model of societies:

Suppose that the criterion length of the D-curve arc is the same between the two pairs of societies' definitional points, $S_i \cap S_{i+k} = S_i^* \cap S_{i+k}^*$, $k = 1 ...$

m-2, although the *donor* societies are defined at two different points, $S_i \neq S_i^*$, one below the other on the D. The pertinent question then is:

Q2: Can our decision-makers tell which of these two *donor-recipient* systems, with the same quantifier of risk, would feature greater long-term socio-economic and socio-political wellbeing and environment more conducive to other long-term deals following from amicable societal interaction? To put it in terms of risk-of-conflict category and related overall systems disutility the question simply is: which of the two *donor-recipient* systems would produce lower cumulative overall disutility (in the long run)?

We shall do our best to answer these questions in the following paragraphs. Right now we think that a little reflection on the matter of "cumulative risk in conflicting socio-political environments" might be in order.

In **DEFINITION 2.6** we claim that the occurrence of major composite business (trade and/or banking) problems in *recipient* countries always increases the intra-societal heterogeneity because it will negatively affect the social and political spheres as well. Political dissatisfaction, hopelessness in the society, and social and political (eventually religious) activism, and political (eventually armed) conflicts are the main problems we can expect to happen there. If combined with religious radicalism and the export of terrorism, the hole we dug ourselves in these countries is indeed very deep. Elements of our methodology should be able to handle most of these pitfalls via **the conversion tables** combined with a data-base of real-life occurrences.

5/2   Conversion Tables for Risk in Conflicting (Exogenous vs. Indigenous) Socio-Political Environments

5/2/1   Introductory Remarks and Discussion

Let us start with **DEFINITION 2.9 and** some notions from Chapters 3 and 4 to which we shall add some personal experience [42].

It is a well known—but not necessarily always acted upon—fact that the behavior of any socio-economic system is based solely on the (standard of) behavior of the people in the given society. Even in a most repressive despotism, there are still people in that society that could make the difference given the basic "law and order" instincts and decency of their societal interrelations.

Thus, a **necessary but not sufficient, condition is that a transparent legal system**—above all the substantive law and code of conduct, inclusive of tailor-made to the individual society sanctions and punishment scale—**is installed, be it imported or compiled from outside existing legal systems, in a society.**

To make the condition sufficient, a lot more is needed. As long as (by definition) everybody is corruptible [35], [36] and [38], inclusive of law enforcers and other assorted watchdogs, a logical approach of every member of the *recipient* society towards the law (particularly the substantive law) is clear: the code of conduct does not pay at all; in fact, every law-violator must expect not only zero sanctions but a high reward. From all of the above, a viable proposition can be charted.

In the previous two chapters we have seen that the three groupings of societies on the D-slide curve differentiate mostly in so far as the quality of legal system, and above all the substantive law, code of conduct and sanctions and punishments is concerned. At the same time **PROPOSITION 5.1, PROPOSITION 4.1 and LEMMA 4.1** tell us about symbiosis between the corrupt socio-political systems and debacle-prone economic environments producing crises more frequently and with greater and **highly unpredictable** negative impact to societies on the tail end of the curve D.

Above all, however, they tell us about the relationship between the length of the arc between the two investigated (*donor* and *recipient*) societies on the curve and the magnitude of socio-economic and socio-political decay of societies, which gets deeper the more the *recipient* societies are allocated closer to the end of the slide-graph.

Then we hear—and see in causal chains **(2.1) - (2.2)**—that more unstable and unpredictable socio-political systems funnel greater socio-economic unpredictability. The vicious circle is now complete. Given all of that, the following proposition and lemma clearly follow:

PROPOSITION 5.2:
Suppose we have two societies: the *donor* one, Si, and the *recipient* one, Si+k, k = 1 ... m-2, on the slide curve D. The risk of conflict and expected overall *donor-recipient* systems disutility (during simple economic aid as well as business transactions)—brought about by their level of incompatibility (or dissimilarity)—is then represented by the length of arc Si ∩ Si+k or (from PROPOSITION 5.1) by the number of intermediate points Sk in between Si and Si+k.

The Crucial Challenge for International Aid

This overall risk of greater conflict for the *donor–recipient* transactions:

(A) <u>Increases</u> either with choosing the *recipient's* partner, say S_{i+k+j}, $j = 1 \ldots n$, $n \neq m$, farther down and to the right of the original society S_{i+k}, which makes

(5.1) $\quad S_i \cap S_{i+k+j}$ greater than $S_i \cap S_{i+k}$

Or, when the original *donor* society improves its intra-societal homogeneity—for example, because the newly elected administration "homogenizes" the society—to a higher position, say S_{i-j}, on the D-curve.

Thus,

(5.2) $\quad S_{i-j} \cap S_{i+k}$ is greater than $S_i \cap S_{i+k}$

And, as a logical follow-up, it doesn't want more political problems with its *recipients*.

EXAMPLE: Russia is now supporting greater stability in Egypt, Iran, and its former (i.e. USSR) republics. She has also tried to find a reasonable *fait accompli* with Ukraine.

(B) <u>Decreases</u> when

(5.3) $\quad S_{i+j} \cap S_{i+k}$ is smaller than $S_i \cap S_{i+k}$, $j = 1 \ldots n$, $n \neq m$

PROOF: The first part represented by inequality **(5.1)** follows clearly from **PROPOSITION 4.1** and **PROPOSITION 5.1**. The second part follows from **PROPOSITION 3.3** and **LEMMA 4.1**, both stressing the fact that both S_{i+j} and S_{i+k+j} are less stable and less predictable societies and therefore the probable cumulative disutility (i.e. risk of this to happen) of ***donor-recipient*** system is greater under ceteris paribus conditions. Inequality **(5.3)** then follows from the proof of **PROPOSITION 5.1** when $S_{i+j} \cap S_{i+k}$ could be approximated by $S_i \cap S_{i+k-j}$ based on greater society closeness of the ***donor*** and ***recipient*** and thus lesser danger of the incomprehensibility between their respective societies. Here is the explanation why the indigenous NGOs—although financed by international NGOs—are "dollar for dollar" much more effective in local aid (than "bilateral aid", i.e. country to country), voiced in [177; p.A14]. NGOs typically have people working at the grassroots levels, building schools, training farmers, sewing up war victims and the like which makes their "communes" much closer to the *recipient* societies.

The lemma following from the above axiomatic has, at this moment, nothing to do with the system we are trying to put in place. It is only the logical conclusion form the algebraic apparatus we have used and as such will serve as a "wake-up call" for the various politicians, CEOs and heads of NGOs.

LEMMA 5.1:
Suppose we define an overall world-wide inter-societal heterogeneity as the sum of every (*donor-recipient*) heterogeneity, graphically depicted as a sum of distances-arcs on the D-curve and denoted by CHAOS:

(5.4) $$\text{CHAOS} = \sum_{i,k} S_i \cap S_{i+k}, \; i \neq k$$

Then we say that CHAOS increases with time.

PROOF: Follows from **PROPOSITION 3.3**, **PROPOSITION 4.1**, **LEMMA 4.1** and **PROPOSITION 5.2 (A)**. We shall return to this result later in the following chapters.

Now, the question is: **How do we transpose qualifiers like "less stable," "less predictable," and, most importantly, "risk (or disutility) increases" into a scale that would make sense to a standard decision-maker who either understands verbal-cum-political categories (diplomats) or balance sheets and profits (businessmen, bankers etc.)?**

The answer, again, lies in **conversion tables**—first mentioned in **DEFINITION 2.9** and also in the Appendix—and of which a practical real-life example is seen in **EXHIBIT 4.3**.

However, before we start some meaningful construction of the risk conversion table we shall need another element of the mosaic to be established first.

To this end we just remind the reader that the crucial element of the high probability of the risk-of-conflict raised through the transactions between *donor* and *recipient* societies is the non-existence of 'law and order' system comparable to any *donor* society and the impossibility to enforce any of the existing legal norms—least of all those concerned with substantive law—in developing (*recipient*) countries. Last but not least, there is the fact that the "reigning" oligarchy is "untouchable" by the society's legal institutions (if they even exist). To this we add a valid point. Even in the most pro-Western Moslem country, Sharia Law (i.e. traditional religious instructions of general behavior the way the local clerics interpret the Quran) is the law of the country and as such supersedes any other international protocols, conventions and legal machinery. If, in fact these clerics, as is the case in Iran, are the oligarchy, they can even legally do as they please.

This is crucial because fraud in the sphere of government hurts the society most: First, because the money has been removed directly from the society's future expenditures and secondly, because part of the same money is used to perpetuate further corruption, as illustrated by this statement from a Burmese dissident [74; p.2]:

> The real benefits of investments now go to the military regime and their connections. They go to small, very privileged elite. And the people get very little.

Second, because it takes specialized expertise to discover especially crafty violators. Such an expertise may not exist—not at the required quantity and quality anyway—in many transitional and newly "liberalized" societies for perhaps as long as several indigenous generations' life-times, if ever.

In the meantime, **two possible ways of remedy may be found feasible and practical:**

First, it may be worth considering importing that missing specialized legal expertise—both practitioners and academics—from the countries of the upper groups (of the D-curve) until fully educated indigenous generations take over. The problem with this approach is that it may assure the proper legal system but not necessarily a fair and universally upheld one. After all, there is still the untouchable oligarchy in the game.

A classic example is, again, Saudi Arabia and other Gulf oil-rich states that have been importing legal professionals for some time (provided that they are Arabic speakers). However, they can only introduce basic mercantile law points into the business agreement between the two corporate (usually one local and one foreign) entities. In every other instance—including overruling even these business basic agreements if it suits them—they have left Sharia Law in place, making international law subject to the indigenous paralegal clergy. Also, they have not incorporated especially draconian punishment for violators—this is where the oligarchy tries to sabotage any such action that would contradict its interests [42]—and obviously set different standards for different classes in the society. Typical, in this context, is the claim of the Indonesian Finance Minister [80; p.1]:

> In reality, if you want to nail someone you must be more powerful than the one you're trying to catch.

This is something that is very difficult to achieve in many autocratic regimes.

A different situation exist in the Central and Eastern European 'transitional democracies' unless they are already in the EU, which is—via the EU Court in Strasbourg—the only chance for the recovery of the basic principles of the Napoleonic Code and the civilized behavior of yore [171; pp.55-58]. If not, problems abound. Import of 'law and order' professionals is hampered, first of all, by language barriers (see **PROPOSITION 5.2 (B)**). In these countries, only very few people can be understood in anything other than their mother tongue. Conversely, you find very few professionals speaking the Slavic languages living in the West and willing to relocate (even for a couple of years). On this topic, several scenarios have been analyzed [102]; one based on the assumption that new generations will absorb new, ethical and lawful conduct in the society whereby the problem of lawlessness in the society will cease to exist. Feedback, in terms of many letters and other means of communications, tells us that the society does not believe in this theory, saying in effect:

> Once the children recognize that crooks and liars always end up on top, nothing can sway them from imitating these 'qualities' they believe to get them there too.

Then there is the question of cost. For poor developing countries, where basic education, let alone university education, is in short supply with very few skilled educators about and no money for import of expatriate specialists or educators of any kind, this alternative is clearly a non-starter. Similar problems hold for many a transitional society too. For both, due to the prohibitive cost and fear of the loss of power, the corrupt elite has therefore kept virtually a free hand not only to milk and destroy its society—as seen in scenario **(3.8)**—but also to let the destabilization spill over into the region and eventually make problems for *donors* as well. Typical in this respect are some pauperized developing countries in Africa, otherwise very rich in natural resources. In literature [88] we read:

> The result is that, in order to acquire military power, those who rule ... have not needed to develop the economy ... or establish an efficient and honest administration capable of collecting and handling taxes with which to pay for military forces ... they have only to grant a concession to a foreign country to make a hole in the ground and pay for taking away what is found.

The second alternative is theoretically more feasible, yet also strongly politically charged and thus not very "palatable." It calls for federalization (or as the Swiss model calls it cantonalization) of the two neighboring intra-societal heterogeneous societies-states in which the lower-lying (on D-curve) transitional state steps into some sort of socio-political union with the developed one next door. The same or similar language is a necessary assumption there (see **PROPOSITION 5.2 (B)**), just as willingness to let the professionals from the *donor* society take over the introduction of the comparative substantive law (and legal institutions and legal system generally), and take care of enforceability of existing legal packages to all citizens inclusive of the indigenous oligarchies. To a certain extent, and with the above reservations, this is what the European Union (EC, EURO and Brussels) is all about. Similar models were traced throughout the history of humankind, where several federalized multi-ethnic states in which the application of a single legal system and its absolute enforcement made them last for centuries (e.g. Roman Empire, Austro-Hungarian Monarchy, British Empire etc.). In modern times there was the reasonably successful implanting of the former DDR into the FRD—with reservations—while some other "candidates," such as unified Korea and Vietnam, are still waiting. From the above discussion, some general ideas—and, subsequently, feasible policies—about lowering the risk factor in the interaction of two, or more, heterogeneous societies can be established.

5/2/2 Tools for Minimizing the Risk Factor

We have said that the real damage stemming from risky transactions and deals in conflicting socio-political environments always follow the initial economic and/or political shocks caused by the indigenous oligarchy. **Whether the economic shock was caused entirely by indigenous factors or the unscrupulous exogenous multinationals played a role in it as well is largely immaterial**. What is important is this notion.

When such an overall damage possibility appears on the horizon, all **the corrective actions** we plan, such as: emergency international loans, aid transfers, etc. might become much more effective when **negotiated with the following propositions in mind**, starting with the one pertaining to the general situation and a subsequent one dealing with extremities:

PROPOSITION 5.3:
Let us take for granted that increase of intra-society heterogeneity is a function of time. Then, to reverse this axiomatic phenomenon, the society itself (with outside help and/or advice) will have to install and legitimize a society-friendly indigenous administration and a legal system that is fair, acceptable to all the society's social strata—also such that it is transparent with "checks-and-balances" in play so that the administration cannot revert to the old oligarchic ways—and enforce it, even brutally if need be. Only then we will ensure sustainable socio-economic and socio-political growth of the society.

SCHEME OF PROOF: We have shown in Chapter 3 that a society has a future only when the key conditions of scenario (**3.7**) are firmly imbedded in

Risk Assessment of Conflicts

its behavior. For the sake of clarity we are reprinting a graphical image of the subject from Chapter 3 in **EXHIBIT 5.1**. The major issues are:

"learning process of how to play the social roles," "implicit rules containing the accumulated tacit knowledge of past generations," and "adherence to a complex system of moral codes ... as well as a system of punishment for violators ... a system under which bad men can do least harm."

EXHIBIT 5.1: Learning Process Scenarios

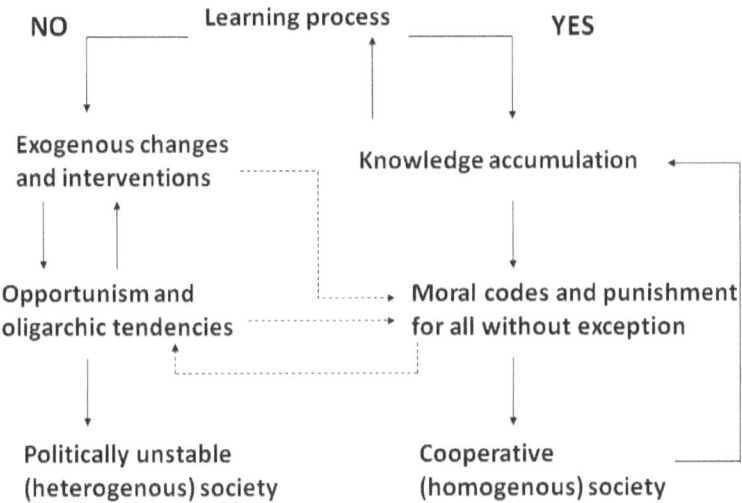

We note that there is no *"learning process"* or *"accumulated knowledge of past generations"* (of how to behave responsibly; note by M.K.) in the tacit society assumptions in **PROPOSITION 5.3**. Therefore, **the indigenous administration**, that will use the chosen (improved indigenous or imported exogenous) legal system and will enforce it (brutally, if needed) until it becomes the moral and ethical standard of the society—denoted by *"exogenous changes and interventions"* in **EXHIBIT 5.1**—**must play the role of proxy for these missing historical behavioral links**. The transparency of the whole political-administrative process and, above all, the moral, ethical (or at least popular) esteem the administration is held in by the society then assures that the one-way dashed arrow *"exogenous changes and intervention"* → *"moral codes and punishment for all without exception"* is a correct expression of the socio-political process.

DISCUSSION: This is why the people-friendly "autocrats" of the caliber of Putin (e.g. Fidel Castro) have been far more preferable (in their own societies) than whatever half-baked plans to exogenously force "democracy" of the British, American, or French style upon a society that has had no experience with either and probably no stomach for it.

And then there are **rogue societies**—North African "khaliphates" for example—**that actually pose a grave danger to the rest of the world**. As these are based on extremely poor (and/or extremely politically-cum-religiously naive) society elements and therefore ideal breeding grounds for armed warriors of any extreme religious and/or political persuasion—bent on installing a reign of terror wherever it suits their leaders' long-term goals—they represent not a nation- or society-state but the second coming of the Wild West, where the warlord with stronger "enforcers" and heavier weapons temporarily rules. Therefore, a vastly different solution must be found to contain this danger, perhaps along the following lines.

PROPOSITION 5.4:
Assume that a strongly intra-societal heterogeneous society—whose code of conduct oversteps by far even the most lenient criteria of general human behavior—poses a grave risk of a possible devastating "socio-economic and political collapse" domino effect to the whole region. Assume that PROPOSITIONS 3.1–3.3, 4.1, 5.1–5.3 hold, but we also note that simple installation of the (new) legal system and its indigenous enforcement is not working at all, as PROPOSITION 5.3 describes.

Then, to stem and alleviate the risk, the combined forces of exogenous entities (NATO and developed societies' peace-forces) must fulfil several conditions simultaneously:

(1) To physically seal the border—inclusive of international banking, postal and major information channels—with letting in only the NGOs' personnel, monetary, and consumer goods (inclusive of groceries) aid.

(2) To snuff out the power of the corrupt oligarchy and the militant religious-cum-political autocrats who were kept in power by their own 'militants-cum-militia,' the country's indigenous militants have to be overrun by exogenous military forces from NATO and neutral countries. [NOTE: as this is the NOW-OR-NEVER battle—in so far as there is an entire world at stake and the militants are no regular army, killing whole families in their "ethnic cleansing"—the ideal outcome would be complete annihilation of the militant "army."]

(3) To immediately elevate the status of women and increase the living standard of the society.

(4) To substitute the corrupt oligarchy with an indigenous (or "quasi indigenous" of indigenous expatriates) administration either in the form of historically palatable moderate (parliamentary) autocracy or moderate religious hierarchy with a parliament.

(5) To enact a legal system that is fair, acceptable to all the society's social strata—also such that it is transparent with "checks-and-balances" in play so that the administration cannot revert to the old oligarchic ways—and enforce it. This enforcement may be brutal if need be, by new indigenous police and indigenous armed forces specially recruited from the loyal indigenous population.

(6) To leave the exogenous administrators and the exogenous armed forces in situ until the situation becomes stabilized.

SCHEME OF PROOF: The first two conditions are tantamount to solving problems in any developing and/or transitional society and are therefore covered by **PROPOSITION 5.2 (B)** and **5.3**. The third condition follows from the causal chains **(3.17)** - **(3.18)** of the so called "devil's spiral" and is set to alleviate political tensions in the given society. To that aim, it has been proven time and again in all the least developed countries that the womenfolk form the most stable and, at the same time, most entrepreneurial strata of any (whatever primitive) society [178; p.A15] because of their built-in drive for safeguarding the family (and, thus, the young generation).

To make the heterogeneous society's peaceful coexistence permanent so that it can heal, the first two conditions must be met unconditionally. To this end, for the sake of simplicity, let us assume that the world can be modeled by a two-dimensional space in which one society—economically marginal but politically and socially highly polarized, armed, and possessing suicidal militancy allowing its citizens to hate other societies more than they love life [162; p.6]—can affect the rest of the world in a way leading it into certain socio-economic and moral destruction. **Assume also that there exists a third dimension, accessible to the "rest of the world" because of its strong self-preservation instincts and resolve matched by appropriate economic and military power.**

As anecdotal explanation of higher-dimensional spaces (4th, 5th, ...) vis-à-vis the lower ones (in any basic physics text) assumes the ability of "inhabitants" of the higher space to elevate any object from the lower-dimensional space and let it hover temporarily outside of its original domain, this is what is bound to happen: **(a)** The political power of warlords (i.e. political and/or religious gurus) will be marginalized because of **(a.1)** loss of funds from foreign "bankrollers," **(a.2)** loss of "hired guns" from foreign staging grounds and, **(a.3)** their own physical incarceration (eventually liquidation, if they stage armed rebellion against the monetarily well-endowed armed forces of the administration); **(b)** Once the ideological pressure is removed, the society and particularly its women will, under their socially, politically and economically strongly elevated status—this is where condition **3** comes in—**(b.1)** take over, with the help of a vastly revamped school system, the rearing of their children, and **(b.2)** make sure that the basic human principles of intra-society behavior will, for the sake of their families, prevail. To this end, only conditions **(2)**, **(3)**, **(4)** and **(5)** of **PROPOSITION 5.4** are necessary. However, it is only in conjunction with conditions **(1)** and **(6)** that they are necessary and sufficient.

To illustrate **PROPOSITIONS 5.3 - 5.4**, we use several real-life examples.

EXAMPLES: In the first one, William Pfaff [126; p.8] writes:

> The war drove Taliban from power and uprooted the Al-Qaeda organization ... but substantial 'stability cost' (in terms of large peacekeeping and police force, not to mention government; added by M.K.) must be added to those, since the outcome has led to 'warlordism,' banditry, and (revived) opium production ... in some areas virtual anarchy prevails ... the new Afghanistan is more chaotic and less stable than the old.

In another one, Defense Secretary Donald Rumsfeld [127; p.4] asks:

> The question is, do you want to put your time and effort and money into the International Security Assistance Force—go take it from, say, 5,000 to 20,000 people ... There's one school of thought that thinks that's a desirable thing to do.

In the third one, the ***Washington Post***'s article "Lessons from Cambodia" [136; p.4] we read:

> The United Nations sent in a peacekeeping force that numbered almost 16,000 (compared to 4,000 in Afghanistan now; M.K.) ... but UN staged elections before disarming the combatants ... Hun Sen (the Vietnamese backed strongman) lost the election.......when the foreign peacekeepers had departed, Hun Sen ... chased his rivals from the country ... killing about 100 other opponents ... in the next election ... Hun Sen won, to nobody's surprise.

The last example uses the 1857 Sepoy Rebellion in India as a show of successful risk containing. In May, 1857, Indian sepoys in the Bengal army mutinied at an army station in Northern India. In the process they shot their (British) officers and marched on the old capital of Delhi with the intention to restore the Mughal Empire by expelling all foreigners from India. The rebellion spread very fast to the urban and rural communities of upper and central India while establishing full control over the Indian subcontinent took Western troops the better part of year to accomplish (see [180; p.A16]).

For the previous 50 years, the British had been imposing a large-scale transformation of Indian law, governance and society: too drastic changes for a mosaic of many different ethnicities and religions that has always revered its traditions. So, for example, some traditional institutions were banned, and formerly independent states were annexed. This eventually led to the belief that Christian evangelists were part of a plot to eradicate indigenous religion.

A valuable lesson was learned by the British. The most immediate result was the **India Act of 1858** transferring any semi-private power (for instance of the East India Company) to the direct rule of the Crown. Also, and more importantly, **they learned that Indian traditions must be respected and elite groups conciliated**. All this supports conditions **(4) - (6)** of **PROPOSITION 5.4**.

DISCUSSION: From all of these notions and experiences clearly emerges the absolute necessity to change the tack of the new indigenous—but not necessarily democratic at all costs—administration and to isolate the country physically: In other words, to seal the borders. In [128; p.4] we read, for instance:

> One important lesson to be drawn from East Timor is the need for a strong peacekeeping force with robust rules of engagement ... the UN forces were able to stop militia raids into East Timor from West Timor,

Later, in other source [129; p.8]:

> The United Nations went into Sierra Leone in 1999, for example, with an inadequate force of 6,000 that was humiliated by the country's limb-chopping rebels. Now the UN force there has been bumped up to 17,000, and the troubles have died down.

To put the economically ailing and socially deeply stratified societies on a better financial footing, eventually by annulment of their debt, is an idea being heard from many sides. Kofi Annan, former secretary-general of the United Nations says [132; p.1]:

> Globalization risks a devastating boomerang effect if the world's elite fail to increase spending to battle poverty in developing countries ... if more money is not spent on reducing poverty, some poor countries will collapse into conflict and anarchy and become a threat to global security and international business.

In another source [133; p.9] we read:

> And what developing nations? In a system that claims to advocate common peace and prosperity, it is almost laughable that there are developing countries devoting 60 percent of their GNP toward paying just the interest on some of their debts.

Mr. K. Courtis, vice-chairman of Goldman Sachs says [123; p.4]:

> There is a Himalaya of debt that is crushing the economies at a time of recession and deflation.

And, finally, Bob Geldof, writing in ***The Daily Telegraph*** [134; p.6], suggests forcefully**:**

> Debt is largely a by-product of the old world order. The Cold War was a mask for oppression and kleptocracy ... superpowers wrote large checks to dictators and asked no questions. And now we want that money back, the same money that was spent on brutalizing the population. No. That money should be used to help rebuild the state. When the debt is forgiven on conditions of ... accountability, it works.

In short, **PROPOSITION 5.4** debunks the theories that most major NGOs, such as UNMIK, NATO, UNDP, Euro Aid, etc., can succeed under the present policies.

While the "stick" and "carrot" policy is still a viable option for some, virtually peaceful and basically ethical, poor **SOUTH** societies (Caribbean, South Pacific Archipelagos, Central Asia, etc.), in the civil war-torn societies of the Middle East, and North and Central Africa a "huge stick" must be applied (according to **PROPOSITION 5.4**) by exogenous forces on the ruling indigenous warlords, religious ideologues (fomenting the civil wars), and warring insurgents and "liberation" fighters (from both sides) in Somalia, Sudan, Angola and, most recently, in Central Africa, Libya and Syria. The only "carrot"—and a big one—should be applied to women, children (unless they already enlisted into fighting forces) and a *bona fide* peaceful part of the indigenous men folk. The **NORTH**-based activists—do-gooders, and NGOs supporting "rebel fighters" (the code-word here is: 'liberation' fighters), of which some are actually financing the hard-core terrorists—are making the situation simply unmanageable.

The following axiom then stems from all the above propositions (particularly from **PROPOSITION 5.2 (B)**) and subsequent discussions.

AXIOM 5.1:
If our goal is to exert an influence on a specific socio-economic and political entity to rebuilt itself in a way that basic moral codes and constitution assures the same rights (and necessary obligations) for every single citizen, then the aforementioned "carrot" and, if need to be, a "stick" should be wielded by a peace-force and the temporary administration made of the nationals that are culturally, religiously, historically and language-wise close to the "society-in-healing." Then and only then there is a chance of sustained political and economic rebuilding of the society.

Earlier in human history, whenever these two alternatives (i.e. "carrot and stick" and "big stick only") came to a showdown, the former policy always prevailed. One of the most typical examples was the total implosion and collapse of the communist states of Eastern Europe (i.e. COMECON) in the 1980s. Even if we look far deeper into history, we came to a similar conclusion. We find that several practical applications of just the one condition of the **AXIOM 5.1** have already been not only tried but tried successfully in the last half of a century in Europe and in the Far East and one, just recently, in the Indian sub-continent.

The European examples started right after the end of WWII in 1945 when the Western European countries had been ravaged by the war and, with virtually all industrial and most of their agricultural production extinct, the peoples of Europe expected little more than an enduring hunger. At the time an international organization UNRRA started, under the auspices of the allied military commands. Through military channels it completely circumvented the societies' political structures and distributed unused military rations, shipped to Europe for much larger and longer campaigns, by which action the danger was successfully averted. This was the first truly international aid that did not acknowledge individual societies' structures or countries' frontiers; in fact it was administered by the exogenous agents: the Red Cross or the allied occupational armed forces.

Next came the reconstruction phase, also in Europe, through the *Marshall Plan*. The gist of this program was that individual governments (not firms or groups of societies) were offered by the United States what amounted a direct road to economic recovery for all countries, East and West, exhausted by the war. As these programs were completely, even unexpectedly, successful—remember, for instance, that the totally devastated economy of the West Germany got under full steam in a little less than 10 years.

While we are at the historical application of local oligarchy-substituting feature of **AXIOM 5.1**, we should not forget post-war Japan. In a similar economic situation as post-war Germany, with a political environment based historically on the dictatorship of the emperor and his clique, General MacArthur, a *de facto* American Viceroy in the country, single-handedly resuscitated not only the Japanese economy but virtually stripped the Emperor and the ruling classes from power and installed the stepping stone to what might become a parliamentary-democratic political system. Here, we have to stress that McArthur represented a typical "enlightened monarch" as we noted to be the only condition of success in **LEMMA 3.2**.

Another example of a socially heterogeneous but politically and/or religiously absolutely homogenous society is Saudi Arabia which has an autocrat, an all-mighty monarch, trying his best to keep the country—with extreme social disparities while religion-wise, the country is also the birthplace of the most radical Islamic sect of all times, the Wahabis, and, last but not least, the al-Qaeda leader, the late Osama bin Laden was born there—not just together but on the social upswing as well. In that, he is incredibly lucky because not only the population is religiously homogeneous but the well-armed indigenous Bedu tribes—which the Saudi armed forces mostly come from as well—are totally loyal to the royal family. Hence, there is really no need to apply **PROPOSITION 5.4** as most of its attributes are already in place. To suspend the monarchy and physically isolate the country (even if it were technically possible, which we doubt because of the oil demand) would make no social improvement in the Saudi society.

It is quite possible that the society will continue along the statement of **PROPOSITION 4.1** for a long time, as medieval behavioral traits are fairly difficult to bend let alone to break. The following **LEMMA 5.2** should summarize the situation.

A practical, and historically successful, application of **PROPOSITION 5.4** might find its model in the political entity, known throughout human history as a **"protectorate"** and discussed in **DEFINITION 2.14**. Here a rationale being that if a (temporary) protectorate was set up over any deeply economically (and hence) politically troubled society, some of the major socio-political obstacles, such as: socio-political polarization of society, rule of the gangsters, warlords, terrorist-bandits etc. rather than one of the law, and perceived loss of individual rights and liberties, should in time completely disappear.

Some examples can be found in recent publications. In one [131; p.6] we read:

> Nation-building is a blunder-prone business, but it can succeed. In 1992, Mozambique was forlorn and war-ravaged, but with military

Risk Assessment of Conflicts

and civilian help from the UN it has become one of the fastest growing economies in the world ... likewise Uganda was one of the world's horror stories in the 1970s, and now, after a push by Tanzanian troops in 1979 to evict Idi Amin, it is among the stars of Africa.

On the other side, real-life examples of enormous importance—where the combination of **PROPOSITIONS 5.3 - 5.4** should have been applied, but wasn't—can be made out of virtually **all** transitional and "fast" developing societies around the globe. The most glaring blunders of the 'free-market' campaign in all former COMECON countries in the last decade are personified by Ukraine, Czech Republic, Hungary, Central Asian republics, Serbia, Montenegro etc. None of these countries could enforce the law, let alone punish violators, and thus their intra-societal heterogeneity has been rising all the time. In some of them, such as Kyrgyzstan and Uzbekistan (not to mentioned Kazakhstan) it has already reached a level that is dangerous to the region.

Another risk-lowering strategy stems from the following notion. The economic, social, and hence, political necessity—since, as we showed in Chapters 3 and 4, only economically prosperous society are politically stable under whatever regime; classical example here is Saudi Arabia where up till now only the petro-dollars kept the Bedouin tribes firmly behind the monarchy and, hence, the country is more or less politically stable—tends to strongly favor the integration of small independent states into economic (first and, possibly, political later) blocks. The formation and economic success of BENELUX, after WWII, opened the door to the idea of the politically-charged EU later on. **NOTE:** Actually, any recent and future social, economic and, above all, political crises within the EU are the best real-life proof of: **(2.1), (2.2), PROPOSITIONS 3.2, 3.3, 5.1, and 5.2 (B)**.

The necessary condition of any such economic or political block follows, among others, from **PROPOSITIONS 5.1** and **5.2 (B)** and we formulate two lemmas concerned with this situation.

LEMMA 5.2:
The necessary condition for much better chances of successful co-operation among the blocks of developing countries appears to be when and only when the block is formed from "generic" societies, i.e. those with the same (or similar) political, tribal and/or religious stratification and approximate weight of each strata in their socio-economic and political environment.

PROOF follows, from causal chains **(2.1), (2.2)** and **PROPOSITIONS 3.2** and **3.3** that yield **PROPOSITIONS 5.1** and **5.2 (B)** and we can only add that by not heeding this necessary condition we virtually assure that completely contradictory socio-economic (and, above all, political) trends started by a simple economic shock could take the block and any further co-operation apart for a very long time. There is not any better illustration of this than in the history of Europe when the **EU 9**, in 1979, opened the door to, eventually, 20+ strong memberships. Besides, **LEMMA 5.2** effectively squashes any envy between the two peoples (usually a strong political argument of ruling oligarchies; even, and especially, in today's EU).

A logical follow-up of **LEMMA 5.2** (based on the same preambles) dictates another development-policy axiom. Using the very same logical steps, the following lemma can be proved.

LEMMA 5.3:
The economic and social aid, technology and know-how transfer to crisis-stricken *recipients* should be sought to come from better developed socio-economic entities (*donors*) that are historically, behaviorally, politically and religiously closest to the *recipients*, rather than from the very best technologically, technically and cognitively super-developed *donors* that are (historically) so inter-societal heterogeneous that are not able to comprehend the culture, traditions and behavioral make-up of the *recipients*.

PROOF follows from **PROPOSITION 5.1, 5.2** and **LEMMA 5.2**. For better 'digestion' of this basic truism that helped (or destroyed) the rulers from the Macedonian, Hellenic, Roman, and all others in the history of humankind we re-insert an example used in **PROPOSITION 5.1**: Russia is now supporting greater stability in Egypt, Iran and its former (i.e. USSR) republics. She has also tried to find a reasonable *fait accompli* with Ukraine.

5/2/2/1 Present-Day Terrorism Enhances Heterogeneity between *Donors* and *Recipients*

The problem of modern-time mobile and globally organized international terrorism—enhanced by social networking—might be already spotted in the fairly recent example of political application of a part of **PROPOSITION 5.3** in Pakistan. There in October 1999, a coup orchestrated by General Pervez Musharraf deposed the former prime minister of the country [61; p.B4]. The point of this occurrence is that, although a "democratic regime" had been apparently substituted by a "dictatorship," it was done with acknowledgment, previous tacit approval, and backing by all leading NATO and/or developed countries. The rationale was explained in the above mentioned source: *"many Pakistanis so loathed Mr. Sharif's* (totally corrupt; added by M.K.) *regime that the coup may be a democracy of* *sorts."* Thus, in the interest of calming down a possible political destabilization on the Indian subcontinent the *'immobilize-the-ruling-oligarchy'* strategy was arrived at.

The current problem is that internationally-bred radical Islamists have permeated the political underground and have been using Pakistan as a staging area not just for terrorist actions in Kashmir, India and Afghanistan but the whole world as well. *As the whole region became a bona fide powder keg (and point of origin) the importance of a strict adherence to both conditions of* **AXIOM 5.1** *becomes even more important.*

The principle behind the most recent politically charged instabilities in various societies is that the ruling classes (i.e. the oligarchs) have been using a mix of ideology, religion and relatively well paid army, police and mercenaries from the rest of the world to acquire absolute power. At the same time, they keep the rest of the society in complete isolation from the educational, scientific and, generally, cultural strides the world at large has made during the last several decades. In these societies—some of them are still communist countries (see e.g. Cuba, North Korea) or freshly independent yet impoverished former colonies in Africa or Asia or, on the other side, ostentatiously oil-rich yet socio-politically and cognitively poor countries of the Arabian Gulf—where (especially if both of the two antagonistic sects of Islam, Shia and Sunni, are living in the same country or on the border adjacent to another) there are due to be intra-societal heterogeneities at such a high level that a comparison to the proverbial 'powder keg' is not only valid but frightening too. [**NOTE:** Right now the only possible stabilization element in the whole Gulf is Saudi Arabia with religiously homogenous population and well armed indigenous Bedu tribes loyal to the royal family].

Societies with extra high intra-heterogeneity status when encountering whatever NGO deal that would not immediately enrich the ruling oligarchy—which means the enrichments will have to be squeezed from the already poor population—are the most probable trouble spots in the world today. For illustration we present an excerpt from Mark Bowden's ***Black Hawk Down,*** a book on the Somalia fiasco and now a very successful film, which reads [130; p.44]:

> This was Somalia ... a country in a state of violent anarchy and economic ruin. A United Nations initiative ... had evolved into an ... attempt at nation-building ... the head of UN mission was determined that some sort of coalition government should emerge ... what stood in his way was the cunning and ruthless figure of Mohamed Farrah

Aidid, the most powerful warlord in the country, a man capable of stealing his own people's UN food aid in order to tighten his grip on them.

This paragraph suggests that the possible and perhaps feasible policies to improve the life of the poor and reduce the base of possible terrorist conscripts didn't work at all. When cases of bombing subways, sports events (such as the Boston Marathon) and family restaurants full of children, building rocket launchers in school yards, cutting heads of hostages and large-scale religious cleansing are exponentially growing, there is nothing much humankind can do except completely and forever insulate or take out—with drones if necessary—these terrorist tribal chiefs as condition (2) of **PROPOSITION 5.4** insinuates. Some similar ideas are discussed in the last chapter.

5/2/3 Construction of the Risk-of-Crisis Conversion Table

5/2/3/1 Construction of the Basic "Risk-of-Impending-Crisis" Warning

After discussions on the importance of the "red flag" or "risk-of-crisis" warning—when dealing among two or more inter-heterogeneous entities, based on the physical distance of S-points on the D-curve and transformed into verbal assessment—against the **systemic and cumulative disutility** in any investigated *"donor-recipient"* system, we have to introduce, for the sake of the policy-makers, some sort of conversion table for monetary (financial and fiscal) quantifying of this "red-flag" warning.

We have postulated (see **DEFINITIONS 2.4 - 2.8**) that any transaction within heterogeneous entities (i.e. *donors* with heterogeneous *recipients)* has the propensity to become crisis-prone in conflicting socio-political and political entities. Then, **DEFINITION 2.9** and a detailed discussion in the Appendix tell us that the **monotonic sequence of intervals within which the risk-of-crisis warning are mapped provides a useful methodology of conversion of qualitative (verbal) factors into quantitative (monetary) ones in a** *recipient* society.

As risk-of-crisis is viewed to be a more important factor than most we have to start with conversion of its **potential "disutility"** which can be transformed [46; p.54] first into the bounded scale of any rational numbers and, in the next step, into the expected real-life financial and fiscal changes.

As we have already used rational numbers in labeling the physical points S_i, **i = 1, 2, ... 9, on the D-curve, we can easily use intervals of their numerical differentials**—as these differentials (in Chapter 4) were used to label potential over-all disutility between the numerically assessed definitional expression of the given socio-economic entity's intra-heterogeneity level—**for this first step.**

In the realm of **conversion tables** (see **DEFINITION 2.9** of Chapter 2 and the more detailed discussion in the Appendix) the quantification of the term "worth" is crucial. In our case, "worth" will have to be, obviously, translated into the numerical level of the "risk-of-crisis in the *recipient's* society."

NOTE: In the following text, only basic principles of the risk-of-crisis warning assessment and quantification will be presented and their results investigated. Basically though, we can postulate—within the logic of the D-curve in **EXHIBIT 4.3** and how the distance between the individual *donors* and *recipients* negatively affects the *recipients'* social, economic and political well-being—that only the simple principles of Chapters 4 and 5 will be followed in this step.

Let us now set up the conversion table in **EXHIBIT 5.1** based on: (a) the original conversion table in **EXHIBIT 4.3**, (b) **PROPOSITIONS 5.1** and **5.2**, (c) points on the D-curve which are graphical transpositions of **EXHIBIT 4.3**, and (d) the "worth" scale which ordinarily takes on 6 verbal levels: "excellent," "good," "fair," "poor," "bad" and "worthless" quantified in this step by the following rational numbers 1.0, 0.8, 0.6, 0.4, 0.2 and 0.0.

After changing the verbal interpretation of 1.0, 0.8, 0.6, 0.4 ... 0.0 into "No Risk at all," "Small Risk," "Fair to Considerable Risk," "Bad Risk," "Very Bad Risk," and "Do not Consider (Such High) Risk" we present the first risk-warning conversion table in **EXHIBIT 5.1**.

NOTE: It is necessary to keep in mind that here we are focusing on the problems from the *donors'* perspective. Thus, **the biggest problem is the societies on the lower-right tail of the D-curve** in **EXHIBIT 4.3**; those denoted and defined as S_7, S_8, and S_9. These countries feature the greatest intra-society heterogeneity and thus their allocation also shows significant inter-society heterogeneities (vis-à-vis most *donors* located higher up on the D). Hence, a typical risk score for a transaction in these societies should be somewhere within the interval **< 0.0, 0.4 >** in this conversion table; the political repercussions are denoted by single, double and triple asterisks.

Now, the conversion table in **EXHIBIT 5.1** is really nothing more than a first iteration on the way to develop numerical mapping and modeling of the verbally defined monotonic sequence of inter-society-heterogeneity-driven levels of systemic risk-of-crises in socio-political-entities (*recipients*), as it stems from individual generic *donor-recipient* transaction problems. It is based on the socio-political "ladder" of intra-societal heterogeneities defined in the original conversion table in **EXHIBIT 4.2 with feedback from real-life historical economic and political effects from various** *donor-recipient* **systems.**

EXHIBIT 5.1: Conversion Table for Risk Level Score

Interpretation	Verbal Assessment	Score
No Risk at all	Donor is S_1 and Recipient is S_1-S_2 Donor is S_2 and Recipient is S_2	1.0
Small Risk	Donor is S_1 and Recipient is S_3 Donor is S_2 and Recipient is S_3 Donor is S_3 and Recipient is S_3	0.8
Fair to Considerable Risk	Donor is S_1 and Recipient is S_4 Donor is S_2 and Recipient is S_4 Donor is S_3 and Recipient is S_4 Donor is S_4 and Recipient is S_4	0.6
Bad Risk *	Donor is S_1 and Recipient is S_5-S_6 Donor is S_2 and Recipient is S_5-S_6 Donor is S_3 and Recipient is S_5	0.4
Very Bad Risk **	Donor is S_1 and Recipient is S_7 Donor is S_2 and Recipient is S_7 Donor is S_3 and Recipient is S_6 Donor is S_4 and Recipient is S_5	0.2
Do not Consider (Such High) Risk ***	Donor is S_1 and Recipient is S_8-S_9 Donor is S_2 and Recipient is S_8-S_9 Donor is S_3 and Recipient is S_7-S_9 Donor is S_4 and Recipient is S_6-S_9	0.0

* economic crash leading to political unrest;
** economic crash leading to strong political unrest and, eventual, armed uprising;
*** economic crash leading to all-out armed uprising and civil war.

We know that there are many completely imponderable factors—at the time of forming the original verbal definitions—in the conversion table in **EXHIBIT 4.2** and its graph in **EXHIBIT 4.3**. These will have to be made more explicit in the second and subsequent iterations. Now, however, some of the highly behaviorally-based negative effects can be successfully alleviated by practical application of **PROPOSITION 5.4** (see e.g. [10] or [4]) and embodying scenario **(3.7)** by temporarily suppressing the given society-country's socio-political roots of ruling oligarchy. This, for instance, means to make sure (see [80; p.1]) that the given entity will have more power to catch and nail everybody who's cheating.

Suppose, for instance, that by massaging a lot of past *donor-recipient* final effect data we can find some redeeming factors, in terms of practical *donor*-based policies, that would lower the systemic risk of socio-economic crisis in *recipients* and thus ease off the original risk assessment. **Then these upgrades of the numerical scores (in the third column of the table in EXHIBIT 5.1) would act as correcting (i.e. improving) elements to the original numerical scores** and would be added to the scores in column 3 of **EXHIBIT 5.1**.

DISCUSSION: In our previous analyses, we have established that one of the mightiest corrective tools for a severely socio-politically disturbed society is **"neutralization of a *recipient* society for a certain period."** It might come as a perfectly legal political vehicle called "protectorate." Because cultural and religious differences between the *donor* society expatriate personnel and the *recipient* society indigenous population could and have been playing a political role especially when fomenting these cultural and religious differences—the latest split along these lines is labeled **NORTH** vs. **SOUTH**—we have assumed two variants of the individual scenario; one with **"cultural and religious acceptability"** and one without it (**in bold font**) in the scenario table in **EXHIBIT 5.2**).

Needless to say, virtually all expatriates—businessmen, professionals, peace-keepers and members of NGOs—are, by definition, the **NORTH** religious enemies and shortly to become the most despised part of any indigenous **SOUTH** *recipient*. The never-ending series of bombing of the **NORTH** (*donor*) facilities: compounds, embassies and consulates, military barracks, navy ships etc. everywhere in the Middle East, Africa, Malaysia, Philippines and so forth are just a small illustration of the problem. **Hence, typical local conflicts escalate into serious international ones.** And, as usual, indoctrinated militant ethnic and/or religious parts of any society on the lower right end of the D-curve, **usually (but not always) poor and uneducated**, are typical examples of where the danger to the world has always lain throughout human history.

EXHIBIT 5.2: Conversion Table for Risk-Correction Scenario Score

Recipient Society Scenario	Correction Score
Opposition (democracy-seeking) powers inside a society neutralize to a large extent the power of local OLIGARCHY; mostly economic and some political pressure from IMF and allied NATO-style, inclusive of DONOR, societies brings the economic & political system to a standstill; society is ready to accept exogenous help from other culturally acceptable societies in restructuring its socio-political trend alongside DEMOCRATIC scenario **(3.7)**; the socio-economic trend is going to feature a stable, long term (although slow) growth.	Up to +0.6
The same premises **but help from culturally or religiously unacceptable societies is not restructuring the socio-political trend** very successfully and scenario **(3.7)** conditions are very slow in changing; yet some improvement show stable trend.	Up to +0.4
OLIGARCHY has the political system under control with only parts of society's opposition alive; to neutralize powers-that-be requires tough IMF-imposed economic sanctions and political retooling) and observers from NATO-type (inclusive of the DONOR) societies; even then the total and successful conversion to scenario **(3.7)** is questionable; imported professionals from culturally acceptable societies can, within the medium-to-long-term time scale, simulate conditions of scenario **(3.7)**.	Up to +0.4
The same premises **but help from culturally and/or religiously unacceptable societies is only restricted to presence of localized observers** and it may take a long time before, at least, some of the conditions of scenario **(3.7)** are met; to reform or slash the power of oligarchy is again dependent on DONOR's (perhaps even armed) observers.	Up to +0.2
OLIGARCHY has the political power under total control; virtual absence of society's opposition makes import opposition-view expatriates or other professionals (without supporting personnel) practically impossible; to neutralize powers-that-be would require an all-out political and economic pressure (i.e. toughest IMF conditions + some embargo combined with military and civilian administrators); even then to sustain conditions at least approximate to scenario **(3.7)** would require **constant presence of these "observers"** and military personnel.	Up to +0.2
It is almost certain that when the perceived intruding personnel—deemed to be generally politically and religiously unacceptable—leave the society, the original conditions (with increasing political unrest) return.	0.0

The conversion table in **EXHIBIT 5.2** above represents a straightforward attempt at translating assumptions and propositions about **the composite risk level** from which the **overall systems disutility** stems. The **systemic**

disutility is the function of inter-societal heterogeneous societies among which business and/or non-profit transactions are to be negotiated. The intra- and inter-society heterogeneity is defined by disparities in the realm of their socio-political, socio-economic, cultural, cognitive and economic systems that have been originally defined in **EXHIBIT 4.2**. Finally, it is worth stressing that the above conversion table should be taken only as an illustrative example of how the methodology generally works.

We have suggested, and **shown graphically, that the extent of these disparities**, and hence the assessment of the risk level (of the expected overall systems quantitative disutility) attached to the proposed deal, **can be measured as the length of an arc between the two societies-countries definitional points on a hyperbolic curve in EXHIBIT 4.3.** As the transformation of these disparities into verbal definitions and their subsequent numerical conversion in **EXHIBIT 5.1** goes on to show that, for example, "**fair to considerable**" risk level has a numerical "worth" score of **0.6,** pertaining to the interval from 0.41 to 0.6, we should not forget that the original verbal definition of the two (or any other for that matter) societies' systemic heterogeneity comes from scenario definitions of our basic conversion table in **EXHIBIT 4.2**.

Therefore the conversion table in **EXHIBIT 4.2** is actually not only the stepping-stone, but also a necessary and sufficient condition for the whole risk-assessing iterative methodology. Of secondary importance is the fact that **the "worth" score emulates the (credibility, confidence, or support) interval estimate of risk** as seen above, in an example of definitional intervals of inverse risk function in **(5.3)**.

Also, and more importantly still, by employing elements like "worth" scales and "importance of any kind of transaction" for both the *donor* and *recipient* societies, we have entered the realm of decision-making theories and practice. And it is about the right time and place to do so. There is no business without decision-making and there is hardly any decision-making that would not have a business either clearly attached to it or hidden somewhere in its agenda. We are, thus, going to pursue this topic with a vengeance in the next chapter.

However, at this point a few explanatory words should be written about the "correctional score" (to the one in the third column of the conversion table in **EXHIBIT 5.1**) as it appears in the subsequent conversion table in **EXHIBIT 5.2**.

The scenarios show two correction levels; one for culturally—that is ideologically and/or religiously—acceptable help that has been imported into the *recipient* society (be it professionals, educators, support teams etc.), and a much lower correction factor for the **culturally and/or ideologically unacceptable help** in whatever shape, form and manner.

As we already alleged, the term *"culturally acceptable"* does not necessarily mean just **culture** *per se*. Obviously, the true indigenous Muslim peoples do have somewhat different life-style, inclusive of traditions, customs, etc. from, say, a typical Scandinavian. This, however, does not necessarily mean that the Scandinavians cannot serve as a valuable workforce of specialists, merchants and other professionals in Arab countries—in fact they have been doing just that for decades—and vice versa. That said, we should immediately put some sort of disclaimer forward. "Culture" is a term also used with a much less innocuous connotation. Without going into cumbersome explanations, one example should do. Commenting on the Tokaimura nuclear debacle (in Japan) [53] we read:

> It may say something about Japanese **safety culture** (bold by M.K.), where some claim that workers place too much emphasis on consensus and too little on thinking for themselves.

More serious problems, however, start when politicians of various nationally-political—nation (or better still "tribe") is here taken in line with the narrower alternative in **DEFINITION 2.2**—persuasion and agenda, are putting their own interest, such as independent statehood and with it various well-paid government and ambassadorial posts for them and their cronies ahead of their own people.

These problems become unmanageable and outright dangerous—see e.g. **PROPOSITION 5.2 (A)**—when the specific political and/or religious ideologies are made an official doctrine and the only basic law of that "new" entity combined with the single political power-party. This is when various indigenous and exogenous elements of society (expatriates of different religions and from different countries) are being used as scapegoats to explain socio-economic problems of the society by these unscrupulous politicians-cum-future-dictators. And this is also when their own failings are becoming causes of tensions, discontent and even physical confrontation within that society.

Examples abound:

Lenin and his Marxist-Communist ideology that eventually absorbed not just the USSR but all of the East European states, Hitler's Germany with his NSDP party ideology, North Korea, North Vietnam, China, all with an ideology modeled after Stalin. Together they exterminated well over 100 million of their own citizenry.

Here we should especially note the fact, mentioned in the previous paragraph, that all these socio-political upheavals have been based on, and with the executive help of, the "poor and uneducated" masses in their respective societies.

Again, *"non-essential parts of the society"* here means the minority-peoples or even majority-peoples that do not belong to that narrowly defined nation and that all together form a multinational society-state. A typical example is the 35% German minority in pre-war Czechoslovakia (not to mention the case of German Jews in Nazi Germany) or the Hutu majority in Tutsi-governed parts of Sub-Saharan Africa.

In this context these **culturally unacceptable** are all other people that "do not belong" to the chosen few and whose apparent goal (in the words of those ideological spin-masters) is to undermine the well-being of the ideologically-pure "nation." Within the society this unacceptability is corrected, as noted above, by mass extermination. Vis-à-vis external peoples, one of two alternatives takes place: either a war or hatred fomented by spin-doctors.

That this behavior prevailed in 19th century Africa (and, after making a full circle, it is, again, in full bloom there now), in the first third of the 20th century in Europe (Nazi Germany) and in the late 20th century Arab states (Syria, Iraq, Afghanistan, Libya, Egypt) is not, perhaps, too surprising. This is especially so when we realize that all these societies, with the exception of Germany, belong to the developing world.

At the end of the 20th century such a behavior was much more conspicuous in societies that used to belong (and perhaps they still think they do) to the developed world. And yet, bizarre as it is, it is true.

One example should highlight it sufficiently:

After the Soviet (and other Warsaw Pact) military invaded Czechoslovakia in August 1968 about 60,000 young or youngish people left for Western societies. Of them, probably 70% were university graduates, some of them already in top management positions in the "Prague Spring" ideological inertia. Many of these became academically, professionally and entrepreneur-wise extremely successful during the next 21 years.

Then, after the communist regime crumbled in 1989, quite a few of them were ready to help the new society. After all they had all been successful professionals, consultants and advisers to Western governments, heads or top managers of various giant corporations, big banks, etc. and all that at a time—actually the "time" is still on—when there was virtually nobody in the new "post-communist" society who had any Western-world knowledge and/or experience; not just business experience but even general holistic view and understanding of the functioning of the Western society.

Now comes the weird part: The new rulers—we must call them "rulers" because the proponents of the old regime: former top communists and a few naïve neo-democrats successfully formed a **very powerful "velvet revolution" oligarchy** that has, since then, ruled in a similarly lawless state (some law experts calls it actually worse than the communist one before [55]) as the one they "de-communized"—**decreed all of these (political) emigrants to be virtually "culturally unacceptable."** As a next step they prohibited them first from taking back their citizenship (the revised law allowing this was passed in October 1999; ten years after the "non-communist" society has been established) and by doing so prevented them from being elected to or nominated to any government position whatsoever. The Czech Republic (formerly Czechoslovakia) thus became the only former COMECON state of Eastern Europe to virtually bar their own citizens living abroad (who were perfectly willing to return and re-settle there) from helping them to navigate the intricate world of today's business, finance and politics.

It is certainly no surprise that, according to **EXHIBIT 4.3** and **PROPOSITIONS 5.1-5.3**, and in view of recent articles, such as *"Czech Communist Talk of a Comeback"* or *"Head of Czech Bank Quits Amid Fraud Investigation"* [84; p.8] and [75; p."Europe"], the Czech political, social and economic system was, in the 1990s, deemed to be among the worst out of those post-communist societies of Eastern and Central Europe—with the exception of the former USSR societies—with very few willing *donors* on the horizon. This practical illustration of **LEMMAS 5.2** and **5.3** is now complete.

The next comment will support our lowest scenario in **EXHIBIT 5.1** together with zero-correction lowest scenario of **EXHIBIT 5.2**. In *The New York Times* [56] we read:

> Within the last fifty years the so called international aid has neither helped the economic growth nor saved the great number of poor societies (those on the lower rungs of D-curve in **EXHIBIT 4.3**; added by M.K.) from bankruptcy, decline and chaos."

And then, finally, comes the ultimate threat to the world—that we already touched upon in Chapter 4 and **PROPOSITION 4.2**—in the "war of civilizations" as Thomas Friedman so aptly put it in [162]. He claims that as dangerous as the Soviet Union was, it was always able to be deterred by a wall of containment and US and NATO nuclear weapons because, at the end of the day, the Soviets loved life more than they hated the non-communist world. Despite their ideological differences, both antagonists agreed on certain bedrock rules of civilization. He continues:

> With the Islamist militant group, we face people who hate us more than they love life … this poses a much more serious threat than the Soviet Army because the human bombs (and here the parallel to the Tamil "bombers" is striking; note by M.K.) … Attack the most essential element of an open society: trust … without trust, there's no open society because there aren't enough police officers to guard every opening in an open society ... which is why suicidal Islamist militants have the potential to erode our lifestyle" **and with it, indeed, our whole civilization.**

5/2/3/2 Assessment of the Actual Financial and Fiscal Crisis Effect on the *Recipient* and its Over-all Effect on the *Donor*'s Socio-Political Environment

The previous section **5/2/3/1** dealt with the first part of the paradigm; assessment of the risk-of-impending-crisis (in other words the risk of total disutility in transactions among heterogeneous entities of the *donor-recipient* system).

The goal of the entire paradigm, however is to avoid embarrassingly high overall disutilities in a *donor-recipient* system stemming from emergency aid operations, know-how and technology transfer, and, eventually, from direct business transactions (at a later date). **Losses that involve real economic quantities as well as changes in *recipients'* behavioral and socio-political environments, illustrated by unrest, riots and armed uprisings, usually culminate in acts of international terrorism.** Ensuing fatalities and chaos in *recipient* societies will add to the systemic monetary (and political) disutility. These losses–assume an unsuccessfully "controlled and thus abandoned" *donor-recipient* system: all international business contacts are terminated and the *donor* will lose its exporting outlet and, usually, its political clout as well–**will have to be summed up by the *donor*'s policy-makers to present the total disutility,** that will affect the *donor*'s domestic political issues, such as higher unemployment, lowering of the standard of living, increase in political instability and such. We shall briefly introduce this second and more important part in this section (and in subsequent chapters).

The necessary condition of success of this part of the paradigm is the large and well documented data-base of as many as possible past data-series on

The Crucial Challenge for International Aid

donor-recipient systems' **INPUT-OUTPUT** macro-economic coefficients collected from as many as possible *donors'* and **recipients'** entities. (**NOTE:** The most difficult part was the data collection, improvement, test for reliability via methodologies seen in [6], and in Chapters 2, 3, and 6 of [24]):

Having this in mind, we can construct a sort of **Summary Table, EXHIBIT 5.3**, that brings the elements from the previous section face-to-face with some (weighted averages of) real financial and fiscal losses in *recipients*.

EXHIBIT 5.3: Summary Table

(a)	(b)	(c)	(d)	(e)
Abbreviated Verbal Definitions of Societies in EXHIBIT 4.2	Ordinal Numbers Assessment on D-Curve in EXHIBIT 4.3	Levels of Inter-Society Heterogeneity (Length of Arc between Points on D-Curve)	Verbal Assessment of Risk Levels in Column C (from Table 5.3)	Real-Life Quantifiers of Systemic Risk-Induced Crises in Generic Societies (from Chapter 4)
Intra-homogenous society	1	1 – 1 = 3 – 3 = 0	no risk at all	
Less than complete intra-homogeneity	3	3 – 1= 5 – 3 = 2	manageable risk	Lost IMF premium; low interest loans for 2 years
Intra-heterogeneous society	5	5 – 1 ≅ 9 – 7*= 4	bad risk*	Stock market fell by 40%; currency lost 40% and GNP 20%
High intra-heterogeneous society	7	7 – 1 ≅ 7 – 3*= 6	very bad risk**	Stock market fell by 70%; currency lost 60+%; GNP halved for 2 years
Very high intra-heterogeneous society	9	9 – 1 ≅ 9 – 3*= 8	do not consider***	Same as above; situation worsens with time

*   economic crash leading to political unrest;
** economic crash leading to strong political unrest and, eventual, armed uprising;
*** economic crash leading to all-out armed uprising and civil war.

The individual computational steps show that:

(1) First of all, the Summary Table shows the immediate connection between the verbal definitions (of **EXHIBIT 4.2**) and models-points of individual intra-society heterogeneities that are numerically assessed

through ordinal-scale numbers in the graph of the D-curve (in **EXHIBIT 4.3**). This is seen in columns (a) and (b).

(2) Secondly, it demonstrates the logical connection between these models-points and numerical and verbal assessments of the risk of (economic and political) crisis in the *recipient(s)* and between the *donor* and *recipient* entities that have entered into inter-society transactions. The numerical risk characteristics (computed from column (b) ordinals) are seen in column (c) while their verbal assessments are in column (d).

(3) Thirdly, and most importantly, in the table is clearly seen the scheme of application of **one-to-one correspondence between the numerical or verbal definition of a risk level** (in columns (c) and (d)) and its actual societal impact defined in real-life economic numerical characteristics: stock market losses, currencies devaluation, real GDP cave-ins, etc. These real-life numerical evaluations are depicted in column (e). Even more important though is the socio-political correspondence between the conversion table for scenario-defining points S_i" in **EXHIBIT 4.2** and column (d).

These last one-to-one correspondences, between (c) ↔ (d) and (d) ↔ D-curve **verbal definitions** of the social stability of the system, are vitally important for the final part of the paradigm that consists of a decision-making module, in which individual alternatives are subjected to close scrutiny insofar as reliable comparison of real-life cost-benefit factors and "red-flagging" the dangerous ones.

5/3 Final Remarks

To recapitulate, the illustrative scenario tables in **EXHIBITS 4.2, 5.1 - 5.2** with risk "score" definitions in **EXHIBIT 5.1** and graph in **EXHIBIT 4.3** are all summarized in the table in **EXHIBIT 5.3**. Such information can be entered into a decision-making methodology to be discussed in the next chapter. Then, the policy-makers and analysts would have all the information to form a reasonably rational insight into an optimal solution (of how to proceed with the proposed *donor-recipient* transactions). Consequently, they should be in a position: (A) to postulate certain proposed alternatives of the deal as nonsensical, and (B) to explain these alternatives' overall impact and shoot them down before the damage to a particular *donor-recipient* system is done.

The paradigm also suggests several theoretical tools stemming from **PROPOSITIONS 5.1-5.2, LEMMAS 5.2-5.3** and, in particular, from **PROPOSITIONS 5.3-5.4** and **AXIOM 5.1**. These could **be helpful in**

forming a policy to minimize the risk of the *donor-recipient* system's meltdown. Whether some, or all of them, can be practically executed will probably rest with a particular *recipient* society [56] and will be dependent on international co-operation, global political situation and several other factors. Items 1) and 2) hold for the simple cases of economic aid and cooperation while item 3) concerns the direct socio-political help of the stricken society:

1) Close cooperation of the governments of both the *donor* and the *recipient* society on the strategy which would be used for the given economic co-operation. **In the optimum alternative, the (aid, technology, know-how) transfer should be brokered by a third party—an NGO indigenous to the *recipient* society and/or a neighboring country with fairly similar cultural, religious, traditional, behavioral and cognitive M.O. leading to similarity in institutional frameworks, codes and regulation, etc.— which would make the transfer easy and, above all, "palatable" to the *recipient* society.** Note that this condition is just another way to express **LEMMA 5.3** above.

2) For the same reason, the business transaction or whatever other economic deals with the *recipient* society—performed by any NGO and/or administration agency or corporate economic entity—are going to be undertaken according to existing (business) laws, and codes and regulations of the *recipient* country. The newly set up indigenous SME, ostensibly independent, might have all sorts of economic ties with the *donor* society. The key is that, on the one hand, it brings substantial economic well-being and profit to both entities and, on the other hand, it cannot be politically abused and/or utilized by the indigenous political firebrands. The strategy of "farming-out" or "outsourcing" parts of industrial infrastructure from *donor* countries to the developing world's *recipient*s has generally proved to be an unlimited success.

3) Under no circumstances—even if the conditions seem critical enough to force a virtual military and political occupation of the *recipient* country—**no specific exogenous political and socio-political doctrine should be pushed onto the *recipient* society unless the historical trends of the society's cultural, social and political environments are conducive to it**. Rather, the solution should be found in two alternative political tools: "federalization" and "protectorate" (strongly preferable—and highly appropriate—with indigenous moderate administration and power base, if such a base could ever be installed).

These steps would, *de facto*, be tantamount to lifting the *recipient* society off its, probably very low, allocation on the D-curve (just as **PROPOSITION 5.4** suggests) and conducting business-cum-political transactions that would, in the long range, benefit both the *donor* society from unwanted economic losses and the *recipient* society (and not just the ruling oligarchy) from no help at all [56]. In practical terms—just like **PROPOSITION 5.4** suggested to apply in extremely dangerous situations when the wellbeing of the region depends on one society—this is just the definition of the old, and historically well tested, **political concept called a "protectorate."**

At the same time, the *recipient* society's cultural, legal, political and social trends would be left intact in the hope of kick-starting the natural healing process. Robert Kaplan's comment on 'political moralists' [94; p.B5] is typical:

> They can't deal with complexities such as the tragedy in East Timor or the recent bloodshed in Nigeria, which are directly attributable to democratic elections. Without the [imported] democratization of those societies, you'd have thousands more people alive now.

A similar, though reverse, political blunder of Anglo-American armed forces in Central Europe at the end of WWII helped the Russians to 'bag' all the pre-war democratic societies into the communist camp; where they held them for almost half a century.

In the current world of social information-nets and information-driven economies, any society's culturally and behaviorally retardant stereotypes also impede that society's future. If this is only a one-off occurrence happening at a specific point-in-time, the situation would still be not too bad. The major problem here is that the gap between the societies on the upper left end of the D-curve and those on the lower right end is getting bigger all the time. This is what follows from **PROPOSITION 4.1** and **LEMMA 4.1** (not to mention some retarding effects of Information Technology on *recipient* societies discussed in Chapter 2 and "law of increasing the over-all inter-society heterogeneity" presented in **LEMMA 5.1**). Combining this axiomatic with **PROPOSITIONS 5.1** and **5.2** dealing with not just the gap or the overall heterogeneity but with its transformation into the overall risk of conflict—that being the function of the gap's magnitude—we may actually present a new and proven **by-product of the paradigm: The law of increasing risk of unbridgeable conflicts in the world** (discussed in detail in Chapters 7 and 8).

And as we are transcending the horizons of simply economic apparatus that had been designated to deal with the risks-of-conflict between societies up till now, we are wading into the murky world of sociology in which economic shocks, sharp downturns and other perceived perils serve only as an ignition system—or tip of the iceberg, if you wish—of a deep and dangerous-to-society social discontent, unrest or outright armed rebellion and terrorism. After all, in the already mentioned source [70; p.548] we read:

> The crowd delusion of persecution, conspiracy, or oppression is ... a defense mechanism ... The projection of this hatred on those outside the crowd serves not so much, as in paranoia, to shield the subject from the consciousness of his own hatred, as to provide him with a pretext for exercising it.

This situation that started by dismantling half-a-century old totalitarian regimes where everybody but a very few were poor, but where many services as well as basic foodstuffs were free, and ended up as an illiberal 'quasi-democracy' with economic gangs looting everything, stealing from everybody, and nothing is cheap (or available) any more, could not be better illustrated than by the following remark of the Russian political analyst Sergei Markov [101; p.8]:

> If you look at it from far away, the Russian state looks like a big Atlas, full of muscles. But as you get closer you realize that this Atlas is actually dead. Inside, this huge body is full of worms, which are eating the body and feeding off it. Sometimes an arm or a leg moves a little, but that's not because Atlas is alive, it's because the worms have moved an arm or leg. It's a very depressing and ugly state.

Generally, under the conditions of "ruling clique" quasi-democratic standards, it would constitute a very dangerous situation as far as the rest of the world is concerned, given the nuclear arsenal still in place and ready to fly. Fortunately, the Russian "ruler," Putin, knows how to keep the Russian homogenous society on the economic upswing and, thus, extremely loyal to him. Hence, the risk is low at this time as any war or conflict would probably destroy such contentment. The situation may, however, change in a moment's notice. Should he die, Russia may fall into a lawless and strongly economically heterogeneous and ugly morass.

Following this assumption of one enlightened ruler's possible legacy, this is yet another way to illustrate the "**law of increasing risk of conflicts in the world**" (see Chapters 7 and 8).

If this is the case, most of the decision-makers (inclusive of politicians) in *donor* societies are probably too far out of their depth and experience to perceive these dangerous societal undercurrents and their possible repercussions and assess them correctly. This constitutes yet another reason for our belief that the new paradigm would pave a way for better understanding not just the *recipient* countries' societies but, and most importantly, the causal chains which lead from the turmoil and generally serious instabilities in these societies and spill over to the *donor* societies. **Because if we miss this cause-and-effect scenario, the world as we know it may suddenly disappear.**

Some drastic indications, although not very frequent and therefore tend to be quickly forgotten, of such a spill-over effect from *recipient* to *donor* societies have already surfaced all over the world. In most instances the originally economic disparities in these societies have been substituted by tribal and religious hatred between the parts of the formerly reasonably working-together society.

We mean terrorist attacks on conventional airliners (e.g. Lockerbie disaster, downing of Air India jumbo etc.) and on non-military targets: hotels, sports halls, New York Twin Towers in 9/11, churches, restaurants, etc., in developed countries by already mentioned "suicide bombers." What might come next, we can only speculate: nuclear or biological attacks on other non-military targets?

In any case it will constitute a definite erosion of civilization and the way of life that we have been accustomed to up until only about a decade ago. This is why the suggestions—however draconian, expensive and unpopular—contained in **PROPOSITIONS 5.3, 5.4, AXIOM 5.1 and LEMMA 5.3 should be taken very seriously because**, just as these elements and [162] suggests, **eventually it will have to come down to this**:

We cannot change other societies and cultures on our own; but we also can't just do nothing in the face of this mounting threat. What we can do is partner with the forces of moderation within these societies to help them fight the war of ideas. Because ultimately this is a struggle within the Arab-Muslim world, and we have to help our allies there, just as we did in World Wars I and II.

Chapter 6: Practical Use of the Paradigm

6/1 Policy Decision-Making in Risk-Assessment

On the whole we believe that the principles behind decision-making techniques are widely known and understood. Still, we had better start from scratch here and reintroduce particularly those elements of decision-making methodology that play more important roles in our algorithm. The algorithm minimizes systemic (and composite) disutility arising from the conflicts that appear when two or more inter-societal heterogeneous countries—i.e. such with conflicting-socio-political-environments—deal with each other. **By minimizing the disutility, the algorithm maximizes the over-all welfare of the (*donor–recipient*) system.**

In Chapter 5 we discussed the first part of the paradigm. There, we assessed the potential risk of getting into serious socio-economic and, subsequently, even more serious socio-political conflicts with *recipient* societies with which we wanted to carry out transactions. We have started with mapping the increasing sequence of verbally defined intra-societal heterogeneities of a group of generic societies onto a graphical image of a hyperbolic curve. Socio-political characteristics of an individual generic society—this is an imaginary entity that represents a whole bunch of societies with very similar social, political, economic and culturally-cognitive environment—was modeled by a point on the D-curve. Next, we have used these points-models for the important observation: the greater the distance between the two points-models on the graph the greater and more serious conflict we can expect when the transaction goes wrong. We have also shown almost any transaction in *recipient* societies is bound to go "wrong" nowadays.

As an interesting afterthought that has no direct impact on the paradigm as such but serves as a wake-up call to all potential users, the algebraic apparatus (introduced by **LEMMA 4.1, PROPOSITION 5.2** and **LEMMA 5.1**) has also shown that **the sum of bad effects from all these conflicts**—and thus the **overall disutility** of all *donor-recipient* systems—axiomatically **increases with time**.

For better understanding of the systemic (overall) disutility we presented a table in **EXHIBIT 5.3**. There, we can see the scheme of application of one-to-one correspondence between the numerical and verbal definition of the risk levels (in columns (c) and (d)) and also the actual societal impacts of these conflicts defined in real-life economic numerical characteristics: stock market losses, currencies' devaluation, real GDP down-falls, etc.

In the process of quantification of qualitative and/or verbal phenomena we have discussed, in Chapter 4, several tools. Among them: Conversion Tables, Universal Score Function, and a notion of disutilities. We have also listed political instruments, such as: federalization of neighboring societies or setting up protectorates (see **PROPOSITION 5.3** and ensuing discussion in section 5/3) as a way to minimize the risk-of-conflicts' cumulative effects. But a deeper discussion of the mosaic, let alone its final assembly, is still missing.

As, according to general knowledge [47]:

> A fundamental part of risk (of conflict) assessment is to identify the risk (of conflict) in terms of its ... current and future impact on the both societies (donor and recipient), then evaluate what might be the acceptable trade-offs between ... disutility and reward.

any successful practical application of the paradigm-to-be cannot exist without using the elements of a decision-making technique that deals with alternatives and/or scenarios and uses both quantitative and qualitatively-behavioral factors, for both "disutility" and "reward" are phenomena defined in both economic and behavioral sciences (of sociology, for instance.) To this end, we shall first introduce several basic elements of the decision-making technique that should be helpful to the risk evaluation and, eventually, risk minimization methodology.

6/2 Basics of Political Decision-Making

6/2/1 Goal and Alternatives in Decision Processes

In the literature, such as [45] and [46; p.19], we find the following definition:

DEFINITION 6.1:
An alternative should be regarded as a grouping of factors (operating for well-defined purpose) that interacts with its environment (society) through the input and output factors, where the "input factors" are those regarded necessary for every alternative to start functioning as it is supposed to while the "output factors" are in fact products of the alternative functioning and as such they actually evaluate the alternative in terms of current and future pay-off.

EXAMPLE: Assume that a business entity of a *donor* society delineated three alternatives of a business deal. Two alternatives **AI, AII** were to open subsidiaries in two different developing (*recipient*) countries. One of them is close to S_9 on the scale of conversion table in **EXHIBIT 4.2;** the other is fast approaching S_5 (from the original S_4 position) on the same scale. The third alternative, **AIII**, would instead use the money for a large-scale investment in a S_1 society.

According to **DEFINITION 6.1** the **INPUT FACTORS** are: *"Cost of the Alternative"*—for the *donor* entity it is the total net monetary cost plus time lost on developing the alternative expressed in monetary terms before it starts to pay off—and *"Risk in Conflicting Socio-Political Environments."* This entails an assessment of possible financial or economic losses plus possible composite negative impact on, both, the *donor* and the *recipient* society now and, most importantly, in the future.

Concern about the environments of both societies is not new. After all, the "holistic" approach to solving socio-economic problems has been widely promoted for several decades [58; p.9].

The term **"Assessment of possible ... losses plus possible composite negative impact ... in the future,"** clearly classifies the risk level factor as a future-bound one. For such factors the following condition holds [52; pp.114-116]:

(6.1) The significant weight of the "future-bound" factor has to be set such that even combined error interference at the rest of the factor utilities could not easily overthrow this pseudo-pivot factor's prominent role as far as the final ranking of alternatives goes.

Thus, attaching the future considerations to the risk factor has actually increased, according to condition **(6.1)**, its importance quite a bit.

OUTPUT FACTORS determine the final effect of the alternative in terms of "Improved socio-economic well-being of the donor and recipient entities (or societies)."

6/2/2 Factor Tree

Now, to be able to choose from among two or more alternatives under a certain goal, we have to be able to assess their potential outcomes in terms of this goal, and we say:

(6.2) To be able to assess meaningfully each of these alternatives' potential outcome or utility, we first have to branch the alternatives into identical factor-trees; then these groups of identical factors (elements of the 'trees') will have, generally, different factors pay-off values assessed (in each such grouping).

EXAMPLE: Each of the above defined alternatives consists of three factors: F_1 *"Total Cost of the Alternative,"* F_2 *"Risk-of-Conflict Factor,"* and F_3 *"Improved Well-being of Donor and Recipient,"* where F_1 and F_2 are **input factors** and F_3, which branches into F_{31} and F_{32}, is an **output factor**. The appropriately simplified factor-trees for the three alternatives are seen in **EXHIBIT 6.1**.

EXHIBIT 6.1: Factor Tree of "Risk-of-Conflict Alternatives"

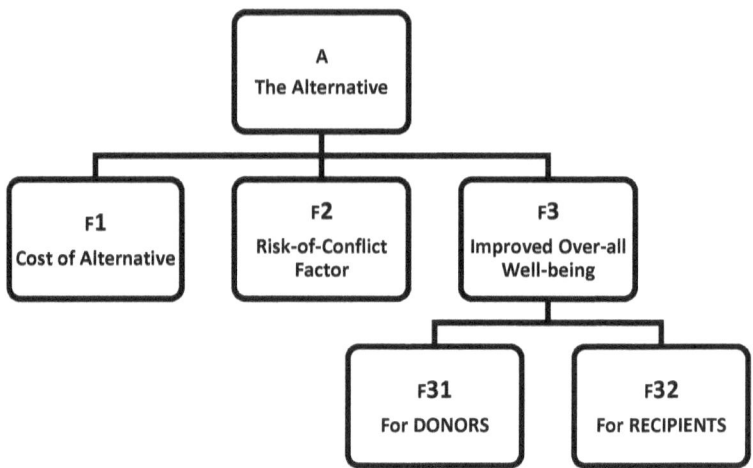

To be able to improve the assessment, and thus the distinguishing ability of individual alternative, we seek factor(s) which can become the stem(s) for further branching and which we shall call **"pivot factors."** *"Improved Well-being"* is a typical pivot factor (in **EXHIBIT 6.1**) and it is not dissimilar to a factor *"Total Welfare of a Community"* seen in source [58; p.19].

6/2/3 Assessment of Factors' Utilities

If all the factors were of uniform-scale (i.e. if they could be measured by and defined on one quality scale, such as money), we would not anticipate any serious problem in comparing alternatives, and problems would be solved quite rationally by choosing the alternative yielding the greatest money-gain or the least money-loss.

At this point, the only important thing is to realize that even a simple alternative, as for instance the one in **EXHIBIT 6.1**, presents mostly multi-scale factors, such as: "monetary cost," "risk-of-conflict," "well-being" (in monetary terms, in social, educational, political and sociological terms), which in any case suggests at least two scales: a quantitative and a qualitative scale.

A common denominator was found [52; pp.43-54] in a numerical scale, and we say that:

(6.3) Universal score function (USF) is the relative (both arithmetic-relative and rank-relative) value of utility of any factor expressed in the same numerical scale. It is assessed with regard to all other phenomena of this kind only. 'Utility'—in case of we assess the "risk-of-crisis," the factor's label is 'disutility' (and then we use its inversion) is then taken in relation to the investigated alternative.

NOTE: For arithmetic operations with USFs apply the same formulas as for computation with "cardinal" and "ordinal" numbers; basic algebraic tools can be found in the Appendix.

The **Universal Score Function** then transforms the "**worth**" of every factor into the bounded scale of rational numbers between 0 and 1 as seen in conversion table in **EXHIBIT 6.2** [52; p.54, Table 3.1]; also [168; p.252] as we discussed the mix of behavioral and numerical phenomena in Section 4/3/2, or the domain of risk level in conversion table in **EXHIBIT 5.3**.

EXHIBIT 6.2: Conversion Table for the phenomenon "Worth"

Score	Interpretation
1.0	Excellent
0.8	Good
0.6	Fair
0.4	Poor
0.2	Bad
0.0	Worthless

NOTE: Details of USF assessment methodology inclusive of equidistant and uneven calibrated scales are seen in the Appendix).

6/3 Analysis of an Alternative

6/3/1 General Methodology

It has been noted above that the term "alternative" is tantamount to the term "scenario." Therefore it might be inferred that alternatives differ only marginally from each other. Nothing, however, can be farther from the truth.

Some alternatives may have reasonable similarity in only one **OUTPUT FACTOR. However,** they may, on the other hand, differ significantly in all of their **INPUT FACTORS**.

Let us therefore start from the structure of an alternative in **(6.1)** where understanding of the structure of the group of investigated alternatives, described by their factor-trees (in **EXHIBIT 6.1**), emerges as an important condition for solving a decision problem. Important elements of this structure are the **significant factors**, which we define **as factors that do not initiate any further sub-branching.**

EXAMPLE: The factor-tree in **EXHIBIT 6.1** has significant factors: F_1, F_2, F_{31}, and F_{32}. From what has been said until now it should be clear that:

(6.4) The assessed factors' USFs can help us to rank individual alternatives only when we assume equal preference or importance for each factor (in a given factor-tree).

Since the assumption in statement **(6.4)** is not only logically incorrect but contradicts condition **(6.2)**, we have to look for another conversion mechanism (similar to the table in **EXHIBIT 6.2**) that would **transform** or decode **the level of importance** we are assigning to each factor **into another dimensionless, and also necessarily, numerical scale**. There is one feature of the importance level that we shall need very badly. It will have to express—from as much historical data as we can obtain—the expected total financial losses (and, eventually, subsequent changes in social and political climate) in relation to both expected costs and profits.

One such conversion table has been used for some time in management science [57] to help determine the total feasibility or applicability of some complex technical projects. We present it in **EXHIBIT 6.3**.

Thus, after deciding on the appropriate "level of importance" for each factor of an investigated factor-tree, we use the conversion table in **EXHIBIT 6.3** to obtain its numerical value.

Why should the scale in **EXHIBIT 6.3** be so extensive? Since the weight-tree is directly tied to a factor-tree—which contains under normal circumstances any number of heterogeneous factors—we should match this variability in kind by greater variability, and thus the better choice, in scale of one-of-the-kind-only quality. Besides, when we want to express the expected total monetary losses under certain 'risk-of-conflict' factor level and compare it with cost and profit elements, the nine-point scale comes useful for being able to refine the importance (as it is our subjective reading of the world) of the given factor as much as possible.

EXHIBIT 6.3: Conversion Table for the Factor "Importance"

Weights wj	Level of Importance
1.0	Extremely Important
0.9	Highly Important
0.8	Very Important
0.7	Important
0.6	Fairly Important
0.5	Probably Important
0.4	Of Some Importance
0.3	Of Little Importance
0.2	Of Very Little Importance
0.1	Unimportant
0.0	No Importance Whatsoever

The big question now is: **How to combine both these numerical scales—one denoting the utility, f, of a certain factor and the other its relative importance, w—so that we obtain some meaningful number to rank or judge the alternative upon?**

In the Appendix there is a derivation of the **weighed arithmetic average** formula that provides the answer:

(6.5) $$a = \sum_i w_i \cdot f_i / \sum_i w_i$$

where **a** is a composite utility of the alternative **A**, **f** is the USF (or utility) of individual factor **F**, **W** is weight (of a factor) and **i** denotes the **i-th** factor, where $i = 1 \ldots m$.

EXHIBIT 6.4: Weight Tree for the Investigated Alternative(s)

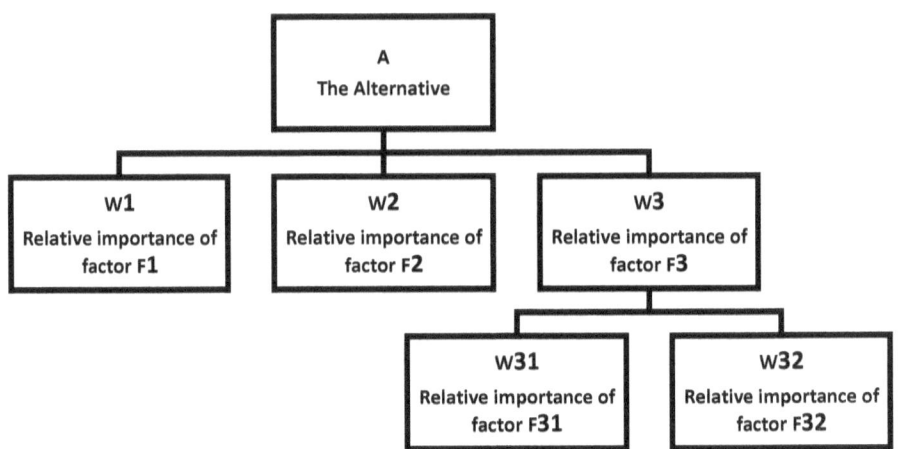

EXAMPLE: As we now have a factor-tree and an (importance) weight-tree in **EXHIBIT 6.4** we shall, for the sake of computational clarity, re-design the alternative **A** in **EXHIBIT 6.1** so that it contains both quantifying elements of these trees.

The resulting factor-tree for a composite utility **a** (of the alternative **A**) that is the product (of multiplication) of both elements **F** and **w** in each factor cell of the factor-tree graph. This is seen in **EXHIBIT 6.5** and represents, in fact, the graphic display of numerical formula **(6.5)**

EXHIBIT 6.5: Graph of the Composite Utility for formula (6.5)

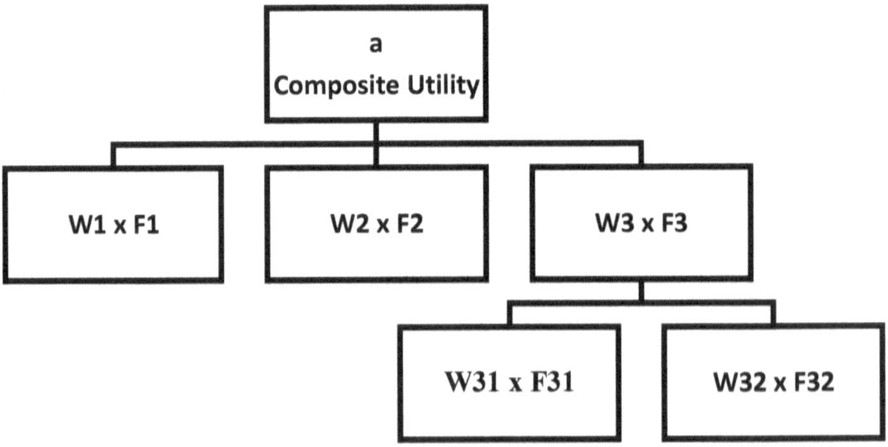

Taking the significant factor as the major improvement on the way to composite utility, as presented in the Appendix, we arrive at the following formula for calculation of composite utility for alternative, say **AI**, in **EXHIBIT 6.5**.

(6.6) $a(I) = w^*_1 \cdot f_1(I) + w^*_2 \cdot f_2(I) + w^*_{31} \cdot f_{31}(I) + w^*_{32} \cdot f_{32}(I)$

where $f_1(I), f_2(I), f_{31}(I), f_{32}(I)$ are USFs of significant factors in **EXHIBIT 4.4** and where w^*_1, w^*_2, w^*_{31}, and w^*_{32} are **significant weights**, computed from the following formulae:

(6.7) $w^*_1 = w_1 / (w_1 + w_2 + w_3)$

$w^*_2 = w_2 / (w_1 + w_2 + w_3)$

$w^*_3 = w_3 / (w_1 + w_2 + w_3)$

$w^*_{31} = w^*_3 \cdot [w_{31} / (w_{31} + w_{32})]$

$w^*_{32} = w^*_3 \cdot [w_{32} / (w_{31} + w_{32})]$

According to **EXHIBIT 6.3**, first we have to assign a system of weights to every factor in this graph.

Assume now that the following importance weights—set with the help of conversion table in **EXHIBIT 6.3** and upholding condition **(6.1)**, since not only the "risk factor" is future-bound but so is "cost of alternative,"—hold for the combined factor- and weight-tree in **EXHIBIT 6.5**: $W_1 = 0.9$, $W_2 = 1.0$, $W_3 = 0.9$, $W_{31} = 0.9$, and $W_{32} = 0.7$.

Using the formulae in **(6.7)** we calculate significant weights: $W^*_1 = 0.3$, $W^*_2 = 0.36$, $W^*_{31} = 0.18$, and $W^*_{32} = 0.14$, which is correct as their sum is equals one (which is not only our case but a general axiom as well).

NOTE: We shall, obviously, have to hold some discussion on attaching the reasonable importance-weights, set with the help of **PROPOSITIONS 5.1–5.3, EXHIBITS 4.2-4.3** and conversion tables (in **EXHIBITS 5.1-5.2**) and **EXHIBIT 6.2-6.3** hold for the factor-tree in **EXHIBIT 6.4**. But first we should present the alternatives in question in more depth.

6/3/2 Description and Discussion of "Standard" Alternatives

The first alternative AI assumes that a *donor* entity, NATO-type country S_1, will build a giant car factory (comprising both truck and passenger car production) in a *recipient* South East Asian country ranked as S_9 on the scale of scenarios in **EXHIBIT 4.2**. The rationale is that when the whole of Asia (inclusive of China) goes market oriented, there would be a great demand for cheap trucks and cheap passenger cars all over the continent with over 3 billion people. Thus, the comparative advantage of cheaper labor cost and cheaper distribution [46; pp.399-400] are two substantial benefits of the alternative.

Well-being Scenario (WB AI):

The hope is that substantial increase of employment together with the saturation of demand for financially affordable vehicles would improve the living standards of a non-negligible part of the *recipient* society. Also, it is hoped that this project would open the door for other-than-economic inter-societal contacts: cultural, educational and, perhaps, even socio-political co-operation.

For the *recipient* it means: (1) rapid industrialization (with subsequent rapid growth of modern education and modern socio-economic trends) in a society which has not developed much since the end of World War II, (2) export of the majority of the production that would bring increase in personal income per capita, and (3) extra revenue to the state coffers that could be used for building some basic welfare, Medicare and old age pension systems. The *donor* expects increased profit by assembling, and producing cheaply mass produced goods and cutting the transportation costs of exports to the whole of Asia.

Risk Elements (RE AI):

The society is a private fiefdom of the succession of army colonels-cum-dictators; politically a *de facto* totalitarian dictatorship with an invisible "Berlin Wall" built around it. This unworldly political backwater borders with some of the biggest opium-producers and several still unsettled societies. There is no semblance of a comparative business and substantial law (to any international standard) and whatever law packages they have are unenforceable. Specifically, the oligarchy is functioning above any law whatsoever. Any future development of the society towards even the essentials of democratic reform is very difficult to imagine. Historically, under similar circumstances and in comparable societies, the risk of serious economic crisis triggering societal unrest and thus the collapse of the comparable transaction can be derived from column (e) in **EXHIBIT 5.3** where for "very bad" and "do not consider" risks we find:

stock market declined by 70%; currency devaluation—60%, GNP effectively halved and situation may worsen.

It is also an environment where the society is strongly religiously charged and if needed could be turned, by local oligarchs, against non-Moslem (or other religious minorities). These minorities then become scapegoats for any (fairly certain) economic downturns with ensuing political (possibly armed) upheavals, civil war and all manner of effects that would be very dangerous to the whole region.

The second alternative AII calls for building a giant petrochemical refinery-cum-chemical-combine. It should produce not only refined light and/or high octane motor and aircraft fuels and oils but also a host of other industrial organic and inorganic chemical products, such as: tires, other rubber products, bio-degradable plastics, agricultural systemic sprays, some pharmaceutical products, etc. The *donor* entities are partly the same S_1 country, figuring alternative AI, and partly the Middle East oil-rich countries of S_5 variety (in scenario table in **EXHIBIT 4.2**). The *recipient* would be a European society, originally ranked as S_4, recently slipping fast into $S_5 - S_6$ ranking.

Well-being Scenario (WB AII):

The *recipient* society has a relatively skilled workforce for such a high-technological endeavor. The project will then increase the employment of (or stop the unemployment slide for) this part of the workforce. The export of final products into Eastern and Central Europe, later on perhaps into EU, will generate substantial fiscal inputs into the state coffers. Furthermore, it is assumed that a project of this size—with sub-contractors from all over the *recipient* society—would bring: (1) indigenous firms and professionals to succumb to internationally comparable substantive laws (and legal systems in general) and (2) eventually, the total enforceability of the legal package, which would then become the norm. This would suppress the growth of oligarchic tendencies and the society will be in a good entry position to join the EU. For *donor* societies, it would mean profit taking from a cheaper and skilled workforce, tax havens, and shortening export lines. Also, there would be relatively cheap import of crude oil from the Middle East by tankers practically to the refineries as well as new outlets for the Middle East oil. This is important because: (1) other oil exports are bound by OPEC quotas and trade agreements, and (2) there is a chance to become a major supplier for the EU.

Risk Elements (RE AII):

The oligarchy in the *recipient* society does not recognize international substantive law (in fact, any legal system, generally) and is, therefore, virtually "untouchable" by the society's legal institutions. This has frozen up and set back the functioning of any healthy political (let alone democratic) process. It is, therefore, entirely possible that the electorate having lost its high hopes may turn the regime into further left or even far-left, eventually into some kind of dictatorship not unlike the refuted communist—or even "national-democratic" as in pre war Germany—regime of yesteryears.

Future improvement is likely; but only in the distant future. In the *donor's* other (developing) parts of societies a possibility of another conflict on the Arab peninsula still exists, not to mention the religious zealots-terrorists' actions that can be expected. In economic terms, comparable transactions in similar (generic) societies have yielded, according to column (e) of **EXHIBIT 5.3**: *"40% short-term downgrade of stock market, 30 – 40% devaluation of local currency and 20% drop of GNP."*

The third alternative AIII is strictly business between or within S_1 NATO-style societies and concerns a straightforward investment, albeit on a large scale.

Well-being Scenario (WB AIII):

For the *donor* there is no particular societal impact, let alone improvement since mergers, buy-outs etc. usually mean increase of unemployment; the *donor's* presumed profit (even if there resulted greater productivity and cost-efficiency) would, on the whole, be lower than at **AI** or **AII** and easily taxable (because of transparency) too. For the *recipient* the results are practically the same.

Risk Elements (RE AIII):

In Chapter 2 we have discussed the systems situation among *donors* and *recipients* in intra-societal and inter-societal homogeneous groups. We have summed them under the label of "generic" (developed) society and, as such, assumed to be "societal risk-less." There are no unknown or hidden systems risks seen in **EXHIBIT 5.1** (see **"excellent risk level"** with score 1.0). The possibility of wrongly assessed profit potential of the investment always exists, however.

6/3/2/1 An Alternative based on Isolation of Indigenous Oligarchy

The "standard" alternatives, **AI**, **AII**, and **AIII**, investigate the *donor-recipient* system from the particular *donor's* perspective. There is another angle to look at it from, however. Consider the **"law of overall or 'world-wide' heterogeneity increase"** formulated in **LEMMA 5.1** and assume that an international organization of *donors* (UN, EC, NATO, etc.) decides upon the necessity of improving the well-being in seriously political polarized *recipient* societies presently low-lying (on the D-curve). These are the societies that represent the potential 'powder-keg' in the realm of the world's peaceful coexistence and cooperation.

Thus, following the recipe of **PROPOSITION 5.3**, we "lift" the specific *recipient* society in alternative **AI** off its allocation on the D-curve to be able to conduct whatever business and/or economic and social aid transaction would benefit both the *donor* society (from unwanted economic losses) and the socio-economically rejuvenated *recipient* society (by reaping the economic and social windfall which would normally go to the ruling oligarchy). At the same time the *recipient* society's cultural, political and social environments would be left with a positive trend due to the natural healing process and, obviously, the region (or the world) should be a bit more safe too [56]. This new alternative will henceforth be denoted as **AI***.

However, for **AI*** to achieve peace and progress, extra monetary outlays will be needed for setting-up and running successful **protectorate administration and infrastructure**: peace-keeping corps, schools and social facilities and basic regional business enterprises in the *recipient* society. The scheme should be reminiscent of the old Marshall Plan with much stronger political strings attached: Meaning, all the organizational and direct distribution of the "package" cost of the infrastructure would be the *donors'* responsibility). And, the overriding assumption would still be—which in case of official designation of the given society a 'temporary protectorate' is axiomatic—that the indigenous oligarchy will be completely neutralized and a new administration, combined expatriate and indigenous professionals, would take over. Then we can easily imagine the following importance weight tree : $W_1(I^*) = 0.4$, $W_2(I^*) = 1.0$, $W_3(I^*) = 1.0$, $W_{31}(I^*) = 0.9$, and $W_{32}(I^*) = 0.7$, leading to the significant weights : $W^*_1(I^*) = 0.18$, $W^*_2(I^*) = 0.41$, $W^*_{31}(I^*) = 0.23$ and $W^*_{32}(I^*) = 0.18$.

6/3/2/2 Further Analysis of the Alternatives' Utilities

The time has come to calibrate the significant factors F_1 ("Cost of the Alternative") for all alternatives. From the start it is obvious that, just like with "risk" factors, to follow the axiom of "higher utility → higher USF" we must use inversion cost function here.

There is no detailed information on individual "cost" factors [52; pp.131-133]. We might, for the sake of simplification, therefore assume that roughly the same monetary outlay is available for each alternative.

Thus, we start assessing the USF (or "utility") for factor F_1 in each of the three alternatives. It can be derived from the heuristically constructed—on the basis of historical cases and current expertise of many professionals; hereby simulating the conditions of source [91])—conversion table "cost of alternative" → "worth" [52; pp.56-57]. It is based on money available to the donor without excessive borrowings, and on the principle of diminishing return (or over-financing the alternative). To this uniformly shaped utility we have to add future-bound corrections. To make the correction algorithm clear and simple, we assume that the longer we "pour" money into the recipient country in alternative **AI**—without costly political and economic "counter-checks"—the faster it disappears in the pockets of the ruling oligarchy. In the case of alternative **AII**, the situation is not that serious, but it still requires some extra precautions. Relevant discussion follows.

EXHIBIT 6.6: Conversion Table for Cost of Alternative

Cost of Alternative in billions	USF Interpretation	"Worth" Score
$2.00 - $2.40	Excellent	1.0
$2.41 - $2.80	Good	0.8
$2.81 - $3.20	Fair	0.6
$3.21 - $3.60	Poor	0.4
$3.61 - $4.00	Bad	0.2
$4.01 - $4.40	Worthless	0.0

Without undue simplification (and using the conversion table in **EXHIBIT 6.6**), let us assume that for the significant factors of the **first alternative** the original projection of its "utility" was $f_1(I) = 0.9$ and for the second alternative $f_1(II) = 0.8$. However, we have to consider extra costs associated with risk element (RE) in alternative **A1**. With this in mind, we make both factors USFs in RE **AI** and RE **AII** equal to 0.8 while the third alternative (because of some counter-bidding due to an announced hostile take-over) has utility level $f_1(III) = 0.6$.

The next significant and future-bound factor, **F_2 ("Risk-of-Conflict Factor for the Alternative")** is, however, the major element of the decision-making. As such it is unique for each alternative.

For the assessments we shall use scenario table in **EXHIBIT 4.2**, D-curve in **EXHIBIT 4.3**, risk scenario table in **EXHIBIT 5.1**, risk-corrective scenario table in **EXHIBIT 5.2** and partitioning the risk domain in **(5.3)**. Also, we shall use the brief risk element scenarios in RE **AI**, RE **AII** and RE **AIII** already mentioned in this chapter.

Following our postulates about the risk scenarios, the risk score at $f_2(I)$ is—because of the unacceptable high risk in scenario table in **EXHIBIT 5.1**—**equal to zero**. Its theoretical maximum possible elevation is 0.2. However, we noted that in **EXHIBIT 5.2** substantial extra-budgetary costs should be spent on initial political and other 'real-time' actions. In that case the "cost" utility for $f_1(I)$ decreases to, say, 0.6. Thus:

(6.8)   If $f_2(I) = 0.0$ then $f_1(I) = 0.8$, and
         if $f_2(I) = 0.2$ then $f_1(I) = 0.6$

The risk-element "score" for the second alternative RE **AII** is also a bit more complicated. The political situation in *co-donor* and *recipient* societies needs some preliminary political 'leg-work' and, initially, very tight control and frequent control checks later. Thus—see scenario tables in **EXHIBITS 5.1 and 5.2**—to achieve utility level $f_2(II) = 0.6$, quite a bit of extra time and money will have to be 'shelled out.' Algebraically speaking:

(6.9)   If $f_2(II) = 0.4$ then $f_1(II) = 0.8$, and
         if $f_2(II) = 0.6$ then $f_1(II) = 0.6$

The risk factor $F_2(III)$, because all of this is happening in S_1 society, is at the lowest utility level $f_2(III) = 0.8$.

The next significant factor is F_{31} **"Convenience and Well-being to the Donor."** It could be derived from the "Well-being scenarios," denoted earlier as WB **AI**, WB **AII**, and WB **AIII** and from an imaginary conversion table in **EXHIBIT 6.7**. In real-life these scenario tables should, and obviously would, deal with real-life scenarios and data.

Given all these supporting sources, we can rate the utility (**USF**) of factor $F_{31}(I)$, denoted by $f_{31}(I)$, not higher than, say, 0.4. For factor $F_{31}(II)$, we can foresee $f_{31}(II)$, perhaps, at 0.6, similar to the last factor's utility, i.e. $f_{31}(III) = 0.6$.

EXHIBIT 6.7: Scenario Conversion Table for "DONOR's WELL-BEING"

Verbal Assessment of Donor Well-Being	Score
Thirty percent net **profit rate** on the original "Excellent" investment (in **EXHIBIT 6.6**); project is on-stream starting 21th month; the projects mushroom into other projects with over 25% profit on the smaller investment; **DONOR**'s presence in the region improves drastically and is expected to be long-termed (25 years+)	1.0
Same as above except that **DONOR**'s presence is expected be shorter lived (10 – 15 years)	0.8
Same **amount of net profit** (as in the first scenario) on the originally denoted "GOOD" investment scale; the project mushrooms into other countries in the region; **DONOR**'s presence is expected to be safe for 10 – 15 years	0.6
Same **amount of net profit** (as in the first scenario) on the "Fair" investment scale (in **EXHIBIT 6.6**); this is one-off business deal with no markedly improved regional 'visibility'; **DONOR**'s presence is expected to be safe for maximum 10 years	0.4
Same as the previous scenario except that the **DONOR**'s presence may antagonize the **RECIPIENT** society and therefore could be unilaterally revoked any time after 5 years	0.2
Nothing can be taken for granted; third and fourth scenario could well apply as well expulsion a a moment's notice	0.0

The last significant factor F_{32} "**Well-being or Total Welfare to the Recipient**" can be derived from all the above sources in this way:

If F_{32} (I) simply calls for no significant increase in the society's economic welfare but, at the very most, only slight improvement in political well-being. Then its utility, f_{32} (I), could be about 0.4. For the second alternative, while there might be a chance to improve the socio-political welfare a bit, we assess the utility f_{32} (II) at 0.6. In the case of factor F_{32} (III), the *recipient* is, probably, not better off than before the take-over or merger, but possibly a lot worse, as unemployment, wages freeze, etc. kicks in. Thus, f_{32} (III) = 0.4 might be a reasonable assessment.

Finally, we reassess the factors' and significant factors' utilities for the alternative with a danger of serious socio-political conflict **AI***. Since we are using now a completely different set of criteria, the utility f_1 (I*) could easily be 0.2, given **EXHIBIT 6.7**. Then, utility f_2 (I*)—using similar logic in reverse as in **(6.8)**—should be, say, at 0.8. The stress on the system's well-being yields f_{31} (I*) = 0.8 and f_{32} (I*) = 0.8 up to 1.0.

6/3/2/3 Results of the Analysis of the Alternatives and Discussion

At long last, we apply formula **(6.6) - (6.7)** to obtain ranking of the three (actually four) alternatives. For better insight into the problem we assemble all the significant weights and significant factors' utilities into the **analytical matrix** [46; pp.85-94].The formula then yields **"composite utilities" of all the alternatives** in the last column of each row. For better insight into the algorithmic relevance we add extra rows of significant weights* and significant factors* utilities for the conflict-ridden alternative **AI***.

The results in the analytical matrix implicitly encompass formula **(6.6)** for each of the alternative's composite utility to the society [52; p.102]. They clearly show that **under no circumstances we should be getting into alternative AI**. Its composite utility is simply too low relatively to the other two alternatives. And, worst of all, not even the "risk-of-conflict" factor is playing any part in it.

DISCLAIMER: PROPOSITION 5.4 introduced in the previous chapter has brought in one important exception, however. **When we treat this alternative as a "savior" of the whole** *recipient* society **or**, more seriously still, the whole region from socio-economic and socio-political crises that might end up in armed uprising, civil war or, worse still, in international terrorism on the large scale, then **we treat the** *recipient* **as a (temporary) protectorate**.

Also, before we go into detailed discussion, one thing should be said. The author has not come across a single instance in which—under similar or roughly the same circumstances—any developed country *donor* has ever seriously entertained such a business proposition. Unless, that is, the circumstances allowed the treatment mentioned above and denoted as alternative **A I*** (e.g. in **EXHIBIT 6.8**). This fact alone all but proves that the risk factor and its assessment is one of the most important and, at the same time, serious element in the matter of business ventures in general and those in developing countries in particular.

There might, on the other hand, be some discussion as to whether the difference in the alternative composite utility—which we shall denote **d**—is big enough to claim that alternative **AIII** is the only one to consider. Let us introduce the appropriate **analytical matrix**:

EXHIBIT 6.8: Analytical Matrix for 3-alternative Risk-Decision Problem

Significant factors	F_1	F_2	F_{31}	F_{32}	Composite utility
Significant weights	0.32	0.36	0.18	0.14	
Alternatives AI	0.60 [0.8]	0.20 [0.0]	0.40	0.40	0.392 [0.394]
AII	0.60 [0.80]	0.60 [0.40]	0.60	0.60	0.600 [0.592]
AIII	0.60	0.80	0.60	0.40	0.644
Significant weights*	0.18	0.41	0.23	0.18	
AI*	0.20	0.80	0.80 [1.00]	0.80 [0.728]	0.692

A simple technique of analyzing possible errors or the margin of such errors in alternatives is likely to help here.

6/3/3 Errors in Analyzing the Alternatives

In the preceding section we have judgmentally assigned factors' USFs to equally judgmentally constructed factor-tree and an importance-weight-tree. As long as the weight-tree is reasonably assessed—and the eleven levels of importance in **EXHIBIT 6.3** should assure this—the question of alternative ranking can be formulated as:

(6.10) What maximum error (or deviation) is tolerable for a particular significant factor's USF (or significant weight) so that the given ranking remains unchallenged?

To analyze the ranking of alternatives technique we start with the analytical matrix in **EXHIBIT 6.8**. That matrix contains significant factors' USFs and significant weights for all three original alternatives **AI, AII, AIII**. The fourth alternative, **AI***, has been added to highlight the world's rather than the system's problems with composite disutility.

The magnitude of tolerable error can easily be answered via the right-hand-side column of the analytical matrix. This is where the composite utilities of compared alternatives reside.

As alternative's utility **a (III)** (= **0.644**) is greater than **a (II)** (= **0.600**), we denote

(6.11)   a (III) minus a (II) as d (III,II)

and say that d (III, II) is the numerical difference between the two composite utilities.

We use composite utility formula **(6.6)** in which we substitute for **(6.11)** obtaining

(6.12) $d(III,II) = [f_1(III)-f_1(II)] \cdot w^*_1 + [f_2(III)-f_2(II)] \cdot w^*_2 +$
           $+ [f_{31}(III)-f_{31}(II)] \cdot w^*_{31} + [f_{32}(III)-f_{32}(II)] \cdot w^*_{32}$

The essential thing now is to know: How much room for error is there that—when we fumbled the assessment of some USF(s)—**(6.12)** still holds, meaning algebraically:

(6.13) $d(III, II) > 0$

DISCUSSION: Let us revert to the above numerical example. We assume that there are two significant factors whose USFs might be subject to erroneous assessment. Factor F_1 **"cost of the alternative"** and F_2 **"risk-of-conflict factor."**

Here, it is interesting to note that both factors' utilities are inversion functions of their respective arguments. This we have already explained in previous chapters. There, we needed all "utilities" to have a uniform growth trend. We must change "the over-all disutility" into individual utilities by a simple inversion.

Take the first investigated factor f_1 (II). From the discussion about the "cost of the alternative" vs. the "risk factor"—denoted by "what-if" terms **(6.9)** and from the tenets of condition **(6.1)** we have put extremely high utility on its cost at 0.8. **Yet the composite utility at 0.592—in brackets below the original utility in EXHIBIT 6.6 came even lower than the original one at 0.600.**

An implicit supporting point in the discussion is this. If the "cost of alternative" would be so prohibitively high (because of the inversion of "disutility"), there would be virtually no investment in the U.S. and other "NATO societies."

Consider now the possibility of erroneously assessed risk level in those two alternatives. To put in another way: The values of f_2 (II) and f_2 (III) are quite open to variability in interpretation and thus assessment.

The author has, over the years, acquired very detailed knowledge of both the European *recipient(s)* and Middle Eastern *co-donors* and used to work on strategies for similar deals. It is his contention that the actual "risk-of-conflict factor" utility of f_2 (II) should be, at the very best, set at 0.6. There are number of supporting facts for this. Not only has the *recipient* society in question currently one of the lowest trends of foreign investment in the whole former COMECON block of countries, but, in the last few years, a score of foreign firms sold their holdings and left. That said, we have to add that socio-political environments can be—given the time and right people—revived and substantially improved.

It is also worth mentioning that even if f_2 (II) is set at the extremely favorable, and highly improbable, risk level 0.8 this would be quite "catchy" for other societies within the same Central European region. The combined utility of this alternative would then just surpass the combined utility of the third alternative by 0.028. In other words, the results would be a toss-up between the two, with the probability of something going wrong strongly on the side of **AII**.

The questionable element thus remains the "risk-of-conflict factor" in *donor* society**:** F_2 (III); **e**specially its disutility f_2 (III). Here we must assume that an explicit "hard-wired" menu contains information about known spill-over effects from similar *donor-recipient* transactions. We may, for instance, visualize a correspondence table similar to the one in **EXHIBIT 5.3**. In column **(e)** of that table we find an increasing sequence of the spill-over effects (in a generic donor society) enumerated in real numbers. Therefore, it is surely within the combined knowledge, experience and intelligence of any of the *donor's* entity leaders (president, CEO, prime minister, etc.) to choose a transaction with low-level disutility.

6/3/4 Concluding Remarks on Methodology and Results

The inclusion of the risk-of-conflict element and possibility of its assessment in, both, macroeconomic and socio-political terms has brought a new dimension into the problem of strategic decision-making. This is particularly over the viability of transactions of economic and socio-political provenience in the almost unknown environments of the *recipient* (developing) countries.

Risk analysis has been an indelible part of doing business ever since free-trade system began in earnest. It was only the large-scale banking crunch in 1997 and subsequent economic hardship, as well as the increase of political instability in virtually all societies of South East Asia, the Balkans and former COMECON countries, that firmly introduced the element of risk-of-conflict-and-crisis and its grim aftermath into the picture.

As all banking and trust investments are interdependently global, one unnecessary risk might have nowadays much larger consequences than Mr. Leeson's coincidental destruction of the Baring's (Bank) quite a few years ago. The domino effect is much more pronounced nowadays. Also, unfortunately, it is much faster.

Contrary to global banking and information infrastructure, the political environment tends to become more and more fragmented along ethnic and sometimes even tribal lines. This contradiction has become the primary source of unrest, upheavals, and other features of polarization of societies and their destabilization.

In terms of real-life cause-and-effect, the following sequence usually happens. When the *recipient* countries' oligarchies start to siphon off the proceeds with economic crashes resulting, the society takes note and as the despair mounts, the society is bound to take action (see [78; p.1], [79; p.5], [80; p.1], [88; p."Op/Ed"]). And they usually do take action. It may start as simple unrest, graduate to armed clashes and end up as a full scale armed civil war. Political (or religious) ideology can be brought in from outside together with arms.

To become more aware of the mechanics behind the decision-making—where substantial risk of intra-societal conflict, leading to inter-societal heterogeneity, may be involved, yet not quite recognized—we shall recapitulate the causal chain of the proposed methodology.

Inter-societal heterogeneity has been graphically depicted as the distance or the length of the arc between the point-models of the investigated *donor* and *recipient* societies on the D-curve. It is not just the risk analysis *per se* but the whole decision algorithm—i.e. whether to do it and, if so, how to do it best—about the proposed (financial, economic and/or social aid) transactions between the *recipient* and the *donor* societies we are after. That's why we introduced the decision-making technique that works with alternatives into the problem in the first place.

Any such technique works with the combined utilities (or combined welfare) for both *donor* and *recipient* societies as a point of reference. On top of that we have also to add into it a system with feedback that recognizes symptoms of trouble (i.e. red-flags potential inter-societal and, above all, intra-societal crises in the *recipients* (in the making)) in any investigated transaction between the two. The feedback-loops are easy to imagine through the summary table in **EXHIBIT 5.3**. When we start from the last column of actual real numbers we can check whether the monotonically increasing or decreasing sequence—each element of which is entered in an individual row of the last column—fits with the sequences of ordinal numbers or the verbally defined phenomena in the first and fourth column.

It is then and there where we actually see the problem changing from the intra- and inter-societal homogeneous (with *donor* and *recipient* societies' points-models close to each other) into inter-societal heterogeneous. In this inter-societal part, the distance between the definitional points on the hyperbola grows. Eventually, the resulting risk characteristic should be in sync with societal definitions of **EXHIBIT 4.2** and macroeconomic damages of the risk-of-conflict entered in column (e) of **EXHIBIT 5.3**.

Speaking of "risk in conflicting socio-political environments" importance weight, **w**, it is worth remembering that its high importance is not constant in every situation. If, as we said in the previous paragraph, in the *donor-recipient* system, both societies are inter-societal homogeneous, the "risk-of-conflict" factor has obviously lower importance weight than in the inter-societal heterogeneous system. And again, the bigger the physical distance between the points—depicting system's societies on the hyperbola D—there is this added weight on the factor's importance. More importantly though, we have postulated the **"Law of increasing risk of conflict in the world"** in **LEMMA 5.1**. This is just another way of saying that the sum of physical distances between the definitional points keeps growing over time. Hence, the importance of this factor should also keep growing.

For confirmation we do not have to go very far. Let us take a look at the analytical matrix represented by **EXHIBIT 6.8**. We immediately see the situation. If we ignore the column of factor F_2 (risk-of-conflict in and between the societies), or substitute the column with another less dangerous factor, the alternative **AI** would look much more appealing, virtually indistinguishable from alternative **AII**; while alternative **AIII** would look like a clean winner. As is the case, however, it is alternative **AI*** that clearly illustrates the danger of ever-growing risk of conflict in the world today. Also, it shows the necessity to start seriously thinking about ways to resolve these conflicts.

EXHIBIT 6.9: Flow-Chart of the Risk-of-Conflict Assessment Paradigm

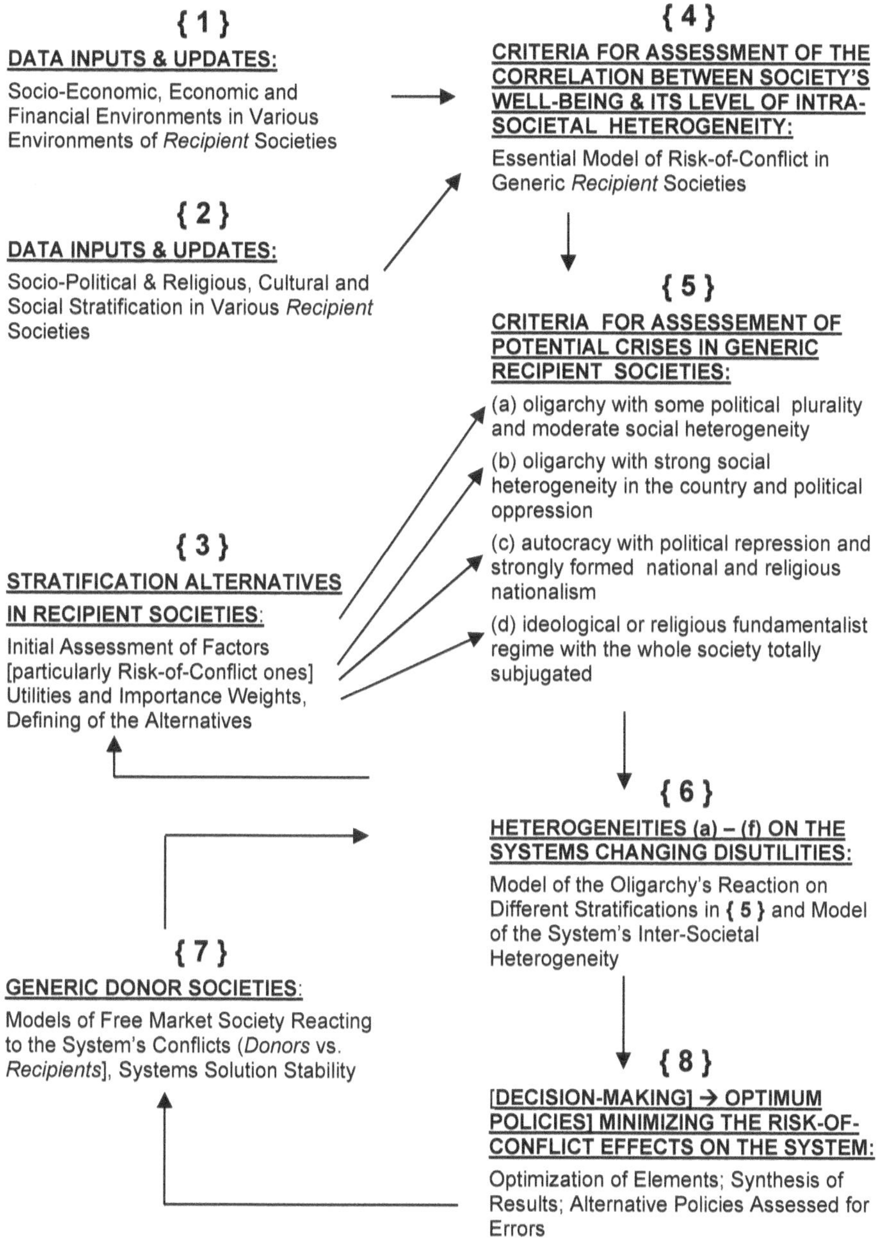

{ 1 }
DATA INPUTS & UPDATES:
Socio-Economic, Economic and Financial Environments in Various Environments of *Recipient* Societies

{ 2 }
DATA INPUTS & UPDATES:
Socio-Political & Religious, Cultural and Social Stratification in Various *Recipient* Societies

{ 3 }
STRATIFICATION ALTERNATIVES IN RECIPIENT SOCIETIES:
Initial Assessment of Factors [particularly Risk-of-Conflict ones] Utilities and Importance Weights, Defining of the Alternatives

{ 4 }
CRITERIA FOR ASSESSMENT OF THE CORRELATION BETWEEN SOCIETY'S WELL-BEING & ITS LEVEL OF INTRA-SOCIETAL HETEROGENEITY:
Essential Model of Risk-of-Conflict in Generic *Recipient* Societies

{ 5 }
CRITERIA FOR ASSESSMENT OF POTENTIAL CRISES IN GENERIC RECIPIENT SOCIETIES:
(a) oligarchy with some political plurality and moderate social heterogeneity
(b) oligarchy with strong social heterogeneity in the country and political oppression
(c) autocracy with political repression and strongly formed national and religious nationalism
(d) ideological or religious fundamentalist regime with the whole society totally subjugated

{ 6 }
HETEROGENEITIES (a) – (f) ON THE SYSTEMS CHANGING DISUTILITIES:
Model of the Oligarchy's Reaction on Different Stratifications in { 5 } and Model of the System's Inter-Societal Heterogeneity

{ 7 }
GENERIC DONOR SOCIETIES:
Models of Free Market Society Reacting to the System's Conflicts (*Donors* vs. *Recipients*], Systems Solution Stability

{ 8 }
[DECISION-MAKING] → OPTIMUM POLICIES] MINIMIZING THE RISK-OF-CONFLICT EFFECTS ON THE SYSTEM:
Optimization of Elements; Synthesis of Results; Alternative Policies Assessed for Errors

To show how the whole risk-of-conflict and crisis assessment methodology should fit into the larger picture of top-level financial, economic, and political decision-making, we have presented the whole system in graphical form in **EXHIBIT 6.9**. As we said earlier, the graph makes the causal chains, together with feedback-loops of the system, instantly recognizable and their importance acknowledged. The graphical form may also serve as an initial design-form for computerizing of the whole methodology.

6/4 Discussion of the Risk Assessment Methodology Cast into the Systems Analysis Framework

We have cast the risk-of-conflict assessment methodology into the systems analysis framework. This notion, presented in a flowchart in **EXHIBIT 6.9**, shows some interesting features. Despite several independent techniques having been forged together to achieve the goal we have set for this study, the causal chain arrows in the flowchart tell the story:

On the one side, two single directional flows, from { 1 } and { 2 }, go into block { 4 } in which the over-all rating of the countries (societies) is stored. It appears in the form of scenarios converted into image points S_i on the D-curve. An example of the technique is seen in **EXHIBIT 4.2** and in columns (a) and (b) of **EXHIBIT 5.3**. In this module the real importance of intra-society heterogeneity begins to unravel. We can spot it as the one-to-one correspondence between the point of the generic society on the D-curve and its real-life socio-economic problems. This is established through the correlation between a society's well-being and its level of heterogeneity.

Needless to say only the most credible and latest data and information updates flow there from the databases in blocks { 1 } and { 2 }. These are also the ones that visually update the criterion of the D-curve. They do it by **altering the position of the *donor* and *recipient* societies' image points S_i, $S_{(i+1)}$ on this curve with the new reading of the reality**.

Also, only one flow goes from block { 4 } to { 5 }, the "risk-of-conflict assessment" block. This is because the transformation of "distance" (between the two societies-points on the D-curve) into "risk-of-conflict factor" is based on a causal chain which is unidirectional and independent of any changes in "risk assessment." The importance of this factor is also a function of the "distance." Thus the same unidirectional trend holds here too. The directionality of block { 4 } → block { 5 } assessing methodology is depicted by causal chain: column **(b)** → column **(c)** → column **(d)** in **EXHIBIT 5.3**.

On the other side, there are two very important feedback loops in the scheme. First is the loop among the risk-assessment block { **5** }, model of the heterogeneity of the system in block { **6** }, and initial assessment of factor disutility, importance weights and preliminary definitions of alternatives in block { **3** }. Block { **3** } is virtually the same quasi-input block as presented in **EXHIBIT 1.1**. It has only added tools for definitions of alternative systems heterogeneities, through changes in intra-society heterogeneities. This loop is, for example, useful for choosing an appropriate socio-political tool. In potentially regional welfare-threatening *recipient* societies it helps to decide between federalization and protectorate and, in any case, helps improve the assessment of the risk factors relative to the remaining ones.

The loop reflects the ever-changing nature of the basically subjective—although corrected for illogical claims, subjective suggestions and notions as much as possible—nature of factors and risk assessment. In other words, the feedback loop makes sure that the bigger the distance between the points S_i, $S_{(i+1)}$ there is, the greater importance weight should be attached to the "risk-of-conflict" factor. It also reflects the iterative problem-solving scheme known in Popperian philosophy [64; pp.14 -16] which in this case serves to make the assessment and the final decision as objective as possible. An illustration of this loop would entail running a check on the correctly ordered sequence of row assessment of **EXHIBIT 5.3**'s columns **(c)** and **(d)** through the real-life data sequence in column **(e)**.

The second loop starts with another quasi-input factor { **7** } in which we have set the standards for generic *donor* societies. This is done so that the modeling of systems heterogeneity in module { **6** }, arrived at through the first loop { **6** } → { **8** } → { **7** }, can be meaningfully reassessed (if needs dictate). The final product of the iterative process in the first loop provides the ready-made factor and importance trees for the decision-making module { **8** }. The solution flow from module { **8** } checks back with the standards in module { **7** } to see whether the optimum selected alternative is stable enough to withstand possible inclusion of errors (in factor utilities and importance weight assessment). The final part of the loop is the confirmation of the selecting of the optimal solution for a system in crisis.

Let us take this last suggestion about the "iterative solving scheme" into the realm of our original numerical example. There we denoted the "risk-of-conflict" factor F_2 with its disutility (USF) f_2 and importance weight w_2. Numerically we have established—on the basis of the first batch of information—that the importance-weight will, through **EXHIBITS 6.3** and

6.4, be $w_2 = 1.0$ with the significant weight $w_2(A) = 0.36$, as opposed to significant weight for "cost" factor $F_1 (= w_1(A) = 0.3)$ in **EXHIBIT 6.7**.

Assume now that new information reached the decision-maker.

EXAMPLE: Political upheavals in the investigated *recipient* society have changed into an outright civil war with the prospect of the destruction of the whole socio-economic fabric (see e.g. Egypt or Syria; to illustrate the domino effect add Afghanistan). At this point, we might and should feel compelled to increase the disutility of the significant weight $w_2(A)$ from 0.36 to, perhaps, $0.4 - 0.45$ at the expense of the output factors' significant weights, $w_{31}(A) = 0.18$ and $w_{32}(A) = 0.14$. This is all in **EXHIBIT 6.7**. The upgrading of the originally constant weight-tree then becomes part of the iterative improvement of the decision-making module via the loop of modules { 3 } → { 5 } → { 6 } → { 3 }. These loops reflect the famous quotation in this excerpt [46; p.99]:

> By decision I do not mean the act of choosing between alternatives whose character is felt by the chooser to be certainly and perfectly known to him in all respects which matter to him. To make a decision is to commit oneself to the first step in an action-scheme about whose relevant consequences the decision-maker has in mind a plurality of rival (mutually exclusive) hypotheses none of which he regards as impossible. How does a person choose amongst several action schemes open to him, when the outcome of each is uncertain in this sense?

The "uncertain outcomes" which prominently feature in the above quotation are, indeed, both implicitly contained in the assessment of an individual society's position on the D-curve criterion graph. They have also been the reason for all the feedback loops going to and from the risk-assessment and the decision-making modules.

The decision-maker would certainly like to be as sure as possible that the D-curve in module { 4 } has both societies of interest, the ***donor*** and the ***recipient***, correctly placed on it. This is as much as "correct" means in the world of cognitive, ordinal, and mixed ordinal and cardinal values.

Equally eager would the decision-maker be to have assurance that the ranking of alternatives—stemming from his own preferences—as a product of decision-making module produces a stable solution. Here, being "stable" means that only major reassessments of factors and importance weights values can move the worst or, even, bad alternatives to the winning position. It also implicitly means "stability in a certain time frame."

But reassessment is the thing one has to do any time new information comes to light; especially **reassessment with regard to the future**. We may feel

Practical Use of the Paradigm

lucky that the basic qualities of ethics and behavioral make-up of society—so important in scenarios **(3.7)** and **(3.8)** and hence in criterion module with D-curve and graphical display of societies as points on it—are, generally speaking, reasonably close to being constant. At least this holds among societies (*donors* and *recipients*) on the upper left part of the hyperbola D.

This is why we stressed the "deterioration" element in the risk-of-conflict factor. It is particularly important for long-term strategic forecasting, assessment and decision-making. Once we build these variable-dynamics "deterioration" trends into the systems algorithm, we might be able to get a better grip on the real-life problems.

A typical example of a "deterioration" effect is seen on the fast deteriorating socio-political and socio-economic situation in parts of Central Asia (Kyrgyzstan, Uzbekistan) and Zimbabwe [89; p.1] at this very moment. To model it takes nothing more than to change the allocation of the "deteriorating" society point on the graph. We can also use features of **PROPOSITION 3.4** and find some other society lower and more to the left on the D-curve whose verbal definition would be closest to the situation in the "deteriorating" society. This, of course, jump-starts the loop among modules { 3 } → { 5 } → { 6 }. The feedback should reassess far greater importance weight (of disutility) to the "risk-of-conflict" factor as we already discussed in the numerical example in the previous paragraph.

The major part of any reassessment—apart from enlarging the distance between the *donor* and *recipient* points S on the D-curve and its effect on the disutility of the risk-of-conflict factor—should therefore concern more quantifiable or better ascertainable matters and issues in a *recipient* society. There may be many changes: First of all, change of the decision-maker and that of the *donor's* goals. Then, there are changes in socio-political priorities and economic policies importance weights. Also, the probability of a dramatic change in political milieu of a *recipient* society which almost always reflects the political trends in neighboring societies and the rest of the world. And, last but not least, there are changes in market conditions, exchange rates, balance of payments, etc. A classic example of sudden **strategy re-evaluation** and re-assessment is the "oligarchy isolation" strategy presented in the simple numerical fashion in section 6/3/2/1, in subsequent sections and in **EXHIBIT 6.7**.

Most of these issues are fairly well known. Thus, taken together, they make the problem a bit easier for the decision-maker to enter into the computerized system whose output would assist in any further strategic decision. If these other "matters" add up to further downgrading the society's position on the "slide" curve, so be it. It could, however, only be accomplished successfully after another round of careful analyses.

This brings us back to the very *raison d'être* of the whole, just presented, paradigm. We have proved that it is very important for governments, commercial banks, multinational firms and other entities and societies (we have summarily called **donors**) to assess the risks of conflicts involved in international deals and operations with inter-societal heterogeneous **recipient** countries.

Paradigm or not, the standard risk assessing methodologies still operate along the paths depicted by source [59; p.213] as:

> Although no method of assessing country risk is foolproof, by evaluating and comparing countries on the basis of some structures approach international lenders have a base on which they can build their subjective evaluations of whether to extend credit to a particular country ... **Institutional Investor** magazine surveys international bankers twice a year seeking their evaluation of country creditworthiness. The bankers are asked to rank each country on scale from zero (for least creditworthy) to 100 for most creditworthy) ... It is interesting that the United States has always been the top-ranked country until the September 1986 survey when **Japan passed the United States**.

Here, we can immediately see the shortcomings of the still current-standard methodology of risk assessment. We shall show it in two methodological issues that can be made from the above excerpt.

First, that **all** ranking is done by "invisible hands" with virtually no connection to the specific **donor** and/or specific **recipient** and although the quantitative methodology of pooling information and data (known also as the Delphi Technique) is a valid tool in collective decision-making, individual decision-makers may well wonder what kind of, and how deep and well-founded, reasoning lies behind those assessments.

Second, and more serious, a flaw can be spotted immediately from the statement about Japan passing the U.S. (albeit more than two decades ago). Under no circumstances would the paradigm presented in this study, in either the graphical or the numerical output, rank Japan over the United States; not even in the 1990s. The socio-political and socio-economic criterion of D-curve "democracy vs. oligarchy" in module { 4 } would not simply attach much credence to Japan's internal socio-political, social and socio-economic environments' stability. Not to mention complete alien

Practical Use of the Paradigm

socio-cultural conditions [76; p.9] or [90; pp.1 and 4]. In fact, the intra-societal heterogeneity in Japan vs. relative intra-societal homogeneity in the U.S. should put Japan in every possible assessment of module { 4 } way down and to the right from the U.S. on the D-curve. The **danger of forgetting to put a time frame on any conventional wisdom** (as noted above) is clearly visible here.

Still, on the positive side, an appealing feature of the paradigm is the total transparency of the computational process and all its elements. Let us again list and specify—eventually comment on the credibility of—at least the major ones:

- Assume a certain conversion table (in **EXHIBIT 4.2**)—with criteria definitions of societies' graphical images in terms of points S_i placement on the D-curve—entered as a menu in magnitude and importance of the risk-assessing software. Then, any investigated *recipient* society's definitional point on this hyperbolic curve, given the most recent information available, is unique.

- The scenario definitions are 'hard-wired'. Since they are products of historical but documented real-life cases, the risk-of-conflict assessment intervals **(5.3)**—with the help of conversion tables in **EXHIBITS 5.1, 5.2** and **5.3**—simulate the probabilistic estimates of risk and the appropriate credibility (confidence, or support) intervals.

- The user does not have to wait for upgrading the scenario definitional criterion only when new information reaches the decision-maker. Since the menu in block { 4 } crops up anytime the system is used, the invitation to virtual continuous upgrade is implicit.

- In block { 5 }, the conversion tables for individual alternatives or scenarios of the risk-of-conflict assessment (seen in **EXHIBITS 5.1** and **5.2**) are, again, accessible and upgradeable from pop-up menus. There is an inherent assumption that the user should become much more involved (if not totally immersed) in the design and development phase of these menus' conversion tables. After all, it is this particular decision-maker whose risk assessment vis-à-vis the *donor* subject is sought. It is, also, where the major strategic re-assessment (see our example with the "oligarchy isolation" strategy) is taking place.

- Similarly, a combination of the designer-user inputs and real-life data combine in models of systemic inter-society heterogeneity (and thus of overall systemic disutility following from the risk-of-conflict factor level) in module { 6 }. This is where the final factor-trees and importance-weight trees are assembled for each alternative and then enter the decision-making module { 8 }. While for most generic situations some standard 'hard-wired' decision-tree might be found in automatically-popping-out-menus, specific situations might occur. This may need some extra deliberation, perhaps on the strategic planning unit level. Similar reassessment and, at long last, the stability of the solution are taken care of in the loop among modules { 8 } → { 7 } → { 6 }.

Producing the input menus—for factor utilities and importance weights—are left to the user's own expertise, expectation and priorities. Only the decision-maker should be able to assess the *donor* society's objectives and priorities impact of known or imaginary conditions on the *donor*'s well-being. For the users' benefit, feedback among blocks { 3 }, { 5 }, { 6 } checks periodically on the credibility of the weights, utilities and risk criteria of the systems factors. On the other side, the iterative steps of blocks { 6 }, { 8 }, { 7 }, make a sequence of still better models of the decision-making. This iterative technique is not dissimilar to the famous Sir Karl Popper's argument about the direct ratio between degree of corroborability of a model (or hypothesis) and its empirical content, verbally expressed in the following excerpt [24; p.78]:

> This corroborability (or reliability; added M.K.) can be achieved for instance by fixing the upper bound of degree of corroboration (of a hypothesis, theory, mode; added by M.K.) at its empirical content, and by allowing evidence to raise the corroboration of the more informative theory (or mode; added by M.K.) above the maximum level of corroboration of the less informative one.

The only area which may pose some uncertainty is assessment of potential conflict impact of *donor's* operations on the *recipient* society. But this problem has been inherent to the paradigm from the beginning. It could be (and has been) solved by designing of 'hard-wired' generic scenarios in module { 6 }. They would be based on known past impacts of virtually the same operations between the generic *donor* and a generic *recipient*. And again, here we should take advantage of the computer's vast memory capable of storing, arranging, massaging, retrieving and analyzing enormous amount of information in virtually no time at all. A simple example of a real-life database—where macro-economic damages to the generic society are arranged into increasing sequence of "quantitatively → verbally → macro-quantitatively" expressed disutilities—is presented in column (e) of the table in **EXHIBIT 5.3**. Information of this kind could be collected, collated and verified with the help of new and hopefully more enlightened Internet-based modeling systems in "real-time."

Chapter 7: Macro-Economic and Micro-Economic Implications of the Paradigm

7/1 Macro-Economic Issues in the New Paradigm

7/1/1 Intra-Societal and Inter-Societal Heterogeneity

We have, so far, dealt with a problem that is fast becoming a nightmare in international relations with highly oligarchic and religiously autocratic societies, which include the former underdeveloped societies of Asia, Africa and the Middle East as well as all the former COMECON countries. **This is because the spin-offs from intra-society social and political conflicts—inclusive of political and armed upheavals and subsequent export of terrorism in the region and, eventually, to the rest of the world—are real and increasing** (see e.g. **LEMMA 5.1**). They are real, not too easy to fathom and, worst of all, ready to be triggered by any apparently innocuous bi-lateral transaction, such as monetary, technological and technical aid, know-how transfer and similar ventures.

In the world of science, a paradigm is valid only when its cause-effect reactions are repeatable.

This means that given the same or similar data, environment and input we should expect the same or a similar output every time. To assure this maxim, we have collected, collated, statistically massaged and tested specific behavioral data from many developing and transitional countries over the span of several years.

In **DEFINITION 2.4** we postulated that if in some (two or more) societies-countries there existed social, political and socio-economic environments in which a sound moral foundation, law abiding behavior, high quality legal framework and law enforcement capability, respect for human rights, freedom of religion, and credibility of the legal institutions and of the government prevailed, then we can call each of them intra-societal homogeneous and for the whole group we use the term **inter-societal homogeneity**. This holds irrespective of social and sometimes even political stratification.

There exist societies in which the **ruling autocracy has absolute power**—especially when the isolation of the society from the rest of the world realities is total—whose **social order is deemed by the general population to be "the only way possible."** Consequently, the pseudo-homogeneity of such societies is high and, at the moment, virtually risk-of-conflict free. In such countries, just as in all historically democratic and law abiding societies, **the risk of inner political conflict—based on the economy turning bad, unless the "bad" becomes "unbearable"—is minimal if it exists at all.**

One would, therefore, imagine that the general trends of modernization (perhaps via globalization) should lead to an increase of well-being in these societies. Wrong. These trends, relayed by the instant global information systems, such as the internet, TV and social networking, make the society slowly (but surely) realize the oppressive character of its ruling oligarchy and political problems soon commence when the built-in behavior starts to change.

To put it in proper perspective, recently a Harvard professor wrote [111]:

> If we learn anything from the history of economic development, it is that culture (for "culture" substitute "people and their 'hard-wired' behavior"; added by the authors) makes almost all the difference.

We have already presented the two all-important causal chains—originally as **(2.1)** and **(2.2)** in **DEFINITION 2.8** and subsequent **DISCUSSION**—at play in every society throughout the history of the world. Here we shall denote them **(7.1)** and **(7.2):**

(7.1) Economic crisis → socio-political crisis, and

(7.2) Intra-societal heterogeneity → socio-political crisis
→ major economic crisis

The combination of these chains then forms a vicious circle of deterioration, pauperization and destitution of the whole society. It is fair to mention that both chains work in reverse.

This means that if a smart oligarch, monarch or government creates full employment by expanding public works and, at the same time, diverts the attention of the masses from political to material and hedonistic values—the principle of "bread and circuses" eventually inclusive of regimented leisure as was known to happen in all communist and fascist dictatorships—then the intra-society heterogeneity radically diminishes and with it the chance for socio-political crisis. A classic example of "circuses" in one of the most president-cum-dictator ruled society, the Republic of Uzbekistan, is represented by this joke circulating among the population:

If you'd like to see Heaven, watch Uzbekistan TV, if you want to sample Hell, go to Uzbekistan.

NOTE: The "hell" was probably too much and lasted too long for Uzbeks because in the latest political move the president virtually kicked out NATO, which many political analysts have seen as a first step toward installing some sort of loose federation with Russia (a move everybody in Uzbekistan would vote for at any time; M.K.). The sociological base of this problem has been discussed in Sections 3/4/2 and 3/4/3 of Chapter 3.

7/1/2 Heterogeneous Societies and Escalation of Poverty

The necessary and sufficient conditions for risk analysis in transactions (however innocuous, such as simple economic aid) between conflicting socio-political, cultural, religious and cognitive environments are, from **DEFINITION 2.3**, two. **The investigated societies must be:**

(a) Intra-societal heterogeneous, and

(b) Feature such socioeconomic, socio-political, political, religious, social and society expectation environments that causal chains **(7.1)** and **(7.2)** come into being.

NOTE: Henceforth we shall call these societies **D-LRH**, i.e. **those on the lower-right-hand (side) on the D-curve**.

In various places in this text we have mentioned that chain **(7.2)** yields, among other economic ills, pauperization of substantial strata of the *recipient* societies. This itself is quite a serious factor in every society. But in economically underdeveloped and socially, cognitively and, above all, politically immensely heterogenized and stratified countries the poverty and further pauperization has—all throughout the history of the civilized world, for instance Russia's Bolshevik terror in 1917—become a base of radical, militant, and hence, armed movement (be it upheaval, civil war, or international armed conflict).

The **phenomenon of poverty** may not be quite so unbearable as it may be perceived in the *donor* countries as long as: **(a)** there is a certain **nivelization of poverty disparities** in the society, i.e. poverty is a general phenomenon in a society with very little social stratification; **(b)** socio-political dialogue within the society is good (i.e. people can easily approach their elders and even, to a certain extent, the ruling elite with problems to be decided or solved); and **(c)** there is a certain **"good feeling" permeating the society with living standards becoming slowly better, and this optimism**

is probably the strongest phenomenon that keeps any impoverished developing society firmly together and politically intact.

EXAMPLE: In Section 3/4/2 we investigated seven post-communist regimes in Central Asia and Trans-Caucasus and introduced and proved—in keeping with the tenor of the paradigm—the hypothesis of a correlation between the levels of high oligarchy rule and the society's feeling of destitution with no hope for any improvement whatsoever. On the other end of the spectrum is the correlation between more democratic and/or transparent governments—acting as if they genuinely wanted the society to get better socially and politically—and perceived "good feeling" based either on **actual** higher living standard **or "perceived" better living conditions.**

The point of this example is that all these societies started practically from scratch, as newly independent states, after the disintegration of the USSR in 1991. There is a great wealth of natural resources in some of them, thriving agriculture used to be in others, and the possibility of making the ancient Silk Route (that goes through most of them) the greatest and most revenue-generating tourism attraction in the world. Despite all of that, the region is one of the poorest (in terms of GDP/per capita) in Asia.

The results confirmed our hypothesis. When the "perceived or actual" (negative or positive) trends in living standards were correlated with the range of democracy, or at least transparency, in these societies—some of them highly centralist, oligarchic-cum-autocratic (and almost despotic) rule of governments implying high social stratification and general despair in the society, some of them on a firm democratic footing with strong privatization drive—the results showed a very highly statistically significant non-parametric correlation coefficient at $r_{s\,(LS)} = 0.83$ (as seen in **EXHIBIT 3.5** in chapter 3, where coefficients r_s and r_p are almost the same for a small sample size).

To prove that the behaviorally-based (and non-quantitatively derived) variable of perceiving of the "actual trend" of living standard **(LS)** in our methodology has merit, we have substituted the data series **LS** with that of Gini Index-based ranked data. The **Gini Index** and the basic data are explained and introduced in details in the Appendix. Here it suffices to say that these indexes are based on simple and straightforward algebraic massaging of the median of the society's poverty in terms of GDP/per capita and, hence, they should describe similar phenomena as our "perceived living standard" data. Sure enough, the basic data matrix table with correlation results, seen in the Appendix **as EXHIBIT A.12**, shows the Gini-Index-substitution (for the original **LS**-series) yields the non-parametric correlation coefficient at $\mathbf{R}_{S\,(GINI)} = 0.67$.

The conclusion is quite straightforward but two-pronged. **First,** it proves that the basic theoretical principle of the paradigm—saying that undemocratic, autocratic rule leads to social stratification, that, in turn, leads to social destitution and pauperization of the society with more serious political and, eventually, armed events to follow—is quite sound. **Secondly**, it suggests that simple algebraic massaging of the social stratification (based on GDP/per capita data in each social stratum; even if it can be measured) will have to be supported by a host of further explanatory behavioral factors, added in a meaningful way to the analysis. Or, ideally, by another set of Gini Indexes measured, say, three to five years later by **the same methodology** and, presumably, by the same institution. This would give us a "sense" of the trend, either positive ("well-being") or negative ("despair").

One of the best examples of this issue is the analysis we call: "Poverty Measure and Its Eradication in Uzbekistan" [163]. It claims that the living standard dropped and general despair in society increased not just because of the fall in output—in comparison with other CIS countries the output decline of the Uzbek economy was negligible—but also, and above all, because of greater inequality in the distribution of income due to its "burgeoning bureaucracy" **(much greater than in the USSR times) and nouveaux riches that never existed ever before**. Thus, the Gini Index— *the higher it is, the greater intra-societal heterogeneity (i.e. social disparity) it declares*—increased from 0.26 in 1991 to 0.38 - 0.40 in 2001. The problem is that in a much shorter time interval (1995 - 2001) the Gini index decreased in neighboring Tajikistan and Kyrgyzstan from 0.40 to a very respectable 0.34 - 0.35 (about the Swiss level).

NOTE: Hence, the problem is in the socio-political heterogeneity bringing in economic disparity and, eventually, crisis, as the causal chain **(7.2)** tells us. Once again, unless they start a meaningful democratization process in Uzbekistan, it is meaningless to talk about using family assets, banks etc. to stop pauperization of the society. The "inequality in distributing of the income" means that the ruling oligarchy (president, his family and cronies) takes Uzbekistan for their own fiefdom and the prevailing sense of despair in the society robs the country of its only productive elements.

Taking this "feel-good" element out of the society means pushing it towards the edge of civil war and further into armed insurgencies. At that point the "militant Messiahs," either indigenous or imported, start sowing the seeds of armed terror ideology into the destitute impoverished masses and this is the beginning of the end of any society. The below cited problems only make the crisis deeper and faster.

History teaches us—and **PROPOSITION 3.5** proves—that, in so far as social stratification is concerned, the politically most dangerous situation in any society throughout the ages has arisen when a brand new strata of *nouveaux riches* suddenly appeared on the social horizon and started charging the rest of the society (sans the ruling classes of course) for not only unnecessary but mostly outright non-existent services.

Society always recognizes historical ties in paying taxes due to fiefdoms (and rulers) but draws a line when a new additional burden suddenly appears. Therefore, enlightened rulers have always waged their fiercest battles against the new "high society" robbers: renegade knights, pirates, mafia families, and the clans of outlaws of any kind. Even Hitler's liquidation of Ernst Roehm's Sturmabteilung (S.A.) in 1934 clearly falls into this category, just as do the bandit-cum-terrorist gangs in the Philippines of 2002.

Remember, if the rest of any society—with the exception of its historical ruling classes (be they the royal camarilla, parliamentary oligarchy, a politburo, Muslim spiritual leadership, etc.)—is reasonably socially homogeneous, such a society is politically much more stable than a society with a much higher median living standard in which the social stratification and, hence, the living standard disparity is greater. **We can, after all, use the previously introduced Gini Indexes (G.I.) for an illustration of this important argument:**

In the first step we conclude (from the list of G.I. in the Appendix) that standard European historical democracies and some of the European transitional countries have G.I. within the interval, that we shall call for short **SED (Standard European Democracies**; probably the 15 countries of 1995 that formed the origins of the EU), where SED = < 25, 35 >.

In the second step we have chosen several other countries from the list of **D-LRH** societies. We picked those in which there have been recent strong political discontents, sporadic or continuous civil war, and assorted armed rebellions and upheavals (not necessarily religiously-related or religiously-fomented). These were: Bolivia, Brazil, Central African Republic, Colombia, Ethiopia, and Papua-New Guinea. We shall call them **Politically Unstable Oligarchies (PUO)**. Their G.I. then delineate for us the PUO interval, where PUO = < 46, 61 >. It is clear that even without religious totalitarians—although some tribal elements have been introduced into the political upheavals in the PUOs—social disparity and poverty-driven despair renders their situations critical. We must dread the situation in which the powder kegs (and readily available arms) of religious fanatics are suddenly introduced into all the social ills in these societies.

In the next paragraph, we shall elaborate on these notions. In the literature cited earlier in the study we see that **"societies tend to work smoothly when economic, social and political activities fit well together. But there is an obvious mismatch in today's global economy, where financial life is centralized as never before but political life is increasingly fragmented along ethnic and even tribal lines."**

7/1/3 Modeling the Societies' Socio-Political Environments

We have already seen that transformation of the qualitative levels of intra-society heterogeneities into the "physical" shapes of points on a graph gives us a chance to model the magnitude of the risk in conflicting socio-political environments. In Chapter 3 we mapped the "generic" intra-societal heterogeneities—via verbally defined scenarios converted into ordinal numbers—by points on the D-curve defined on a plane with two axes.

The highest societies with classical "democracy" ("legitimacy") are allocated on the upper left hand (side) of the curve—henceforth called **NORTH** (in sociological-political lingo)—while the meanest oligarchy-governed "generic" societies with absolute "power control" in the hands of one person or a small circle of "rulers" are situated on the lowest and most-to-the-right end (D-LRH) of slide curve D and, generally, called **SOUTH** societies.

NOTE: This time, however, it is not the "old socio-economic order" (Europe + US + UK + Japan + Australia + New Zealand, etc. **being solely NORTH** and the rest **being solely SOUTH.**)

The physical distance between the "generic" societies' points-models then defines the inter-society heterogeneities. This is a useful characteristic particularly when any two societies and/or entities think about future economic and/or political co-operation. We have seen the simple graph of two dissimilar societies, S_3 and S_7, in **EXHIBIT 3.2**. We show it again in **EXHIBIT 7.1** because of its importance to the paradigm.

DEFINITION 7.1:
In the graph, the developed—historically democratic, free-trade-practicing and virtually intra-society homogeneous—*donor* NORTH societies are represented by points on the D-ULH (i.e. upper left hand side), say, S_1 to S_3 while the *recipient* (of grants, financial aid of all kinds, investments inclusive of technology and know-how transfers, etc.) developing or transitional intra-

society heterogeneous SOUTH countries are represented by points on the D-LRH (i.e. lower right hand side), say, S_5 to S_9.

Then we can assume—and we have proven, e.g. in **PROPOSITION 4.1, LEMMA 4.1** and **AXIOM 7.1**—the existence of the law of increasing magnitude of heterogeneity between *donors* and *recipients*. It says that, graphically speaking, the increase of the distance between, say, S_3 and S_6 (or between any other two points on the graph in **EXHIBIT 7.1**) is, under *ceteris paribus* conditions, only a function of time. The qualifier "ceteris paribus" describes the scenarios discussed below that take a cue from **EXHIBIT 7.1**:

EXHIBIT 7.1

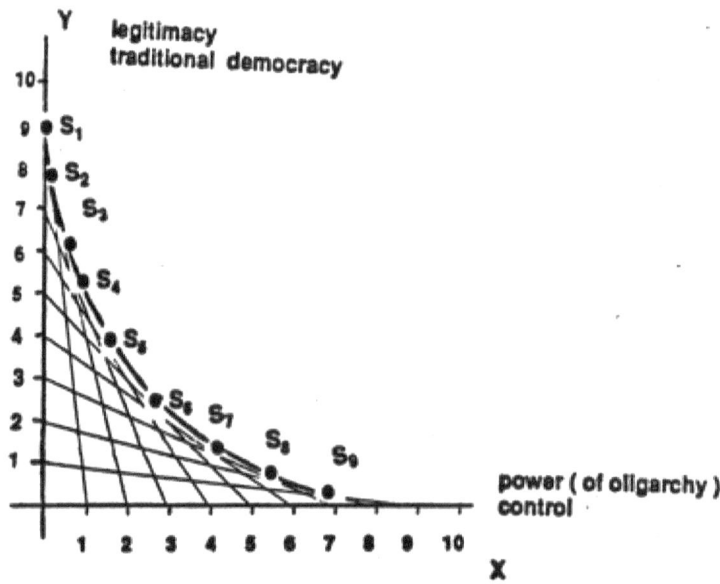

Unless we start promoting soon: **(1)** An efficiently designed set of policies to eradicate poverty (or, at least, to stop its spreading) that are well-thought out and appealing to ordinary (usually meaning the "transitional") *recipient* societies, and **(2)** strategies—mentioned in Section 7/1/4 below—designed for hotbeds of proponents of any kind of radical ideology, **the world as we know it today will fast become a still more dangerous place in which to live.** The causal chain of events is such that pauperization of the whole large segment of developing societies will lead to the growth of political and, in contemporary times of "gun-a-dime cost," armed insurgencies, to ideological and/or religious militancy aimed at the rest of the developed world and, eventually, leading to still more audacious terrorist attacks.

However, it is not just the poverty *per se* that is the problem. It is the complex historical behavior and cognitive traits of, de facto, tribal—in Europe ethnic-cum-national societies spoon-fed a mixture of xenophobia and cheap populism by the ruling classes in most countries of the world. Forget the old **NORTH vs. SOUTH** divide, this new development is much more dangerous and, also, the greatest obstacle to sustainable socio-economic growth (even within such a classic **NORTH** web of societies as the European Union). The first results of the enhanced xenophobic attitudes there are the anti-Roma edits in France, generally anti-Muslim attitude sway in most EU countries, the major divide between the Dutch and Flemish speaking parts of Belgium, Catholic vs. Protestant schism in Northern Ireland and, generally anti-big-banks and big business rallies in the EU **SOUTH** (which is Greece and Portugal, at the moment, but Italy, Spain and, perhaps Slovakia might well be next).

7/1/4 Several Issues Concerning the "Solution"

A practical example of our "new sociology vocabulary" for Europe is this. Germany is, by general consensus, one of the "haves" in the EU. However, due to the historically uneven social, political, ethical and, above all, conscious behavior of society between the two parts, former East and West Germany, we must denote the former West Germany as a **NORTH** society while the former Eastern part has always been **SOUTH**. This split is indeed quite apparent in most of the productivity, domestic migration, behavioral patterns, and/or legal norm observation gaps (and problems stemming from them) in Germany from day one after the merge.

And so, after chapters dealing with various elements of the problem and solutions in terms of "least diseconomy" alternative(s) in the decision module of the paradigm, we come to two major conclusions:

THE FIRST CONCLUSION is **the necessity to drastically amend the axiomatic laissez-faire of Adam Smith and others pioneers of classical free-trade economics, based on democratic socio-political principles, when we deal with socio-economically intra-heterogeneous societies.** This is particularly true for those societies whose historically strong ideological, "cultural tribalism" and/or religious, even gun-toting radicalism—remember the post-WWII division of Europe into East and West, a virtual civil war in Northern Ireland, Serbian war against Moslem Albanians and Macedonians in Kosovo, historical Jewish "Pogroms" in many a European country starting in the 12th century, etc.—is spoon-fed to them by the ruling classes, spiritual leaders, autocrats or oligarchs.

NOTE: This statement has axiomatic range, it has worked everywhere in the whole of Africa in the last decade.

THE SECOND CONCLUSION deals with the practical side, to wit: **How to achieve the actual shielding of the *donor-recipient* systems from potential disasters**—following the domino effect and economic, social and political crises' spurious growth in a region consisting mostly of *recipients* with similar socio-political and economic environment—and, more to the point, what kind of shielding of the rest of the region or, ultimately, the world as a whole would work there?

A possible theoretically correct suggestion, albeit left open-ended, appears in the following source [144; p.6]:

> The specific circumstances and challenges are quite different (from the Marshall Plan; added by the authors). This vision should provide the foundation for a reinvigorated foreign aid program ... much of this new Marshall Plan should be devoted to initiatives that may make some regimes uncomfortable ... including supporting nascent institutions of civil society; promoting pluralism of information and opinions; promoting economic development to reduce the appeal of radical alternatives; and creating modern education systems that give young people in Muslim societies the tools they need to flourish in a world where global connections become ever more important ... where regimes are not open to change, Washington should be prepared to funnel resources to private organizations that are—and to stand up for them if their government interfere.

This comes close to the suggestion found in **PROPOSITION 5.4** and **AXIOM 7.1**, which were derived from behavioral analysis of the "rogue" societies and regimes that endanger world peace. **AXIOM 7.1**, for instance, calls for the unification of global civilized societies and for pooling resources if the "resurrection of such societies" should be successful. There is one point in the above discussion which is both crucial and, at the same time, not very well understood (let alone researched) by either *donor* or *recipient* societies.

It begins with the qualifier **"civilized."** Most of the current rogue societies had not only been very civilized ages ago, but in the 10th and 11th centuries the "madrassas"—the religious schools, that now produce students well versed in the Koran and in the firing systems of Kalashnikovs and various shoulder missiles—used to produce great leaders in the technical and medical sciences, such as Avicenna and many others. As far as this author knows, the downfall of civilization and general intellectual and cognitive levels in these societies during one millennium has not been successfully explained yet by sociologists on either side of the **NORTH-SOUTH** divide. Hence, any preliminary conclusion does not bode well for any serious expectations about the "modern education system" being able to change the, by now, deeply rooted behavioral, cultural and ideologically-religious stereotyped collective minds of these societies any time soon, let alone overnight.

In Section 4/3/2 we presented the hypothesis **that these (very) young generations in these societies might**—due to the globalized information culture of cell phones, BlackBerries, iPods, Tablets, and subsequent social communication (that played such a major role in the so called "Arab Spring"), pop music, TV, movies and media coverage—**slowly accept this unified world culture, which, if we are lucky, will limit the effect of their militant spiritual leaders.**

There are several obstacles to this hypothesis: (a) The poor youngsters would become (with no parental guidance) a very easy target for radical-cum-warrior imams; (b) the (western) educated but unemployed young men would rather drown their angst (against the world and their countries' rulers) in joining the radicals.

In other words: (1) the poverty of the whole young generation in Lower Income Countries" LICs must (and this is very unlikely to happen) be eradicated at the onset of the timetable so that it can start slowly turning the generations from religious hatred of the "**NORTH**-world" to accepting a "**uni-world.**" It might—even for the most intelligent (i.e. second or third well-to-do generation reared and educated in the **NORTH** best schools—**last anywhere from 15-25 years; and this could be a bit too late for comfort**. (2) In source [212, p.79] we read: *"As Fascism and Communism were in their day, Islamism is now the ideology of choice for the world's grievance-mongers."* (3) A social and economic, let alone religiously-political solution that might work faster is not even on the horizon, let alone to be "tried" in the real world.

For a few final words, we show first, as an illustration, one of the above described axioms that showed a remarkable capacity to provide a reasonable, strategic, and very probably sustainable political solution.

EXAMPLE: Assume that we have a society, right in the center of an important European region, in social and political turmoil and the assessment of the risk of socio-political and, even more probable, religious upheavals in module { **5** } of **EXHIBIT 7.1** quickly drops from the original level, say, (**b**) to level (**d**) or, perhaps, level (**e**). This is not just a theoretical construction: the very same trend was witnessed in both Turkmenistan and Uzbekistan over the span of five to six years. **However, the absence of civil war, or any other society upheaval, becomes a tribute to high culture and civilization standards and roots of both indigenous societies.** In any other society the political unrest-cum-full-scale-civil-war would then have been fomented by extraneous bands of armed ideologues and thugs.

At this point, the paradigm yields the following solution: First, we have to be able to ease the tensions and soothe the political and economic environment—which has been proven to be the most important issue. To this end, **PROPOSITION 5.4** urges us to seal the border, take out the most dangerous warmongering and terror spreading rulers and their camarillas, and install a temporary government—as a mixture of moderate and reasonably friendly indigenous and expatriate experts from culturally, historically, behaviorally and cognitively similar societies—and slowly work on improvement of the society's standard of living and on a basic grasp of the democratic political process. In other words, there are not many non-engagement alternatives left.

However, in this case, there is one: the Russian Federation. This is basically because its president, Putin, is seen as the second coming of the Tzar Peter the Great in the eyes of the Russians and to most ethnic nationals from the former USSR.

NOTE: His political pupil Medvedev has just been allowed to do one thing: Let Putin be elected president; probably for life.

Vladimir Putin, who has become the political idol of virtually the entire population of the newly independent, yet also vastly impoverished, republics of the former USSR, uses pro-Russian sentiment combined with free loans and technology transfer but also brutal silencing of political foes on all sides of the political spectrum. This strategy has the potential to produce a stronger and much more united and, even more enlightened political superpower Russia than the former Soviet Union, not to mention the czarist Russian empire, had ever been. **In fact, today's Russia is the most ethnically, socially and religiously homogeneous economic superpower in the world, with a huge surplus of all the necessary non-renewable resources as well as scientific and technological know-how.**

NOTE: China is reasonably homogeneous too, but she is at least decades from the economic prowess—and centuries from the long history of science and arts—of Russia.

Without similar strategies (as in **PROPOSITION 5.4**), we may witness the world, as we know it, being slowly destroyed by the domino effect of the free-fall of the other societies in the region (and, perhaps, eventually in the whole of South-Eastern Europe). All of this is being fuelled by ethnic nationalism or, better still, the ideological (religious) militancy of a relatively small band of followers. One very old example comes to mind. In Cuba, in the Che Guevara days, it (reportedly) took less than a hundred ideologically highly indoctrinated warriors to overthrow the whole government (however corrupt). We believe that one of the more drastic alternatives to **PROPOSITION 5.4** was carried out in Pakistan in the form of the assassination of Bin Laden. He was a one-man "Prophet" of hatred of the **NORTH** (i.e. of all non-Muslims) and also Shiites, as he singlehandedly managed to move the marker **CHAOS** (in **AXIOM 7.1**) quite a few notches towards world extinction.

NOTE: The first author used to know Osama in the mid 1980s. A son of the Saudi king's closest friend, he was *de facto* King Fahd's "nephew" and by far the most intelligent and ambitious Saudi in Jeddah. But, 15th sons hardly ever get their ambitions fullfiled. Had he been made a Sheik and a chairman of Saudi Majlis (i.e. Senate), Bin Ladin might have become a model politician useful to the Kingdom (no Taliban or al-Qaeda ever) and, during Gulf War I, a single telephone call from the American president to King Fahd would certainly have achieved it. (The author, entrusted by the Saudi "underground" consisting of the Saudi elite including a few royal princes heading the major ministries, wrote the final version of a letter requesting just this to George Bush Sr., which was personally delivered by the Saudi ambassador. **No response!**). Instead, the Saudi monarch, after a dramatic *tete-a-tete* with Osama, banished him to Sudan. So, to show to his father and his "uncle" the king how good he really was, he first drove the Russians from Afghanistan and, later, set-up al-Qaeda against all non-Sunni societies. Given his leadership ability, the rest was history.

Speaking of direct-engagement alternatives—even though such a political solution is not exactly politically correct and is by all means only temporary—we shall probably need to install more of the **"enlightened" protectorates** jointly run by the developed ***donor*** societies and local friendly upper classes and/or elders (e.g. Afghanistan now; Iraq previously; none of them very successful). Although fraught with political difficulties, **AXIOM 7.2** turns the operation(s) over to the world's most progressive ***donor*** societies, who, banded together, should have no problem playing this role without political squabbles, overall cost notwithstanding. After all there is only one planet we all have to live on.

7/2 Micro-Economic Effects of the Paradigm on the Society's Homogeneity

7/2/1 Visibly Increasing Intra-Heterogeneities in Developed Societies

We have discussed macro-economic fallouts from economic interrelations between heterogeneous societies; and there is a logical inference that a similar mechanism works at the micro-economic level. **Not only that, if an "economic disease" spreads over a large part of macro-level, the micro-economy will be (and has already) been suffering too; and**—as we shall see in Sections 7/2/2 and 7/2/3—**vice-versa.**

Let us first substitute the term "society" with the term "economic entity." This may define not only a corporate entity (i.e. a firm) but also an entity of individual consumers (i.e. people and/or clients of the firm). After all, Philip Bowring [124; p.7] has said:

> Problems of excessive and unstable capital flows are all too obvious. Little has been done since the Asian crisis (a severe macro-economic crisis in 1999; M.K.) to address these ... the capital market forces that brought recent U.S. corporate (i.e. micro-economic phenomenon; M.K.) debt disaster such as Global Crossing and Enron (two U.S. corporate giants; M.K.) are the same ones that earlier provided absurdly easy money both to Asian corporations and to the government of Argentina.

The disturbing demises, botched takeovers and failing mergers of even the blue-chip corporations that have occurred recently, together with the shaky footing of many high-tech and "dot-com" Web industries in particular, signal one thing. We should look for strong parallels to the socio-economic and sociological phenomena discussed on these pages in the societal and, thus, macro-economic milieu. And if, as the quote from source [111; p. 6] alleges, it is *the culture that makes all the difference in macro-economic* development then we have a good starting point there.

We notice that "culture," which could be substituted by "people and their hardwired behavior" differs in both macro-economic and micro-economic environments. It suggests converting macro-economic factors and elements used in the previous chapters into micro-economic ones and seeing whether the **macro → micro conversion** makes economic and causally logical sense on the corporate level also. Actually, we need not "re-invent the wheel."

Reporting on the case of a Canadian corporate derelict (Biovail Corp. [165]) the columnist ruefully claims that:

> [A]nalysts are getting used to such things. They keep picking nits about aggressive accounting, and stuffing distribution channels to inflate sales revenue. Call these **"cultural differences."** But we in the media are slow learners.

DEFINITION 7.2:
We now apply ASSUMPTION 3.1 onto the D-curve whose attributes were mentioned previously in DEFINITION 7.1. It is immediately clear that even on the micro-economic entity level, the quest for survival requires strong leadership and capable management, together with viable corporate culture, ethics, feedback channels, personnel cognitive level and development policies and wage and remuneration policies and rules that should maximize the entity's efficiency and productivity. Let us for simplicity denote all of these attributes as "the corporate culture of an economic entity" and claim that they can differ as much as the previously investigated societies. Thus, the labels D-ULH (upper left hand side) and D-LRH (lower right hand) would apply here too.

Alan Greenspan lists some basic corporate-systemic dissimilarities [145; p.FP15]. He writes:

> The very technologies that appear to be the main cause of apparent increased flexibility and resiliency may also be imparting different forms of vulnerability that could intensify or be intensified by a business cycle ... in particular, the fact that concepts cannot be held as inventories means a greater share of GDP is not subject to a type of dynamics that amplifies cyclical swings ... a firm is inherently fragile if its value added emanates more from conceptual as distinct from physical assets ... a physical asset ... has the capability of producing goods even if the reputation of the managers of such facilities falls under clout ... the rapidity of Enron's decline is an effective illustration of the vulnerability of a firm whose market value largely rests on capitalized reputation ... the physical assets of such a firm comprise a small proportion a small proportion of its asset base. Trust and reputation can vanish overnight. A factory cannot.

It is apparent that there are big differences in the entities' corporate culture elements, such as: power structures (e.g. pyramid-like rigid managerial scheme vs. lateral, Delphi-like, brainstorming), strategic thinking and using human resources. These phenomena, taken together, should also yield point-images on the different part of the D-curve, exactly like individual societies differing in intra-societal heterogeneities, according to **ASSUMPTIONS 3.1-3.2** in **EXHIBIT 3.2** and, later on, in **EXHIBIT 4.3**.

The big difference from the macro-economic societal analysis is this. On the micro-level, the importance of judging which specific "corporate structure" is more suitable and palatable to the customers than other alternatives is important for the entity's management. **The management should estimate, map and forecast as best as possible the customers'**—eventually indigenous or external competitors'—**behavioral make-up** (i.e. cultural and cognitive traits, expectations, technology trends, etc.) **with the help of the (societal) point-modeling S_i on the D-curve.** Hence, the products of several competing production entities coincide with customers' different tastes and expectations and the product sale-ability is usually dependent upon the quality of assessment of behavioral make-up of the consumers, clients and competitors.

Thus, we can, for strictly compartmentalized micro-economic entities, assume that every such economic entity in its quest for survival inherently behaves as if the maximization of its polity viability (see e.g. **EXHIBIT 3.1** and **ASSUMPTIONS 3.1** and **3.2**) or "corporate culture" was its main criterion. Therefore the usefulness of the D-curve in **EXHIBIT 7.1** can be taken for granted even in the micro-economic climate, with the provision that both axes represent different models of corporate cultures' quality (see e.g. **DEFINITION 7.2**). Hence, we can attempt to formulate some useful propositions along these points.

ASSUMPTION 7.1:
Let us, for the sake of simplicity, assume that any micro-economic entity with lateral management and professional assessment and feedback of employees' and consumers' expectations is better equipped to maximize its sales than an entity with a rigid pyramid-like management structure where only a few owners do all the production, research and marketing decision-making. We call such (and any other major) management differences heterogeneity in "corporate culture."

PROPOSITION 7.1:
We say that the necessary and sufficient condition for a unique definition and mapping of an i-th micro-economic entity is that there exists a point S_i, i = 1......m, on D-curve (in EXHIBIT 7.1) in which the tangent from points OL_i, OP_i touches hyperbola D, where OL_i is, for simplicity, a measure of the "lateral management" with employees' and consumers' feedbacks and inputs into the management process" on the Y-axis while OP_i is, again for simplicity, a measure of "pyramid-like" management rigidity, strictly segregated from the

employees and consumers and their ambitions and expectations. This is on the X-axis. Then we say that S_i represents the i-th entity and that such a representation (of corporate culture) is unique.

PROOF: It follows from the scheme of the proof of **PROPOSITION 3.1**, where again we assume that optimizing the entity's productivity and efficiency calls for achieving the sum of $OL_i + OP_i$ to be maximum. There are other useful statements in the previous chapters, both proven and inferred, that have their roots, if not their mirror images, in the macroeconomic niveau. The problem is that we must completely disregard sociological aspects from them.

PROPOSITION 7.2:
Suppose we have two interacting entities S_i, S_{i+k}, k = 1...n-2—producer of goods or services S_i and the group-entity of consumers or clients S_{i+k}, or two competing or cooperating producers S_i and S_{i+k}—mapped and allocated on the slide curve D. We say that the greater physical distance is between the point-models of those entities-cum-corporate-cultures (S_i, S_{i+k}) along the arc on the D, denoted as $S_i \cap S_{i+k}$, the greater there is a risk of heavy overall financial loss for a single producer S_i when trying to sell to clients-consumers S_{i+k} or when we attempt merging the two producing entities eventually complementing or combining the output of each through one single channel.

PROOF: This goes along the lines of the proof of **PROPOSITION 5.1** with the provision that the distance between the entities' (or an entity and consumers and/or clients) images on D is defined in absolute values to convey the main message here: there is no clear cut criterion of the qualitative label "good entity" as opposed to a "bad entity." We can only infer that the corporate culture, based on a lateral scheme of management with feedback loops to clients and consumers, on Y-axis seems to be: (a) much more homogeneous vis-à-vis the clients and/or consumers expectations, wishes and historical behavior, and (b) much easier to adapt to new ideas, technologies and, above all, the society's socio-economic and socio-political trends—the diffusion effect deemed so important in human progress comes also more naturally to these entities [114]—than the pyramid management schemes on the X-axis.

For illustration of producers S_i vs. customers S_{i+k} heterogeneity and its impact on the producers' financial losses, we use the case of Internet and E-Business in the early days of the new century. On the one hand we read and hear everywhere that businesses that do not switch to e-commerce pretty soon might as well be extinct. On the other hand these same "dot-coms" are laying off thousands of workers and closing shop left and right. Some online sites are losing millions of dollars prompting, in the process, exasperated comments, such as J.D. Lasica of *Online Journalism Review* who wrote [115; p.17]:

I'm getting bored with the Internet. It looks like the Net itself is losing appeal, and the surfing public is becoming dot-bored ... my God, was it all just a meaningless fling?

Clearly the loss of customers is the culprit there—explained by the above statements and ones like: **"the question is, how do we change the culture to get people to switch to the new way"** (of consumers' behavior, added by the authors; and coming from a VP of Raytheon Co.), and "people talked about the Internet as a business revolution ... it is actually more of a business evolution ... the traditional holders of assets are absorbing the Internet and leveraging is as a tool ... the Internet is, though, an instrument of social revolution. It has put power in different people's hands and connected people who have never been connected before ..." [116; p.6].

NOTE: It is necessary to add a flip-side to recent problems with the Internet, problems that shouldn't happen. The major operating system's producer Microsoft seems to have forgotten that the "notebook" should, for the legions of business people, be a replacement for the business PC or low-end workstation. Cramming them full of useless games and ancient and still more user-unfriendly operating systems—typically, the succession of futility of Windows 7, Vista, Windows 8—a substantial loss of students, scientists, and business professional clients shouldn't come as any great surprise.

If we simply substitute "people and their hard-wired, relatively constant, behavior and expectation" for "culture"—as in the culture of a certain socio-economic entity we discussed in previous chapters—we see the real problem. It stems from **PROPOSITIONS 7.2** and **7.3**. Realizing that the contemporary "cool culture" of the Internet (E-commerce, social media, and all the accompanying cell-phone "apps") is one of "geeks making gadgets for geeks," it is immediately clear that there must be a severe clash of "cultures" in the "producer—customers" system. This is why the dot.com industry has, for quite a long time, lost its grip on the national imagination. Put another way: the mere fact that you are on the Internet is no longer something for which you get points for being cool.

One of the best examples of the necessity of estimating the "targeted customers' need and imagination" comes from Mary Lou Quinlan, CEO of a strategic consultancy firm ([166]):

> It's easy to buy into the myth that customers love your brand as much as you do, but business need to wake up and face their **real customer** (bold font by M.K.), not the idealized customer in their heads. In most cases it will be a woman and she'll have a lot to say about how to improve their product or service or retail establishment. Women are

Macro-Economic and Micro-Economic Implications

becoming vigilante shoppers and they expect results. Listen and act, if you're looking to grow your bottom line.

Now, assume that the corporate culture of a production entity and behavioral make-up of the consumers or clients are both based on built-in, historically acquired (in old firms) perceptions, customs and expectations. Then, given the relative constancy of each entity's behavior, it is fairly clear that the greater distance of images S_i, S_{i+k}, the greater the clash of the corporate cultures (or corporate products compared to what the consumers and clients expect) we shall have as the end product of whatever new corporate project. A typical corporate-merger example has been revealed recently when Thomson Corporation's bid for rival Bloomberg L.P. was discussed by Patrick Tierney, Thomson's executive VP [146; p.FP4]. He said:

> Bloomberg and Thomson might not mix because of technical clashes ... Thomson is moving to a business model based on inter-operability while Bloomberg is adopting a proprietary model ... there really are some incompatibilities.

From all of these pieces one can, perhaps, put together another mosaic. This time a proposition running along a similar idea as **PROPOSITION 3.3** (in Chapter 3) can be formulated as follows.

PROPOSITION 7.3:
Let two socio-economic entities of intra-heterogeneous (i.e. within one entity) corporate culture and cognitive level be defined by points S_i, S_{i+k}, k= 1....n-2 on the D-curve and assume that both are subject to the same external economic pressure; be it economic stagnation, crisis or just the emergence of a strong sectoral—maybe multinational—player. Then we say that the entity whose point is located on the D lower-right-side (LRS) of the definitional point of the "control" entity on the hyperbola will end up with greater financial losses.

PROOF: As we assumed that the "enlightened" lateral management with fast and full employees' feedback is much more likely to withstand serious economic pressure we have thus equated it with a macro-economic more socially homogeneous (or less heterogeneous) society. Thus, the formal proof by contradiction of **PROPOSITION 3.3** should hold in this case as well.

It is also natural that the customers—the society at large—with largely constant and predictable behavior clearly need something qualitatively different. That is, qualitatively different from mere information and activities readily available via standard communication media and "your friendly" discount store around the corner. In this case the issues and general public's thinking are:

Why should we bother to fiddle forever with the PC and its Internet applications to get information readily available in the newspaper, on the telephone or on TV or, more pertinently, by a direct visit to the nearest (specific) shopkeeper?

Here is the classical case of the two entities: on one side there are "dot-com" computer geeks and in the other corner there is the general public; far, far different worlds that have just perfectly fit the inherent assumptions of **PROPOSITION 7.3,** and also the results. The "quality factor" is different. The thinking goes as follows: "If I have to bother fiddling with the computer, then I'd like to get something extra for my time spent on it." Nobody ever considers the time spent on shopping as "time spent by free choice among alternatives."

There is a "necessary part of human life traditionally and always spent on hunting for food, clothing and other items of basic human consumption." That is what was special about Napster's idea of free downloading of CDs. That something "extra" for nothing was what made the new activity worthwhile.

Now, for the example of two corporate players as S_1 and S_2 we return, yet again, to the Enron saga. We, however, will not be concerned with Enron *per se* as this entity for all practical purposes withered away. We shall investigate two entities connected in the scandal with a quite different raison d'être: Enron's auditor (Arthur Andersen Inc.) and one firm (say, Sanders Morris Harris Inc.) of the large number of industry analysts who were all selling, underwriting and recommending Enron's stock almost to the end. Let us take the auditor first: Capitalism works on the assumption that managers do all they can to boost profits, much as football assumes players' aggression. Up to a point boards can impose discipline on managers, but directors who meet only infrequently can no more be relied upon to spot foul play than a referee without line judges. This is why the key constraints must come from auditors. These are the experts who get paid millions of dollars to certify that corporate accounts are accurate. The Enron story shows how badly auditors neglect their mission. According to reports, few managers at the company knew the extent of Enron's phony bookkeeping; the board, while knowing something, was also partly in the dark. But Arthur Andersen, the auditor, knew all about the off-balance-sheet partnerships because it had been paid $5.7 million for advice about them. It must also have known about the illusory profits created by the advance booking of estimated future earnings, because it signed off on those accounts. In 2000 alone, Anderson's experts were paid $25 million to understand Enron's finances [147].

Knowing all this, any industry assessor would put the analysts on some point of the D-curve; however, the auditor (Arthur Andersen) would be a lot further down and to the right on the same curve under all circumstances. According to **PROPOSITION 7.3** the overall disutility (lost reputation, financial crisis, etc.) should be therefore much more severe for the auditor. So far, real life supports the theory well. The firm of Arthur Andersen, lost most of its business and suffered very costly litigation, has not returned as a viable business.

EXAMPLE of **PROPOSITION 7.3** and different placement of firms' qualitative markers on the D-curve) has been discussed by Alan Greenspan in the above referenced source [145; p.FP15]:

> The rapidity of ... decline is an effective illustration of the vulnerability of a firm whose market value largely rests on capitalized reputation. The physical assets of such a firm comprise a small proportion of its asset base. **Trust and reputation can vanish overnight. A factory cannot.**

Finally, putting all of the algebraic elements derived from real world (i.e. the sum of the all societies in the world) historical functioning, we come to the important preamble that will be highly significant in the next section on the sub-prime crisis 2008-2009 in the US and the subsequent financial meltdown the world-over.

From all of our previous notions, discussions and real life examples follow the elements of the paradigm, **PROPOSITION 4.1** and **LEMMA 4.1**. These elements have proven two things:

FIRST, every single society shows the signs of more or less perceptible decay over an arbitrarily chosen time span.

SECOND, the inter-society heterogeneity between the *donor* and *recipient* societies (or any two socio-economic entities)—modeled by the physical distance between the points S_1 and S_2 in **EXHIBIT 4.2**—is, axiomatically, an increasing function of time.

From all of our previous notions, discussions and real life examples follow the elements of the paradigm, **PROPOSITION 4.1** and **LEMMA 4.1**. These elements have proven one important 'building block' of this text—**LEMMA 7.1**—without which it would be difficult to understand the micro-economic effect on the whole national economy, and, hence, becoming a serious part of intra-heterogeneity as, for instance, social, political, ethnic and religious elements of the given society.

LEMMA 7.1:
When any serious micro-economic 'depression' involves a substantial part of any society, we have to re-define the impact and call it a macro-economic 'contraction' on the way to macro-economic depression, and eventually, if it persists, a macro-economic crisis.

EXAMPLE: The problems of sub-prime mortgages held by Fannie Mae and Freddie Mac (to be discussed in section 7/2/3) were, originally, only big micro-economic downfalls. As the non-paying mortgagees snowballed to become a substantial portion of the American society the crisis became macro-economic and eventually world wide.

This should drastically change the process of decision-making that has been covered in reasonable detail in Chapter 6. The reccuring words in that chapter were "credibility" of basic data and their "freshness" (i.e. the more recent, the better). However, the more recent data only support and elucidate **LEMMA 5.1** we have proven in Chapter 5 and which is so important that we shall reprint it here as **AXIOM 7.1**.

AXIOM 7.1:
Suppose we represent the overall, i.e. the sum, of all inter-societal heterogeneities between all *donor-recipient* and/or NORTH-SOUTH entities—graphically depicted as the sum of lengths of all arcs on the D-curve—by the label used in Chapter 3 (PROPOSITION 3.2), CHAOS, and we say that the world-wide CHAOS can be made equal to

$$CHAOS = \sum_{i,k} S_i \cap S_{i+k}, \; i \neq k.$$

Then we say that under *ceteris paribus* conditions of the current world economic environment—as depicted by images in the D-curve—CHAOS (i.e. world chaos) increases progressively with time.

The above **AXIOM 7.1** summarizes the *ceteris paribus* conditions of **DEFINITION 7.3** in algebraic terms.

DEFINITION 7.3:
The historically developed spread of societies' images S_1, S_2, ... S_9 along the sliding down continuum of the D-curve (as seen in EXHIBIT 7.1) shows the behavior (defined in DEFINITIONS 7.1 and 7.2) fashioned by the long history of socio-economic relations within world societies. From PROPOSITIONS 3.3, 4.1, 7.2, 7.3 and LEMMA 4.1 we assume, perhaps imperceptible but real, increase of distances between the societies S_i on the Upper Left Hand side of the D (S_i-ULH) and those, S_k, i≠k , on the Lower Right Hand side (S_k-LRH). We call such a behavior a *ceteris paribus* condition of the world economic environment it is also called "the continuous relative pauperization of SOUTH societies vis-à-vis the NORTH countries" and the aim should be to reverse the trend or, at least, to stop the SOUTH decline.

The notion of **PROPOSITION 4.1** and **AXIOM 7.1** about the **axiomatic slide of every society down and to the right on the D-curve**—the speed of the slide being the only truly important factor that affects the magnitude of dissimilarity among societies (as **DEFINITION 7.3** explains)—might be just the best "wake-up call" this paradigm can ever produce. It should make all of us, in the **NORTH** societies, painfully aware of the crucial and universal importance of the tenets and operations manual behind **PROPOSITION 5.4**. They all suggest the mechanics of how to deal with rogue **SOUTH** societies that pose the danger of a domino-like crash of whole regional economies and policies irrespective of their adherence to liberalism, democracy, free trade and their upper-left-hand placement on the SLIDE; in other words to the decent and hard-working **NORTH** as well as **SOUTH** societies.

7/2/2 Major Macro-economic Effect: Sub-prime Mortgage Crisis in the US 2007–2008

The sub-prime mortgage crisis in the US that occurred in 2007-2008 became a threat to the entire world economy. Thus, **AXIOM 7.1** has to absorb "Rogue **NORTH**."

All the above mentioned examples of corporate greed or **heterogeneity in corporate culture and cognitive functions of some managers** came to a frightening cumulative effect in the years 2007 and 2008. The final effect of this **micro-economic cause had led to macro-economic causality** (similar one to **(3.17)** and to a major **world casualty** with political repercussions along the path charted in **(3.18)** will be long remembered the world over, and the changes in banking regulations will, most probably, forever change the character of this industry.

The situation started with the lowering of interest rates after the "dot-com" bubble bursting in 2000. All of a sudden there was a lot of money around and, under the Clinton administration that eased the bank lending standards for potential and existing homeowners (apparently to help low-income and certain racial segments of the society [181; p. 18]), virtually everybody who applied could get a mortgage with virtually no checking of their creditworthiness. **Then the hubris took over**. Owing to a form of financial engineering called securitization, many mortgage lenders passed the rights to the mortgage payments and related credit/default risk to third-party investors via mortgage-backed securities (MBS) and collateralized debt obligations (CDO). The classical case of a clash of two corporate cultures and cognitive levels (three if you add the Feds) as discussed in **PROPOSITION 7.2**.

The reason for the process of securitizing mortgages was that the investment bankers could sell off these "pools" of loans to other financial institutions and investors in a secondary and, mostly unregulated, market. So, basically, instead of holding all the loans they made to home buyers on their books, lending institutions could now pool a bunch of these loans together and sell them in the secondary market to another financial institution or investor. The securitized share of sub-prime mortgages (i.e. those passed to third-party investors) increased from 54% in 2001 to 75% in 2006.

NOTE: Alan Greenspan stated that the securitization of home loans for people with poor credit—not the loans themselves—were to blame for the ensuing global credit crisis. **Apart from being a bit naïve, coming from the supposedly intelligent Alan Greenspan, this explanation still left the problem in the infamous state of "chicken vs. egg."**

As opposed to holding all the loans in the banks' books and being subject to certain regulations, in the case of sub-prime mortgages the derivatives (CDOs and MBSs) magnified the effect of losses because they allowed bankers to create an unlimited number of CDOs linked to the same mortgage-backed bonds. And worst of all, there are **conflicts of interest relating to rating agencies** that are remunerated by the institutions whose assets they are rating.

The problem started with U.S. insurer AIG that has received $182.5 billion in financial support from the government since the company unraveled in September 2008.

NOTE: The Company has been restructured and, in the process, was selling off a number of business units to repay part of the loan. However, it still pays enormous bonuses to its *"(key) people crucial to winding down transactions that are 'difficult to understand and manage'"* [182; p.6].

The key conclusion here is voiced by a very high-esteemed central banker:

> If you did not understand that explanation, you are in good company; large banks writing down tens of billions of dollars in losses may not have understood it either (see **PROPOSITION 7.2**; added by the authors) ... Besides, most people, even fairly sophisticated investors, are not in a position to assess the quality of the assets on a financial institution's balance sheet. In fact, most people don't even know what those assets are.

Similarly, during the 1997 Asian financial crisis, when Indonesia, South Korea and Thailand needed to close or consolidated banks, bankers protested, claiming that that "their connection with borrowers was critical to recovery." [182; p.6].

And then, **a crisis of confidence** that gripped the debt markets, like in the old-fashioned, Depression-era run on the banks—but now with trillions of

Macro-Economic and Micro-Economic Implications

dollars on the line—has taken over. In a bank run, depositors, fearing their bank might not have enough capital to cover its obligations, rushed to pull out their money before it all disappeared. The bank would try to call in whatever loans it could to provide cash and, of course, stopped making loans. If the run was fast and heavy enough, the bank would shut its doors, freezing the accounts of depositors who had not been quick enough to pull out their money and calling in all outstanding loans to the borrowers who depended on the bank.

The backlash is particularly sharp abroad, in countries that were surprised to find that problems with United States homeowners could be felt so keenly in their home markets. Funds and banks around the world have taken hits because they purchased bonds, or risk related to bonds, backed by bad home loans, often bundled into collateralized debt obligations (CDOs). Foreign politicians and regulators are seeking a role in the oversight of American markets, banks and rating agencies. The head of the Council of Economic Analysis in France has called for complex securities to be scrutinized before banks are authorized to buy them.

NOTE: To make our point, in the United States regulators appear to think that the new and often unregulated investment vehicles—which have shrunk the world and sped up business in much the same way as the Internet—are not all inherently flawed. This opinion is captured in an analogy offered by Peter Douglas, the founder of GFIA, a hedge fund research firm in Singapore. He likens using derivatives to power tools:

> If you know how to use them, he said, they are exponentially better and faster for building a house, compared with using hammers, screwdrivers and hand saws. If you don't, "you could drill a hole in your head" (see corporate culture; inclusive of cognitive level).

Analyzing this very serious problem, perhaps critical for the well-being of many countries, through our paradigm encapsulated in **PROPOSITION 7.3**, it is easy to see and explain the major economic and monetary issues that are happening even in very developed **NORTH** societies.

7/2/3 Analysis of the Sub-Prime Mortgage Crisis

Originating in the US, this crisis affected US society and the world.

(A) Starting with **DEFINITIONS 7.1-7.3, ASSUMPTION 7.1** and **PROPOSITION 7.1**, it is natural that any management structure of any micro-economic entity strives to maximize the profit of that entity, be it a bank, grocery shop or car dealership. In this case, the management did what it was supposed to do. In fact, while the cases of ENRON and BIOVAIL were based on falsifying documents, the derivatives in this case, as we briefly explained above, were legal investment vehicles (at the time of their use).

(B) PROPOSITION 7.2 seems to be the gist of the problem. As we have already mentioned:

> If you did not understand that explanation, you are in good company; large banks writing down tens of billions of dollars in losses may not have understood it either ... Besides, most people, even fairly sophisticated investors, are not in a position to assess the quality of the assets on a financial institution's balance sheet. In fact, most people don't even know what those assets are.

Greenspan's explanation [145] claims that there seem to be large cultural and cognitive disparities between the central bank, individual big banks and the basically non-regulated third parties, who mostly "were not in a position to assess the quality of the assets on a financial institution's balance sheet" (as said above) and who used the "securitized" bunch of supposedly low-risk mortgages as collateral for their own investment. These banks lent the mortgages while the mortgage borrowers, who had no clue what was going on with their payments anyway and who, when the economy slowed down, staged the run on banks with catastrophic consequences.

Thus, the more a cognitive and corporate culture—in fact, [147] calls it **"a culture of corruption"—differed on the micro-economic analogue to D-curve in EXHIBIT 7.1 (see also detailed discussion in Chapters 3 and 4), the more money the individual economic "players" lost, no matter whether they almost "took their own bank to cleaners" (which is inexcusable; especially in the Swiss example below) or cooperated in badly maiming a foreign bank in the process.**

The problem, made clear in **LEMMA 7.1, is that the micro-economic analogue of the D-curve becomes, when the micro-crisis becomes a macro-crisis, a macro-economic event which substantially entangles the position of country point S_i vis-à-vis other countries on the D.**

EXAMPLE: By far the biggest non-American loser was the Swiss giant bank UBS A.G. For reasons unknown, UBS employs a third of its staff in the US and its chairman is completely enamored with the American economy, despite losing a bundle on the "dot.com" bubble in 2000. Well, this time his UBS A.G. topped the foreign losers with $30 billion and counting. The chain reaction from this financial catastrophe, unfortunately, is still on and the problems for developed, and more so for developing, countries might well extend into a very serious political quagmire.

There are several points of a possible scenario—we shall call it: "Attack on Validity of **AXIOM 7.1** Scenario."

(C) If we follow **PROPOSITION 7.3**, it is clear that once the **NORTH** countries' banks and other financial institutions in societies perched on the D-LRH-side of the US—and particularly on its tail—lost a lot of money, the social and political differentiations will make it much worse for the great majority of the society. In fact the upward trend of well-being might well be stopped, if not reversed, for the time being (e.g. Greece, Spain, Portugal and even Italy are in this company).

(D) In the **NORTH-SOUTH** *donor-recipient* environment, the **NORTH-***donors*—since their major financial institutions, where the NGOs are banking, were certainly affected by the US crunch; again, see D-curve—would be rolling-down some of their more major investments attributed originally to certain **SOUTH-***recipients.*

(E) From the above two causal chains **(7.1)** and **(7.2)** it follows that political repercussions are next on the agenda. There are several reasons for this: The ordinary people of developed and developing societies alike become progressively poorer to which the "green campaign," see **AXIOM 8.1**, attached almost insurmountable obstacles to revert it. So, with unemployment, drop in wages and salaries—not to mention possible major inflation stemming from governments' bailing out the financial and other sectors by printing money—and even more irritated by their own governments giving bailouts that save the bonuses of the discredited and, generally, totally corrupt managements, social upheavals started in earnest. The final effect (in our D-curve domain) of all this has been **that the NORTH societies have started slipping down the slope to the right, down along the lower-right part of the D.**

The process of continuous dilution of the crucial, and in this paragraph reintroduced, conjecture from Chapter 3, **(3.4)**, may be best illustrated by quotations from professor Kenneth Minogue [96; p.B7]:

> Everybody gets respect for their sensitivities, even sensitivities many of them never knew they had: women, blacks, homosexuals, the disabled. No more Irish or Polish jokes, or sneers about dumb blondes from California or Essex. Human dignity and self-respect—that was the thing. Except of course for racists, sexists, homophobes and a whole cast of other twisted perverts who couldn't measure up to the new perfection … And then, suddenly, it turned out that the class struggle was back in business. Not the **old** class struggle … but a **new class struggle between the sensitive elite processed by the**

universities and the insensitive brutes out there in our society (bold face by the authors) ... the intellectual elite has made the remarkable discovery that everything that is thinkable is, in one sense or another, valid. Truth and objectivity go out the window, except, of course, when we enjoy the truth-dependent conveniences of modern technology ... So, if philosophy and science cannot sustain the political passions of today, what does? The answer is virtue. At the same moment as the whole of Western civilization was thrown into the academic melting pot, the moral dogmatism of political correctness was supplying that stiffening of willful dogmatism necessary to the righteous ... the great ideological project of the early 21st century will thus be the attempt to create a society so **inclusive** (bold face by M.K.) as to be entirely without enemies ... it will be ... like all perfections, it will be dull. It may suit the elite, but it won't suit the masses. And **that is the basic conflict brewing in the West**.

The magnitude of this general discontent may vary from passive opposition (shutting off all donations and as much taxes as possible) in developed countries to political formation of "anti-capitalist" and anti-governmental platforms that, in developing countries, might lead to political upheavals, civil disobedience and armed conflicts. In short, the result of the general economic downturn, which set the GDP loss figure for the world economies anywhere from 6% to 20%, certainly pushed down any country's position on the D-curve by, at least, one peg. But will it stay there and what further trends can we expect?

An *a priori* conclusion might tell us that—as the **intra-societal heterogeneity** of a single society (i.e. the comprehension of the problem, having been left to the hand of the rulers and/or bankers of the same magnitude of greed and ruthlessness before, becomes via the social communication) combines with **inter-societal heterogeneity** (with the same level of corruption and lawlessness)—**the more the NORTH countries may slide down the D-curve, the smaller the gap between the preceding countries' pegs they should expect.** This could be, we may reason, a direct attack on the *ceteris paribus* conditions spelled out in **AXIOM 7.1**.

However, **two monetary flows**—well recognized in the **SOUTH** societies as the backbone of any **SOUTH** financial stability (or lack of it)—**will always keep AXIOM 7.1 (on increasing world-wide chaos) intact**:

First, the **foreign direct investment** (FDI) **is dependent on the health of the origin country's economy.** (The latest WEO projections show FDI inflows in 2009 were falling by almost 20 percent from their 2008 levels; [190]) and

Secondly, the Hon. Nazim Burke, Grenada Prime-Minister, puts it quite clearly:

> Falling remittances from abroad can be expected to hit domestic consumption, and hence revenues from consumption taxes will substantially diminish [191].

As **AXIOM 7.1** has, both theoretically and practically, emerged intact, the quite different situation of "high or low exposure" to the **NORTH** banks rendered some **SOUTH** countries in better financial shape than others.

EXAMPLE: Already mentioned above [182; p.6], concerns the 1997 Asian financial crisis, when Indonesia, South Korea and Thailand needed to close or consolidated banks. As bankers in all three countries protested, South Korea's and Thailand's governments (both countries sitting higher on the D-curve than Indonesia) made a clean sweep and more or less took over the banks. They now are withstanding the global recession much better than Indonesia, where the son of President Suharto closed one troublesome bank but proceeded to continue essentially the same operations under a different bank's name.

On the other hand, at least one country, sitting on the lower end of the D-curve, was not affected by the financial meltdown of 2008-2009: China (and possibly, for similar reasons, India).

China's situation before the crisis was characterized by Lawrence Solomon in [179; FP15] who sees it as:

> not a newly industrialized country with immense technological prowess, but a country of peasants and manual urban laborers ... This is a country of hard-working but ignorant souls, isolated from the world, kept in the dark about their own history, frightened because there is no rule of law (close ties with our macro-economic paradigm; authors) and insecure because there are no property rights. Financial markets cannot function inside China because information cannot flow freely ... neither can businesses invest without securing political protection ... China's Communist party is unlikely to risk a Russian-style perestroika, which led to the collapse of the Soviet empire (and which only recently, as said elsewhere in the text, is being reconstructed; but by the will—almost an "acclamation"—of the former USSR peoples; authors) ... China's leaders will not meaningfully liberalize the economy to keep popular unrest at bay ...

yet without an opening up, the dragon economy that many dread will live in an imagined, and not a real, world.

This is exactly the right combination for "success" in the world-wide financial crisis. **Intra-homogeneous**—because the Communist bureaucracy that opened up to the world market and were underselling everybody with cheap, usually illegally copied products, with the financial sector in central Committee hands (with the exception of 15%-20% of foreign participation), and so many US dollars in the vault that they can virtually buy the US—the Chinese society as a whole does not expect much change, if any at all, in their living standard. This bodes well for a central government that can take care only of inter-heterogeneity vis-à-vis the world at large. Hence, with the financial trove they have at hand, virtually no other economic catastrophe can touch them and therefore this can, and most probably will, only move China some pegs ahead on the D-curve.

7/3 The "Doomsday Scenario" Represents a Serious Threat to Successful *Donor-Recipient* Co-operation

Because of the depressed economies in the developed **NORTH-*donor*** countries (i.e. EU, USA, Japan) they have to scale down all international aid, which is mostly direct financial aid and the administrative support to it. Consequently, the developing **SOUTH** countries those on the lower-right-hand (side) on the D-curve will suffer twice: First, because of the issues (A)-(E), discussed in Section 7/2/3 above, bringing along even worse political discontent, and secondly, because of the limited financial resources (for economic aid) in the **NORTH** countries. The possibility of political unrest in some of them (particularly in some EU members) would just make the whole situation more difficult to provide even the most needed financial aid.

NOTE: These and similar problems were discussed in Section 7.2.3 with the conclusion that whatever slide happened to the **NORTH-*donors*** a "double (maybe triple) whammy" will keep the **SOUTH-*recipients*** in much worse shape, no matter what.

It is obvious that a sudden and prolonged major socio-economic crisis in any **NORTH** society might set the society socially, economically and even politically back quite a few notches down on the D-curve slide, as we discussed in Sections 7.2 and 7.3.

NOTE: We have already mentioned Greece, but Italy and Spain and their major historical, cultural and sociology-wide difference between **SOUTH**

and **NORTH** might be the tip of another iceberg. In Germany, the schism between the nurtured West and former DDR—where for several generations a completely different, let's say, "socialist-outlook-upon-life" was thrust onto generations of East Germans and has not been erased till today—still shows, and Belgium's Flemish vs. Walloons hatred, according to the Belgian king (as of July 22, 2011), might destroy the country and, eventually, the EU in the same wave.

An axiomatic representation could well be assumed for a situation which has actually appeared in the first quarter of 2011, in which serious economic (i.e. financial)—first and then—**social and political damage to** most of the **NORTH donors has been publicly discussed** in the world media:

First, by the racial minorities in the case of economic crisis which, according to **(7.1)** and **(7.2)**, yielded an increase of society intra-heterogeneities and subsequent political riots—probably strongly enhanced by Muslim upheavals in individual *donor* states, particularly within the EU—which the "judicially-politically correct" power practically negates.

EXAMPLE: This is the quote from [212: p. 90]: Anjem Choudary, a thirty-nine British Muslim leader, hailed September 11 as "magnificent" and its perpetrators as "heroes"; he mocked the victims of the London Tube bombing ... and on the BBC, he was asked why he didn't simply move to a state that already has Sharia. "Who says you own Britain, anyway?" he replied. "Britain belongs to Allah. **The whole world belongs to Allah.**"

Secondly, on top of the financial crisis there is still a possibility of the oil crisis—as the **SOUTH** oil producing countries may revolt against their own ruling oligarchies [192], and the subsequent "domino effect" all over the oil-exporting countries—that will send some, or even most, of the **NORTH** and **SOUTH** countries into a deep economic and social abyss.

We can even visualize and assume an extreme case in which **SOUTH** *recipients'* slide down may well assume a quite similar, but not much worse, rate of slide than most of the **NORTH** *donors*. This is when we can seriously produce and defend the *"Doomsday Scenario."*

AXIOM 7.2 "THE DOOMSDAY SCENARIO":
Suppose the behavior described as *ceteris paribus* conditions in DEFINITION 7.3—based on the D-curve images in EXHIBIT 7.1 and recognizing the problems hidden in PROPOSITION 7.3 for the NORTH societies—does apply, but the sum of over-all world inter-heterogeneities which we denoted CHAOS in AXIOM 7.1, remains, in the extreme case, constant as the entire world's societies slide down the D-curve slope at the same relative rate of slide. Then the probability of any SOUTH society's well-being reaching the point of no

return—especially since for many NORTH *donor* countries the long journey through the recessions may take several years, not to mention decades, to overcome—converges to certainty.

FINAL MESSAGE: As the dissimilarity in societal behavior—due to different cultural, religious, political, legal, ethical, and cognitive roots—between *donors* and *recipients* grows progressively with time, at one point (not so far away) economic cooperation of any sort becomes a tool of probable destruction for both cooperating socio-economic entities.

NOTE: The reason for the attribute "Doomsday" is this. In **AXIOM 7.1** (and before in **DEFINITION 7.3** and **PROPOSITION 5.2**) the **NORTH** may hold its S_i position on the D-curve. Thus, this generic **NORTH** still may be able to support the most economically ravaged **SOUTH**. If, however, S_i, i = 1….k, moves down the SLIDE too, the intra-societal (i.e. social and economic) problems in their society will practically prohibit any economic aid to anybody and a doomsday will loom over the expecting **SOUTH**.

EXAMPLE: We have long-existing credit rating agencies, such as for instance **Standard & Poor's with their own credit ratings (SPR)** for the debt of public and private corporations—while rating borrowers on a scale from AAA to D—reflecting their view on the effectiveness, stability, predictability of the investigated country's policymaking, political institutions and, above all, difficulties in bridging the gulf between the political parties over fiscal policy. This gulf we might call the political heterogeneity in an investigated society (country).

As opposed to this approach there is The **Sovereign Wikirating Index (SWI)** that contains a transparent formula taking into account various factors believed to influence the creditworthiness of nations. It contains the following five criteria (with weights):

- Public debt (in % of the GDP) — 50% weight
- Account balance (in % of the GDP) — 20% weight
- Growth rate — 10% weight
- Inflation rate — 10% weight
- Unemployment rate — 10% weight

The resulting value is adjusted by multiplying it with a "scaling factor," which is composed of the Human Development Index (HDI) (60% weight), the Corruption Perceptions Index (20% weight) and the Political Instability Index (20% weight). Clearly this rating, apart from political heterogeneity, takes into consideration the over-all heterogeneity of the society (country), i.e. the cognitive gap between: (1) individual strata of society, (2) people and the governments on all levels, (3) people and big business, and (4) ethnic, religious and behavioral factors due to individual strata of the society. This actually falls into our definition of working intra-societal heterogeneity discussed in Chapter 3 (**AXIOM 3.1, ASSUMPTION 3.1** and **PROPOSITION 3.5**), in Chapter 4 and, summarily, in Chapter 7 in **PROPOSITION 7.2, PROPOSITION 7.3** and **COROLLARY 7.1.** Source [194], **compares SPR and SWI for 12 countries** i; i = 1, 2, ... 12.

In **EXHIBIT 7.2** we list the countries **and the points' differences, Δ,** between both ratings in as

(7.3) $\Delta_i = (SPR_i - SWI_i)$

EXHIBIT 7.2

Country	Δi
Japan	-2.5
France	-3.0
Australia	+1.5
UK	-2.5
Brazil	-2.0
Spain	-2.0
Canada	-2.5
Italy	-1.5
China	-0.5
Germany	-2.0
US	-4.5
Greece	+1.0

DISCUSSION: The surprisingly higher (than expected) negative signs for some countries in **EXHIBIT 7.2** hints at the fact that intra-societal heterogeneity in these countries has already spread into all strata of the given society.

(a) France's second to worst showing indicates the country's sub-par productivity together with escalation of political (ethnic and religious) tensions among the working strata.

(b) Germany is, according to the media, the EU engine but the political and social tension (and productivity-wise difference between the old "EAST" and the "WEST" Germany) saps a lot of money from the German GDP.

(c) Canada is marketed as the only society, apart from Australia, that evaded the Crisis. However, the hastily and without bounds installed, multiculturalism (in the 1970s), made Canada's historical engine, Ontario, a Tower of Babel of cultures, languages, "politically correct" teaching and, hence, no real professionals (in relation to US or EU) to make any inroads into productivity, not to mention legions of the LICs' families that drew on the GDP just like in France.

(d) The U.S. is a boat without a steering wheel (let alone a captain). As the economy stalled due to the bankers' hunt for maximum profit (under tacit nods from the administrations), political tension—(d1) between the population and the government, (d2) population and big business (i.e. banks), (d3) between the North and the South and in the South, (d4) between Hispanic (almost majority) and the Caucasians—increased, especially with double digit unemployment, making the U.S. a seriously intra-societal heterogeneous society that should sit, at best (when we investigate the definitions in **EXHIBIT 4.1**), in the middle of the D-curve in **EXHIBIT 7.1**.

Surprising positive differentials for Australia and Greece and minimal negative differentials for China and Italy are, from the tenor of this study, also reasonably easy to explain.

(e) Australia is a strongly homogeneous society—built and still basically working along the optimized path of **FMSC in EXHIBIT 3.1** in Section 3/2/1—with no political problems, ample natural resources (inclusive of energy) together with food, which also imports. It is also engaged in the Trans-Pacific Partnership talks and ongoing free trade agreement negotiations with China, Japan and Korea (with China as an exporter becoming still more important).

(f) China is still a command economy although the reigning oligarchy understands the need of close (economic) cooperation with the **NORTH** and the developed **SOUTH** economies. No matter that on the "democratic scale" (in **EXHIBT 4.1**) China might be well down, the simple demand of the masses of Chinese for almost everything, the cheap workforce, and the fact that China holds billions of US dollars and tons of gold in its treasury, makes it a less than an average risk country.

(g) Greece, despite astronomical debt and not enough productivity, has three elements that could keep her afloat: (g1) Totally homogeneous society (that has lasted millennia) and is impervious to any serious political upheaval, (g2) society that has been existing from the beginning without any positive co-operation from the government and will do so in future as well, (g3) a lot of governmental assets (in prime tourism locations) that could be sold, rented or swapped for debt arrears, and so on.

(h) Italy, generally the very same case as **Greece,** has a long-standing political problem between the **SOUTH** and the Germans (and Austrians) inhabiting the **NORTH** (and not just geographically). Although very remote, but if it comes to a severe economic (and badly handled) political hardship, political upheavals could flare between industrial northern Italy and the mostly agricultural **SOUTH**. It will not come to the destruction of society, just to create enough problems to give the **Wikirating Index** -1.5, lower than the indices given to the supposedly highly industrialized societies of the EU and the U.S. where the heterogeneity (sometimes even hatred) between the individual strata of the society just use economic crises to foster the society's demise.

7/4 Wrapping up Chapter 7

Chapter 7 is about dissimilarities between the historically induced ethical, moral, and social behavior and cognitive level, rule of law, combined with, also historically formed, legal and political environment of individual **macro-entities,** such as societies, countries, multinational corporations, etc., and between individual **micro-entities**, i.e. intra-national but internationally zeroed economic establishments, that are engaged in social and economic transactions with each other, in order that a certain, usually economic goal could be reached.

One such typical **macro-transaction** is aid, technology and/or know-how transfer between *donors and recipients*; another—and this is mostly a micro-economic transaction—farming-out a production capacity to developing country. The dissimilarities (or heterogeneities) as we called them in the text could be, as said above, in historical, cultural, behavioral, cognitive and social stratification milieu. And also in moral foundations, expectations and ideals, law abiding behavioral make-up, and—in the macro-economic dealing with not just economy but also with political and environmental changes scheme of things. **These are the factors that affect** international social, political and economic relationships and transactions to the point of risking a serious over-all—and sometimes quite debilitating—crisis when the conflicting socio-political and socio-economic environments in the *donor* and *recipient* entities clash.

Cultural difference is, as we have said, a natural occurrence. It can, however, (under the guise of political and religious enmity) become a volatile issue incited by the ruling strata of the *recipient* society and/or entity. The subsequent crisis that hits the *recipient* society first can, and eventually usually does, affect the whole *donor-recipient* system.

Suppose that we leave the **macro-economic plateau** and move to the, assumedly, across-the-board homogeneous **micro-economic** climate of one single developed society. There, we are forced to admit the existence of a **still growing heterogeneity between the anything goes "ethics" of corporate culture and the idealized world of an ordinary citizen even in one single country**.

Here we might, **for example**, mention the financial problems in China's in 2008, in India, and, for the record, in the Russian Federation as well; all societies with whom everybody was trying to do business with. The co-operation has taken place of the globalization or, in other words, farming out the production lines from developing countries (those on the upper-left of D-curve) to downright intra-heterogeneous societies on the lower-right of the same curve. It might already explain a lot of inexplicable economic goings-on in the high-tech (specifically "dot.com") industry and in multinational companies (typical for their farmed-out operations) takeovers, mergers and turnarounds.

Hence, from the above discussion, it is easy to acknowledge the following **COROLLARY:**

COROLLARY 7.1:
All in all, the D-curve graphic depiction and all its practical connotations and applications, seen in PROPOSITIONS 5.1 to 5.4, and 7.2, and AXIOMS 7.1 to 7.3, obviously holds for both macroeconomic (e.g. globally pursued inter-society economic co-operations) and, even more importantly and surprisingly, for micro-economic (i.e. single intra-society operations) that are (a) either harming its own economy, or (b) subsequently "exported" to increase economic and social problems in other societies.

EXAMPLE: Canada's Supreme Court ruling (in June 2014) enacted legislation granting the First Nations, i.e. pre-European settlers, title over the region of 1,750-square kilometers and giving the community control over what development takes place there. This means that—as it is in the province of British Columbia, with agriculture, mining and hydroelectric power lines and oil pipelines proposed for the area—all new development will require consent from the First Nation band that lives there. This Act increases: (a) social, and (b) work-ethical and cultural intra-societal heterogeneity by adding a new, legally powerful strata to the society, strong enough—especially by the domino effect with other neighboring tribes—to close down (via chain **[7.2]** above) any shale-gas and oil pipelines or any other oil-related mining and hydroelectric development, which closure might well close down the Canadian economy as well.

Also, and as mentioned above, the more global economies are intertwined, the *de facto* "micro-economic crisis" in a major ***donor*** country (see Section 7/2/2 and the above **EXAMPLE**) can set back the economic development of ***donor-recipient***-connected ***recipient*** countries quite a bit. It would be the direct effect of the ***donors'*** cutting off unnecessary costs and saving the money for restarting its own economy. There would be, perhaps, a substantial gap in economic aid money and remittances flow to the ***recipients*** among other fiscal and financial problems.

Chapter 8: How to Avoid the Possible "End-of-Civilization" Scare in the "Doomsday Scenario"

8/1 Introduction to the Problem

The **Doomsday Scenario**, in view of the basic assumptions and propositions of thesis in this text (e.g. **PROPOSITIONS 5.1** to **5.4** and **7.2**), should be reinterpreted so that the potential threat can be stressed as much as possible.

The thesis would explain why the present *donor* vs. *recipient* system trying to foster economic aid and political co-operation between two societies—mapped for better understanding graphically on the D-curve—could never really work, let alone well. The two elements (societies) are: *donors*, also called in political shorthand **NORTH**, are the highly developed countries located high on the D-curve; while *recipients* are the poor, developing and low income countries on the lower-right-side of the slide curve D, summarily called **SOUTH**. The idea of the whole exercise of economic aid, and perhaps some political aid, should move *donors* and *recipients* closer together on the D. Instead, every conceivable piece of information tells us that they are, in fact, moving farther from each other.

History has proven that the assumption of the change the habits, customs, ethics, and legal and public governance of societies could not be achieved by a simple economic aid if the *donors* and *recipients* markers on the D-curve were far from each other. It usually means that *recipients*' ruling classes are on complete different wave-lengths. In the following excerpt [143; p6] we read:

> The United States had an interest in overthrowing Communist regimes around the world. The Reagan doctrine channeled major resources to this aim and achieved some successes ... state construction, however, did not follow state destruction (the way Marshall Plan had achieved that several decades ago; added by the authors.) ... the consequences were tragic for American national security.

Let us start from the beginning. The world-wide societies (countries) are mapped—as per their intra-societal heterogeneities that had permeated into inter-societal heterogeneities while all the respective databases could be easily filled by one or more statistical techniques mentioned in the text)—by a point on the hyperbolic curve D. We are, therefore, presenting **AXIOM 8.1** (which follows from **DEFINITION 7.3**).

AXIOM 8.1 (THE CRUX OF THE PARADIGM):
The macroeconomic political entities are "assessed," first according to their intra-society heterogeneities, to wit: by their social, economic, and political (and religious zealotry) stratifications that had put them into their inter-societal heterogeneities' mapping by a specific point-spot S_i on the slide curve D. The paradigm proves that: The greater the distance between the typical NORTH *donor* and the religiously intolerant and belligerent SOUTH *recipient* the more serious social, economic and, above all, political repercussions inclusive of political and religious crises, upheavals, and, eventually armed insurgency, civil wars, international terrorism we can expect in the SOUTH countries. And, they will export all of these social maladies and religious intolerance to the NORTH countries (obviously, at the beginning, in different magnitudes). As the distance between the typical NORTH or SOUTH *donor* and the hostile SOUTH *recipient* grows (according DEFINITION 7.3 and AXIOM 7.1) progressively with time, so does international terrorism—having been exported from SOUTH into NORTH and firmly ensconced there—which in itself represents a much more serious threat to the world than any socio-political crisis. The reason is that here we are talking about the fast destruction of the very fabric of a NORTH country's society.

NOTE: A similar pattern holds for microeconomic national economic entities and global corporations as well. There, issues regarding cultural and cognitive boundaries may arise over job descriptions, work ethics between various (ethnic) groups of workers, and incompatible or unclear lines of work responsibilities which can lead to serious conflicts within organizations and, as we noted in the preceding chapter, sometimes even to the demise of the new strongly heterogeneous merger.

PROOF: The proof follows from **LEMMA 4.1**, **PROPOSITION 4.1**, **LEMMA 5.1**, **PROPOSITION 5.2**, **LEMMA 7.1**, **AXIOM 7.1** and [216].

DISCUSSION: **What the NORTH *donors*' administrations have not understood is the last line of defense the ruling class of belligerent SOUTH has been mounting**. As historical, cultural, and religious differences are objective historical facts, **it is religion that moves the masses nowadays**. So, under the guise of "defending" their political and religious tenets, the ruling class' (i.e. emirs, sheiks, imams) "battle cry" against **NORTH (or SOUTH),** branding them as "infidels" and "mortals enemies," is usually all it takes to provoke an (armed) resistance if it suits the local rulers.

Therefore, NORTH—via the 'spins' of politically and economically 'hard-up' ruling classes in several specifically hostile-to-civilized-behavior *recipient countries*—is perceived in many, free-aid-receiving SOUTH countries, as a politically, culturally and even morally "depraved" socio-political entity that is hell-bent on conquering "OUR" ancient cultural and religious pillars, before they could extinguish "US."

At stake in all of these instances is the only goal the SOUTH's reigning religion-based oligarchies are pursuing, to wit: **Perpetual rule over their fiefdoms.** True, there generally exist historically-based cultural, social, ethical, religious, political, cognitive, and simply economic differences (which are all increasing with time) between a typical NORTH and a typical SOUTH society. But it is also true that these differences—being at the bottom of extreme poverty of some of the SOUTH societies—could be alleviated if both sides were "on the same page."

With no democratic principles in place there are only rulers who—while wanting to rule *in perpetuity*—can decide what serves them better: **(1)** an open war against "infidels" and, at the same time, against the mortal competition within the Islamic faith (Shia versus Sunni); or **(2)** to settle for a policy of sheer ransom:

Either the GOs or NGOs from the NORTH *donors* will channel all the aid through OUR ruling administrations—and suspend all "democracy-promoting" activities—or they, perhaps, might expect armed attacks against THEIR "infidel centers," such as: NGO HQ buildings (schools and recreation centers they built, etc.), their workers and other expatriates from NORTH countries. They would all be put in harm's way by SOUTH rulers who would simply activate the "sleeper" terrorist cells in their countries.

Let us now remind the reader of yet another, already discussed, scenario of the **"Doomsday" AXIOM 7.2** whereby severe economic, financial, and even political crises in one or more NORTH countries—let us just mention possibilities: Greece, Spain with Basque independence in vogue, and France (getting serious with Muslim-origin immigrants on the rampage) and all of them secretly moving illegal immigrants to the U.K.—threaten other NORTH countries, via the "domino effect," with the probability of major economic and social downfall of the whole (Mediterranean) block of EU-NORTH countries.

As this means an almost complete cessation of financial aid from WB, IMF and leading NGOs plus drying up of the remittances of SOUTH nationals living in the NORTH, the social situation of the SOUTH will certainly become bleak.

Sensing that **NORTH** is getting weaker and will not be encouraging too much democratic and "green" ideas to the **SOUTH** (mostly oil producing) societies and, perhaps, even some of their elites, it is high time for the **SOUTH** rulers to start their move. Inciting political (mostly fomented by ideology and/or religion), and, finally, armed conflicts (Muslims vs. infidels) in some **SOUTH** societies is their never-failing weapon. **And the geographic locations for such devastation have perennially been the Middle East and Africa:**

(a) In North Africa (Palestine, Iraq, Egypt, Syria) the economic and, therefore political and religious problems, see socio-political chains **(7.1)** and **(7.2)**, have reached already the 'civil war' level;

(b) The whole of (Central) Africa in which, apart from the perennial Hutu vs. Tutsis hatred, the Muslim vs. Christian "cleansing" probably marks the end for any sustainable well-being for the inhabitants of the whole region for a long time;

(c) Iran is just waiting for further sign of the US 'hands-off-doctrine' to finalize their nuclear armaments their nuclear armaments from unscrupulous dealers in the EU proper and from the Russian Federation. A pre-emptive strike by combined forces of NATO and the Israeli army would, if the worst comes to the worst, be able to erase this threat easily, given that the US president at the time is of Reagan "stock" (see [212], pp. 146-149). There is no other saner and/or safer way when the existence of the world as we know it is at stake, no matter what Brussels' and the UN's "neo-socialist" oligarchs may think.

(d) Afghanistan has been *de facto* forced into penury, as the country is losing the so-called "opium wars" [193].

DISCUSSION: The "opium wars" depicts the society as based on the economically very lucrative growing of poppies used for the production of opium or heroin that has kept virtually the whole Afghan population economically sustainable. Consequently, the **NORTH** professed a good deal of unhappiness with the political situation as their societies are being engulfed by a lot of cheap heroin from Afghanistan. Yet, despite all odds, the Afghan drug lords driven society has entered, pretty well unscathed, the third decade of armed struggle; no matter who called the shots: USSR, Taliban, Al-Qaeda, NATO, or UN. **And in the end, they won**, as the **NORTH** military: U.S., U.K. and Canadian armed forces are leaving.

Hence, it is imperative to try to explain to the 'global saving activist' VIPS of **NORTH-***donors'* GOs and NGOs the danger of abetting the political discontent in the religiously intolerant and religious-zealots-driven **SOUTH** societies. Their "democratic society," "human rights," and "green future" issues, have been already been proven in this text to being responsible for most of the world's human and social disasters in the last quarter of the 20th and all of the 21st century. NOTE: These do-gooders alone can bring the "Doomsday Scenario" of AXIOM 7.2 into being through the back door no matter what we do at the strictly economic "front door."

EXAMPLES:

(a) Remember the July 7, 2005 Tube bombings in London. According to *The Times* of London commissioned poll, 7 percent of one million Muslim in London (half of them under twenty-five) thought that the suicide attacks on civilians were justified (see [212, p. 76]).

(b) "By some accounts, 80 percent of the imams in Canadian mosques are said to be 'extreme'" [212. p. 94]. If this is so, what is the percentage in the UK and the EU? It obviously cannot be lower.

(c) As *The Guardian* reported in London in 2005:

French youth (technically French citizens, but recent second or even third generation French North Africa immigrants, M.K.) fired at police and burned over 300 cars last night as towns around Paris experienced another night of violence in a week of urban unrest [212. p. 122].

(d) And again:

In 2005, a twenty-three-year-old Ahmed Omar Abu Ali (born in Houston and moved to Falls Church, VA where he was valedictorian of his class) **was charged with plotting to assassinate the president.** ... Neither *The Times* nor the AP had space to mention that this typical Virginia **high school Mr. Abu Ali attended was the Islamic Saudi Academy**, funded by the Kingdom of Saudi Arabia. It is on American soil but it describes itself as **'subject to the government of the Kingdom of Saudi Arabia' and its classes are based on the 'curriculum, syllabus, and materials established by the Saudi Ministry of Education** [212. p. 72].

(e) And again:

The famously 'moderate' mullah Yusuf al-Quaradawi was invited to speak at the 2004 'Our Children Our Future' conference. When it comes to children and their future, Imam AL-Quardawi says: "Israelis might have nuclear bombs but we have the children bomb and these human bombs must continue until liberation" [212.p.146].

NOTE: In *The Empty Cradle*, Philip Longman writes:

So where will the children of the future come from? Increasingly they will come from people who are at odds with the modern word. Such a trend, if sustained, could drive human culture off its current market-driven, individualistic, modernist course, gradually creating an anti-market culture dominated by fundamentalism—a new Dark Ages ([212], p. xxvi).

8/2 NORTH's Last-Line of Defense against the Religiously Intolerant and Belligerent SOUTH

This notion is discussed in some detail in **PROPOSITION 5.2** and subsequent discussion. The typical religiously intolerant belligerent **SOUTH**-*recipients* at the end of the D-curve—with usually strongly intra-heterogeneous societies with radical (i.e. fanatical) religious elements from which the "army" of international terrorists are recruited—should be the target of specifically designed international help, such as:

- Taking out (one way or the other) the ruling, terrorist-supporting warlords and their cliques by globally respectable armed NGOs (e.g. NATO plus UN armed forces), and

- Having their border physically sealed, letting in only the NGO personnel, monetary aid, and consumer goods (inclusive of foodstuff) for as long as is necessary to calm the socio-political-cum-civil war extremes.

This two-pronged option is especially important if the situation is combined with religious conflicts such as Sunni Muslims (particularly those of Wahhabi persuasion) vs. Shia Muslims (see lit. [202]), Muslims vs. Jews, Muslim vs. (Coptic) Christians etc., since atrocities against civilians (ethnic "cleansing," and other well defined war crimes) by the warring factions will lead to the inescapable conclusion: **destruction of an important part of the world as we know it.**

DISCUSSION: The threat of international terrorism—originated in the **SOUTH** and, due to "soft international legislation, migrated back into virtually all **NORTH** societies—increases (see [224]). In the history of political science and, strangely enough, in literature, there were several schemes hatched to deal with this problem: (a) To substitute for nonexistent harsh legal **"saving the nation from extinction" acts** we shall have to resort to fighting terror with terror (under specially drafted legislature) and (b) To install, for instance in Northern Canada (or in any vast empty "real estate" in the world) colonies populated with would-be (or have-been) terrorists and the whole underground of helpers, minders, and financiers who should be persuaded to work for wages just high enough to sustain themselves. Guantanamo has been the first step in this direction but there might be much more humane ways to deal with these *de facto* enemies of the world. At the risk of appearing flippant, Cyril McNeil in his **Bulldog Drummond** series of novels [225] put forward the following ideas of using "humanitarian response to the enemies of humanity" a century ago. Here we quote McNeil's "ideal (istic)" way of dealing with such an indigenous enemy.

> The sixty frenzied anarchist (substitute for **terrorists**; added by M.K.) were "gulagged" (neologism added by M.K.) in an uninhabited island off the coast of Mull, presided over by twenty large demobilized soldiers commanded by an ex-sergeant-major of the Guards: every three hours they were all drawn up in a row, and the sergeant-major, with a voice like a bull, would bellow: "Should the ruling classes have money?" Then they answered in unison— "No." "Should anyone have money?" again they answered "No." "Should everyone work for the common good for love?" "Yes." Whereas he would roar: "Well, in this 'ere island there ain't no ruling classes, and there ain't no money, and there's dam' little love, so go and plant more potatoes, you lop-eared sons of Beelzebub."

So much for the thoughts of a novelist. A similar idea, however, occurred even to the British Home Secretary at the turn of the last century. Winston Churchill, in his monthly political summary letter to King George V, wrote in November 1911 (see [227]):

> As for tramps and wastrels there ought to be proper Labour Colonies where they could be sent for considerable periods and made to realise their duty to the State.

8/3 A Feasible "SOUTH-to-SOUTH" Solution

Any transition from the old, socially and politically, oligarchy-based, heterogeneous societal system into even partially open democracy represents a major paradigm shift. The path to democratic system is theoretically based on upholding the law and constitution for everybody. Hence, it is naive to assume that the old behavioral constraints—embodied in the political, legal, and administrative "vassals and/or small apparatchik-cum-serf thinking" *versus* "oligarchic rulers behavior" system—disappear overnight or even in the short future. It is also futile to assume that every poor, developing or transitional Muslim country is hell-bent on starting local religious 'cleansing' let alone to try to drum up an international Jihad on some serious scale.

It would therefore be easier and theoretically more prudent to build a model of society's behavior under its own prevailing sociological constants, the state of legal and institutional environment, society's cultural, religious and cognitive history and society's hopes for a better life, and economic conditions. Such a "block" (see **LEMMA 5.2**) is much more stable and predictable than any other, such as based on wishful thinking about a "democracy" concept which **NORTH-*donors*** have been pushing onto uncomprehending *recipients* for at least a hundred years now.

AXIOM 8.2 (SOUTH-TO-SOUTH cooperation):
Let us consider strictly economic exchange, cooperation or even simple economic aid between a *donor* and a politically and religiously tolerant *recipient* society. We know the overall utility of such an exchange is inversely proportional to the distance of their respective societies on the D-curve, to wit: the shortest distance yields the highest overall utility and vice versa.
MESSAGE: If both societies happen to inhabit: (a) any part of the slide curve D with their S-points reasonably close to each other, and/or (b) the SOUTH-*recipient* is politically and religiously TOLERANT, then the ideal cooperation will be between a (economically sound) SOUTH-*donor* and a needy SOUTH-*recipient*.

NOTE: **AXIOM 8.2** follows from **PROPOSITION 5.1** and as such does not take into consideration most of the behavioral (e.g. expectational, ethical and moral) and/or cognitive differences in the macro-economic (and even micro-economic) niveau, mentioned in **PROPOSITION 7.1**. As far as both societies' populations have similar historically formed ethnic attributes, such as similar reasoning and goals to achieve, ethical, religious, and moral base (i.e. their S_i points on the D-curve being quite close) it should—with the blessing of the ruling class (that should, in this pairing, feel very safe)—instigate closer economic and, perhaps, even political stand-off (i.e. neutrality) if not direct co-operation.

EXAMPLE: The peoples of the Central Asia independent republics are still longing for closer political and economic ties with Russia. They inhabited the "Soviet Empire" under the USSR label for about 70+ years, and ever since indigenous oligarchies took over when the USSR disintegrated their populations' well-being radically changed for the worse. Therefore, if a comprehensive aid plan, similar to the Marshall Plan, could ever be conceived for this region, it has to be initiated and administered by Russia only (i.e. **SOUTH-*donor*** to **SOUTH-*recipients***). A similar plan was apparently formulated by president Putin for the independent republic of Ukraine in 2014 to quell the uprising in Kiev.

NOTE: There is no religious zealotry among the Slavs and other Indo-European tribes in the Balkans and Central Asia. Christian and Muslim populations (apart from observing some basic religious rites) have freely drunk alcoholic beverages together in pubs and intermingled together for hundreds of years. Bosnian Muslims in Bosnia and Herzegovina (B&H) were subject to ethnic-cleansing in the Bosnian war in the 1990s which was aimed simply at splitting the B&H between the Serbs and Croats. There was no a speck of religious issue at stake there.

Here we have to stress that in most cases money to be made by ruling oligarchs via trades with morally, politically, ethically, and religiously tolerant trading countries—of which some part will "overflow" into the society and increase the population's standard of living—usually trumps even serious religious differences. Of course, these traders are not necessarily *"donors"* in the NORTH terminology.

Niall Ferguson made the realm of **AXIOM 8.2**—and thus the tenor of the last section—a wee bit clearer in the following excerpts from his discussion with *The National Post* [189; FP 3]:

> They (Chinese) do not remotely share our ambition to improve the quality of governance in Africa. They couldn't care less. And they have a very different political model, which is neither democratic nor based on law in our sense ... In the eyes of the Chinese, it (Africa) is the place with a lot of commodities and very poor infrastructure. So they have figured out they can access the commodities if they provide the infrastructure ... Given the West has a sentimental view of Africa, which is they want to (help with) water, give it aid, and help Africans by giving them free malaria medications. And China, of course, thinks that's absurd. They want to come in and buy stuff, give them highways in return. And right now that model is working better (for Africa) ... just look at the growth rate, Africa is enjoying, and it is mostly on the back of sales of commodities and the improvement of infrastructure. By comparison, we'd had 50 years of development aid and achieved less. So (in the same vein) it is not pretty in the sense that what China does is bolster regimes in Sudan. They (Chinese) aren't really concerned about people being authoritarian. They are authoritarian, why should they worry about governance in Africa? It is not their vision of what matters, and if they can deliver economic growth and raise African living standards, you can't really blame the

Africans for saying, 'OK, these people ask less of us (than) the aid agencies of the West and governments in the West.'

8/4   Concluding Observations

The **first major conclusion** **of this study** is that throwing billions of dollars into under-developed countries, about which—and of the surrounding regions—the **NORTH** knows absolutely nothing, is not just sheer lunacy but sure-fire suicide.

There are some serious examples of such idiocy in the **NORTH**'s history that changed the world:

EXAMPLE 1: After WWI Woodrow Wilson, based on his strictly personal persuasion, practically ordered ordered the heads of many former Austro-Hungarian societies—mostly against the collective will of the heads of many Central European states each with constantly clashing demographic, socio-political and socio-economic segments of societies—to form independent states. This bevy of incredible nationally, politically, socially and even religiously heterogeneous "successor states," with one nation (Germany, only geographically divided, but still "pugnaciously" homogeneous as everybody was dirt-poor), then gave rise to Hitler and led directly to WWII.

EXAMPLE 2: Same story with FDR during WWII. This time he practically gave the Russians—in the Tehran and Yalta conferences—a *carte-blanche* to usurp the whole of Central and Eastern Europe (and thus inaugurated the Cold War).

EXAMPLE 3: Today the onus lies on the major **NORTH** governments again, and this time—just as in the previous examples—it is "**NOW-OR-NEVER.**" We certainly don't want to be led into WWIII by the do-gooding, yet crazy **NORTH** governments. As the same crucial and exponentially increasing heterogeneities are seen in North Korea, Afghanistan, the whole of North Africa (Iraq, Syria, Egypt, Lebanon, Palestine), former USSR republics of Ukraine, Central Asia and in almost the whole of Central Africa and South America, we have just entered the same "crossroads to hell" again.

The **second major conclusion,** encapsulated in **AXIOM 8.1** and in ensuing **DISCUSSIONS** and **EXAMPLES**, says that unless the **SOUTH**-*recipient* is politically and religiously TOLERANT—and we should, first of all, try every possible policy scenario presented in **PROPOSITION 5.2** to achieve this—the problem of implementation of any sensible **NORTH-SOUTH** cooperation is up to the individual **NORTH** governments, and the world's NGOs must make sure that the *recipients* are interested in help only and will do everything to avoid the imminent "**Doomsday**" **AXIOM 7.1.**

This would work, however, IF and only IF the local warlords, indigenous oligarchs, and/or hereditary rulers agree with this strategy. As we saw in the text, in certain situations they may not. We may assume that the ruling class in the fast-changing world feels that they have only a very short "free grabbing and stealing" (read: from their population) period ahead. Typical examples might be both (or all) Ukrainian presidents being sued for major corruption between 2010 and 2014. If this is going on in a relatively well-developed society, what are the chances that the rulers of the less-developed and much poorer countries will change their behavior at all: None, and the "Doomsday Scenario" is still ON. Then no matter how many UN, NATO, American, EU, and/or any other allied troops you advance into these problem areas, the historical religious tenets, properly encouraged, might still prevail to make life for the rest of the world very difficult.

The developed **NORTH** has, historically, been preoccupied with erasure of poverty and lessening the social differentiation in the **SOUTH** with the aim of a social and political "melting pot." This wishful thinking has, unfortunately, brought instead—alongside free economic aid (to the ruling classes) and lessons in democracy—also virtually unchecked socio-political migration (under the guise of human rights and political persecution) to the **NORTH**.

That has not touched the issue of easing the societal poverty but, instead, has opened up extremely dangerous socio-economic and political minefields in the **NORTH** societies as they have been experienced in Great Britain, France, Spain, Italy, Germany, and in most of the EU states lying in the North, East, West and South.

The <u>**third major conclusion**</u>, having been proven *ad nauseam* in this study, claims that **the greater the social, economic and political stratification, and, above all, militantly charged religious tenets are in the social-economic and political environment of a given society, the more the society is sliding on the D-curve to the right towards chaos and eventual extinction of the society. The logical chain of the appropriate marker on D, [SLIDE TO CHAOS] we describe as:**

(8.1) [SLIDE TO CHAOS] = political crisis ➔ economic crisis ➔ political upheavals ➔ major societal crisis ➔ civil war ➔ possible extinction of society

The [SLIDE TO CHAOS] might be, for instance, kick-started by seemingly innocuous, virtually free migration—but within the EU law and according to the Schengen Agreement—from the **EU SOUTH** societies to the original **EU** 15-member territory. The real problem and the second line and third line of logical chain **(8.1)** appeared during the civil wars in North Africa and Afghanistan. The illegal immigration to Europe via the Mediterranean Sea as a result of Shia vs. Sunni Muslim wars (and ethnic cleansing)—hardly anybody of the **NORTH**'s NGOs or GOs had an inkling that these factions (apart from both despising Palestinians and hating Jews) hold grudges towards each other much stronger than against Christians—has already hatched the **"Doomsday" AXIOM 7.2** scenario.

And, perhaps, as a **fitting epilogue**, we quote **Niccolo Machiavelli** (*The Prince, 1513*) who—and this might be a wakeup call to all the world's developed countries, their governments and major NGOs—said:

> **You must know, then, that there are two methods of fighting, the one by law, the other by force: the first method is that of men, the second of beasts; but as the first method is often insufficient, one must have recourse to the second.**

APPENDIX

A/1 Criterion of Tolerable Error Limits (CTER)

A/1/1 Prerequisites and Problem Formulation

Let us assume that we have a model of an alternative of the **"cause-and-effect socio-political crisis"** that is based on incomplete yet most recent data (called, in **FIGURE 1**, "ORIGINAL INCOMPLETE DATA.") We [6], [24; pp.69-89] have based the *"CRITERION"* (**CTER**) on rational answers of the product of *Ex Ante Modeling* (i.e. preliminary structure based on incomplete data).

We can also say that our notion of "errors" is relaxed and reformulated such that the Criterion emphasizes functional usability of the model. The scheme in **EXHIBIT A1** answers the question of how we can build a fully-fledged *Ex-Ante* model with untested, unproven and/or not nearly complete data. The scheme is based on the following sketch of a **LEMMA** from [6].

SCHEME OF THE LEMMA:

Suppose we have a quantitative model X^* of a real-life situation X. Now, if our database allows us—by purposefully altering parameters of the data inputs into X^* after defining "error limits tolerability" for each specific situation X—to create separate discrete states of X^* (i.e. $X1^* > X2^* > X3^*$ ....) that agrees with what we observe in the real-life X (i.e. that under similar real-life inputs we observe $X1 > X2 > X3$ ....) then we say the data and parameters forming X^* are within the predefined tolerable error interval and can be used for other applications.

The data improvement then follows the circle of methodological elements in **EXHIBIT A1**, except where the extra arrows denote specific loops. Even if the whole data base is suspect and vastly incomplete, we can always start with very simple, indeed perhaps just a bivariate model, and then by trial and error and step by step looping we slowly build up enough usable data information to start using the CTER (i.e. the above scheme) in **EXHIBIT A1** by comparing the modeling alternatives with the real world. Once the alternatives—artificially created discrete states—in the CTER scheme) fit with reality (and the Ex Post Model holds) it automatically upgrades the original database.

The Crucial Challenge for International Aid

EXHIBIT A1: Flow-chart of the Criterion Feasibility in Incomplete Data Modeling

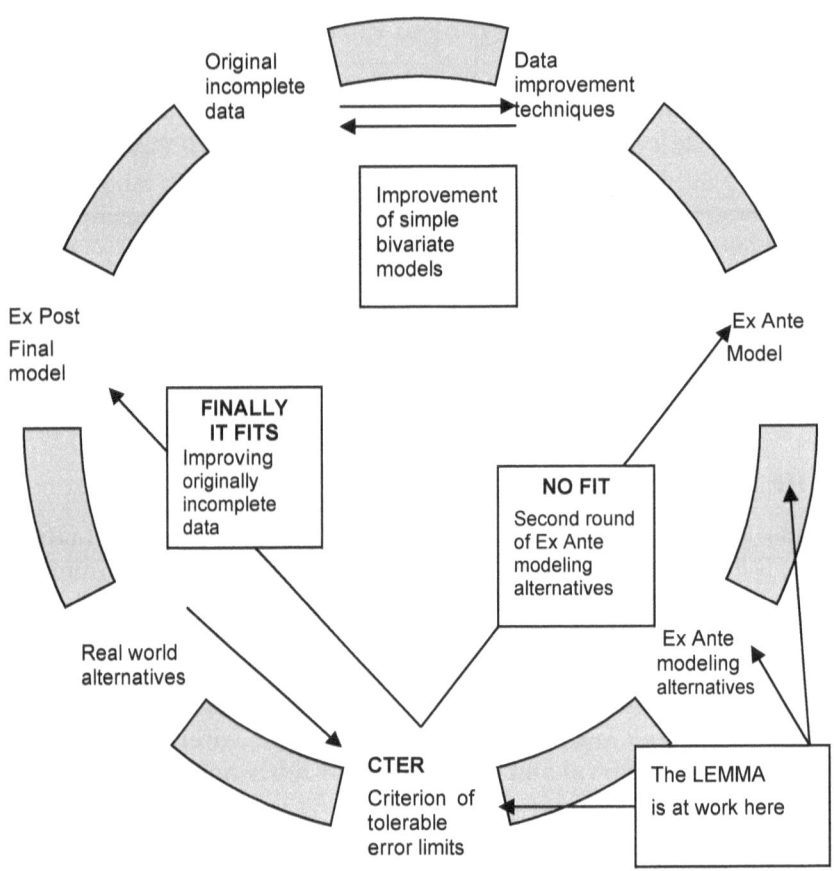

A/1/2 Interval Estimates of Behavioral "RISK" Factors

Further rationalization: As the risk-of-conflict category is to be defined on socio-economic and behavioral sociological terms rather than on economic ones, we should not dwell too much on probabilistic data anyway, since large sample databases do not exist. Instead, small-sample characteristics, combined with decent heuristics, could be developed as specific interval values transformable into an estimable mean or median value of the probability. The theoretical problem of **finite** number of trials (even if that number is large, which in our case it is not) was best articulated by the Russian mathematician Kolmogorov [109; p.267]:

> The frequency concept applied to a large but finite number of trials does not admit a rigorous formal exposition within the framework of pure mathematics.

The essence of this is the limiting frequency doesn't allow for it; and hence the risk concept is used.

If a risk estimate $r*_1$ is defined on the interval $[(r*_1)_{min}, (r*_1)_{max}]$ then for comparable risk estimate $r*_2$, on interval $[(r*_2)_{min}, (r*_2)_{max}]$, holds:

(A.1) $r*_1 > r*_2$ if and only if $(r*_1)_{min} > (r*_2)_{max}$

and

(A.2) $r*_1 < r*_2$ if and only if $(r*_1)_{max} < (r*_2)_{min}$

If, as we mentioned above, the intervals are simply too big and overlap, the rule of thumb holds here and we say:

(A.3) $r*_1 \geq r*_2$ if $\{(r*_1)_{max} - (r*_1)_{min}\} >> \{(r*_2)_{max} - (r*_2)_{min}\}$

where symbol >> means "**much greater than**" which we set, for the sake of simplicity, at a minimum of 3 times greater.

There is one other very important issue accompanied with the assessment, estimation, and/or calculation of the risk level. As we noted above, the risk estimate should be in interval fashion even though the interval may be expressed by a single number from that interval. Therefore, there is no reason why we should not use non-cardinal, i.e. behavioral, hedonic, ordinal etc., data and information for defining the risk level estimate. Even for its actual (combined) disutility level interval. Or *vice versa* as Daniel Suits, in the below conversion scheme (A.4), based on [197], comments on with regard to a slightly different problem:

> We can get by ... by partitioning the scale of a conventionally measured variable into intervals and defining a set of dummy variables on them, we obtain unbiased estimates since the regression coefficients of the dummy variables conform to any curvature that is present.

(A.4) Several methods of quantifying qualitative phenomena, some of which have been already mentioned in the discussion in CHAPTER 2, have been devised to rectify this problem. Each stems from four facts and one assumption [24; pp.41-43]:

(A.5) Dummy variables (i.e. < 0, 1 >) used in multiple correlations have been a well-known instrument in socio-economic statistics for years.

(A.6) The numerical field of the factors, transformed from absolute to relative numbers (i.e. *percentages***) is normalized and generally homogeneous** since we are dealing in relative changes rather than absolute amounts, with all the numerical data falling within the interval between -20 and +20.

(A.7) Morgenstern (in [200]) states that **about 10 – 30% error can be expected in any real numerical economic, let alone socio-economic, datum.**

Interpretation of probability, when applied to practical problems such as reliability and risk analysis, lacks a theoretical framework to justify an application [109]. As we simply have to formally address the problem, interval analysis is probably the safest bet.

Once we introduce **interval estimates** of risk value—probabilistically or heuristically based—its estimable overall disutility to the *donor* and *recipient* system can be evaluated as a system of single-number preferences on the ordinal scale [24; p.42]. For the interval analysis and estimation—here, we can substitute the whole interval for the single-number reference—it is necessary to introduce some evaluation criteria too [87], and we read:

(A.8) Daniel Suits states: "(That we **can** get by) ... by partitioning the scale of a conveniently **measured variable into intervals and defining a set of dummy variables on them**, we obtain unbiased estimates since the regression coefficients of the dummy variables conform to any curvature that is present" [197].

(A.9) "The ordinal values (scales) can be assumed to be monotonic transforms of the actual behavioral factors" [198], [199].

A/2 Basic Formulas, Theorems, and Axioms Used for Conversion Tables

DEFINITION A.1:

Let us graphically express two real numbers: positive, negative, rational, irrational ones and also zero, **a** and **b**, as points on the X-axis (see **EXHIBIT A2**).

Appendix

EXHIBIT A2

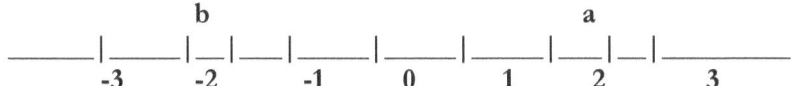

Then we say that **a** > **b** (or **b** < **a**) when and only when the point **a** lies on the right-hand side (RHS) of the point **b**.

DEFINITION A.2:

Let **a** and **b** be two arbitrary real numbers (on the X-axis). Then **a** > **b** (or **b** < **a**) when and only when the number {**a** - **b**} is a positive number.

For any two real numbers **a** and **b** the two operations + (addition) and . (multiplication) each associate unique real numbers, denoted by **a** + **b** and **a** . **b** respectively, in such a way that, if **a**, **b**, **c**, etc. are real numbers, the following axioms hold:

AXIOM A.1:

a + b = b + a

AXIOM A.2:

a + (b + c) = (a + b) + c

AXIOM A.3:

There is a number 0 such that for every real number a,
a + 0 = a

AXIOM A.4:

a . (b . c) = (a . b) . c

AXIOM A.5:

There is a number 1 such that 1 ≠ 0 and, for every real number a,
1 . a = a

AXIOM A.6:

a . b = b . a

AXIOM A.7:

For every real number a, different from zero, there is a number a−1 such that a . a−1 = 1

AXIOM A.8:

$a \cdot (b + c) = (a \cdot b) + (a \cdot c)$

AXIOM A.9 (of Archimedes):

Between any two real numbers, there is a rational number

AXIOM A.10:

If a and b are arbitrary real numbers, only one of the following relations holds:
a = b, a > b, b > a

THEOREM A.1:

If a > b and b > c, then a > c.

PROOF: To be found in [176; Chapter.2, Section 2]

THEOREM A.2:

If a > b and c > d, then a + c > b + d
If a > b and c is an arbitrary real number, then a + c > b + c

PROOF: In [176; Chapter 2, Section 3]

THEOREM A.3:

If a > b and c > 0 (i.e. c lies on the RHS of zero on the X-axis), then
a . c > b . c

PROOF: In [176; Ch. 2, par. 4]

THEOREM A.4:

If a > b and c > d, then a − d > b − c
If a > b and c is an arbitrary real number, then a − c > b − c

PROOF: In [176; Chapter 2, Section 5]

THEOREM A.5:

If a > b > 0 and c > d > 0, then a . c > b . d

PROOF: In [176; Ch. 2, par. 6, (2.3) - (2.8)]

THEOREM A.6:

If a > b > 0 and c > d > 0, then a/d > b/c.
For a = b = 1, we have 1/d > 1/c

Appendix

PROOF: In [176; Chapter 2, Section 7]

THEOREM A.7:

The arithmetic mean of the arbitrary non-negative numbers a1, a2, ... an is not smaller than their geometric mean, i.e.

$$(a1 + a2 + ... + an)/n \geq \sqrt[n]{a1 \cdot a2 \cdot .... \cdot an}$$

PROOF: In [176; Ch. 4, par. 2, (4.20) - (4.29)]

COROLLARY:

Even though the equality in THEOREM A.7 comes about for a1 = a2 ......= an only, we can generally approximate RHS (right hand side) of THEOREM A.7 by its LHS (left hand side).

THEOREM A.8:

For every real number a holds $-|a| \leq a \leq |a|$, where $|a|$ is the absolute value of the number a, and in the first relationship the equality sign holds when and only when $a \leq 0$, while the second equality comes about when and only when $a \leq 0$

PROOF: In [176; Chapter 3, Section 4]

A/3   Scheme of Calibrating the Factor Scales

Let us start this discussion with a few notions about a society's welfare, also (in the text) defined as public or societal (general) well-being. For the further discussion we shall be using quotations from a certain classical economic literature [58; pp.20-27]:

> In this basic attempt to set up empirical categories of **utilities** (bold face; M.K.) and corresponding 'choice parameters' suffice it to draw a distinction between utilities which can be satisfied by (1) individual goods, and (2) collective goods. Similarly, suffice it to distinguish within these categories, 1 and 2, between (1and 2a) '**survival utility,**' does not depend on 'taste' or 'value judgment' ... it is determined here by its biological quality to enable life, and (1 and 2b) '**supplementary utility**' ... Since nobody wants to 'trade in' his life for any other goods. It is therefore, reasonable to make a theoretical generalization that people wish that (1and 2a) be fully satisfied before (1and 2b). It follows that the transformation from individual to social well-being is not dependent on an arbitrary ethical judgment but on

the lexical ordering of utilities whose existence and content can be objectively determined.

Therefore, an **overall well-being** of society WA can be said to be preferable to an overall well-being of society WB if a larger fraction of the population in A (P_A) than in B (P_B) has satisfied 'survival utility' (1 and 2a).

The objection that one man's 'supplementary utility' (1 and 2b) might possibly be higher than another man's 'survival utility' (1 and 2a) and that, therefore, the lexicographical ordering itself implies an arbitrary value judgment is not defensible *"for which a proper place in this rational argument should be found."*

Thus, A (1 and 2a) > B (1 and 2a) whenever $P_A > P_B$, and imposing a lexical (or lexicographical) ordering on the utilities, WA > WB, whenever (1 and 2a)$_A$ > (1 and 2a)$_B$

A/3/1 Maximum Utility Principle

Let "utility" be such a characteristic that expresses the total suitability (value in use or convenience) of a certain alternative regarding a given and presumably well-defined goal. Then the solving of a decision problem could be substituted by seeking the alternative with maximum total utility [52; p.15].

A/3/2 Assessing the Given Factor's USF

Universal Score Function (USF) helps to convert different dimensions (scales) of data needed for our decision-problem into one dimensionless scale. We can assess these data on different intervals, not necessarily just equidistant.

Shackle [1967; p.66] describes the aim of any reasonable decision-making method as:

> Rather than minimize our losses, is it not more reasonable to fix for them some maximum tolerable numerical size, to avoid any action-scheme which would bring losses larger than this within the range of possible or 'too-possible' outcomes, and subject to this constraint to choose that action-scheme which brings within the range of possible or 'sufficiently possible' outcomes, as high a positive success as we can find.

Translating the above quotation into plain language, the paragraph in effect introduces the following **scheme of assessing a factor's USF**:

Appendix

(1) Obtain as much information as you can about the factor's dimension-scale to determine its **"worth,"** where "worth" is defined e.g. by Miller [1970; p.12]:

The general concept of 'worth' is defined as conscious perception held by individual relating to his underlying feeling of preference, aversion and indifference. This includes not only direct awareness of the feelings themselves, but also the entire range of cognitive elements supporting such feelings. Conscious rationalizations, justifications, and explanations would all be included within the broad meaning of 'worth.'

(2) Set the lower and upper limits (or extremes) of the range of the worth of that particular factor upon the linear continuum that models (or represents) the appropriate dimension-scale.

These extremes (limits) can be easily interpreted as the borderline-to-maximum of EXCELLENCE for the verbal scoring in **EXHIBIT A3** and the borderline of WORTHLESSNESS. Graphical interpretation is shown in **EXHIBIT A3**.

EXHIBIT A3: Factors Dimension Scale

WORTHLESS   EXCELLENT

(3) Try to establish such points on the observed dimension-scale that lie on the border of two neighboring levels of the verbal interpretation in **EXHIBIT A3**.

In other words, whenever there is a breaking point—that we shall call a *node*—on the linear continuum which (in our fixed world of priorities and values) would divide two successive verbal qualities of the table in **EXHIBIT A4**; such as EXCELLENT vs. GOOD, GOOD vs. FAIR, etc., mark this tentative spot on the dimension scale.

The process of allocating of these nodes is then called calibrating the factor scale, and some graphical examples of calibrated scales are shown in **EXHIBIT A4** with the cases of equidistant calibrating (in example (a)) and two uneven calibrated scales (in examples (b) and (c)).

The Crucial Challenge for International Aid

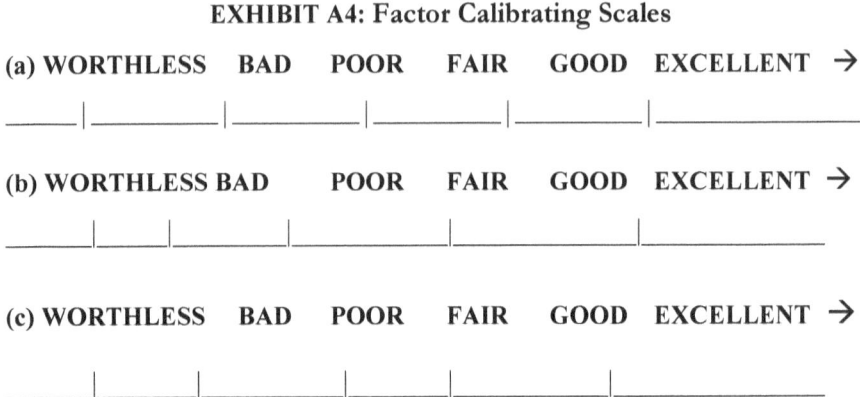

EXHIBIT A4: Factor Calibrating Scales

(4) Place all real data on this particular factor (pertinent to all considered alternatives) upon the calibrated scale and, finally, use the conversion table of **EXHIBIT A4** (or any other similar and/or better one) to obtain the factor's USF for each alternative.

A/3/3 Lexicographical Ordering Scheme

DEFINITION A.3 [24; pp.48–50]:

Assuming that, in general, we have a set of n multi-characteristic elements

$\{ X_j \}$,

j = 1 ... n, and assuming also that, for greater simplicity, we shall consider only the first two characteristics: c (the leading characteristic) and s (the supporting one).

Let the leading characteristic c be ranked such that the following holds:

(A.10) $X(^1) > X(^2) > ...... X(^k)$, k ≤ n

The same applies to elements containing only supporting characteristic s:

(A.11) $X(_1) > X(_2) > ...... X(_r)$, r ≤ n

Assuming that k = r , i.e. length of **(A.10)** = **(A.11)**, and that there can be more than one element with a certain rank k or r, we say that the set (with just two characteristics) is lexicographically ordered when:

(A.12) $X(^1{}_1) > X(^1{}_2) > X(^2{}_2) .... X(\min^k, \in \{n-j\}) > ...$

EXAMPLE: Let us have a six-element two-characteristic set X_j ($^c{}_s$) with the following data shown in the table in **EXHIBIT A5**. Each element is supposed to represent a society.

Appendix

EXHIBIT A.5

Characteristics	A1	A2	A3	A4	A5	A6
GDP per capita rank S	1	3	2	5	5	4
human rights rank C	2	2	3	1	3	3

According to **(A12)**, the bi-characteristic societies $\{X_j(^c_s)\}$ are:

(A.12.1) $X1(^2_1), X2(^2_3), X3(^3_2), X4(^1_5), X5(^3_5), X6(^3_4)$

And, finally, the lexicographical scheme orders the elements $\{X_j\}$, j = 1.......6:

(A.12.2) $X4 > X1 > X2 > X3 > X6 > X5$

A/4   An Alternative in the Decision Process

Suppose we have a full-fledged decision (or policy)-making problem to solve. Any "decision-making" problem has to have the following characteristics:

- The presence of several, but at least two, alternatives
- Clearly defined goals, which act as constraints on the choice among different alternatives;
- A comparison among alternatives and/or the evaluation of their outcomes in terms of total utilities is the general procedure of decision-making; and
- Seeking the maximum total utility is the criterion of a decision-making procedure.

DEFINITION A.4:

Denoting a general term for an "alternative," by capital letter A, we shall call the energy summarily needed for getting the action (alternative) A underway as INPUT, whereas the impact of the action will be summarily called OUTPUT.

A/5 Supporting Data to "Power of Oligarchy" Scale

NOTE: This scale is found in **EXHIBIT 4.1** of Chapter 4 of this study.

The data for "Pacific Rim" societies came as a result of mining existing mosaic-like and very suspect quality sources and information by using the above mentioned CTER, and double-cross-validation of the 43 figures and two tables in study [50]. The final table in **EXHIBIT A6** features the following rankings:

EXHIBIT A6

Country	"Political Rights"	"Concentrated Power"
Japan	8	4
Malaysia	4	8
South Korea	7	7
Indonesia	3	6
Singapore	6	2
Thailand	1	5
Taiwan	4	3
Hong Kong	3	1

A/5/1 Supporting Surveys

NOTE: Questions are denoted by symbol ■

EXHIBIT A7

■ **Maintaining smooth and regular contacts with government is an essential part of doing business?**

CHINA	---------------------------------
MALAYSIA	---------------------------
INDONESIA	--------------------------
JAPAN	-----------------------
THAILAND	---------------

Appendix

PHILIPPINES   -------------
TAIWAN   ---------
KOREA   -------
SINGAPORE   ---
HONG KONG   ---------------------

-2   -1   0   1   2
       DISAGREE   AGREE

EXHIBIT A8

■ There is a high level of government influence in business?

CHINA   ------------------------------
KOREA   ------------------------------
PHILIPPINES   --------------------------
INDONESIA   -----------------------
MALAYSIA   -------------
THAILAND   ---------
JAPAN   ----
SINGAPORE   --
TAIWAN   -----------
HONG KONG   ------------------------------------

-2   -1   0   1   2
       DISAGREE   AGREE

225

EXHIBIT A9

■ In order to be successful one needs to build up a network of 'contacts'?

KOREA	-------------------------
CHINA	-------------------------
JAPAN	-------------------------
PHILIPPINES	-------------------------
MALAYSIA	-------------------------
TAIWAN	-------------------------
INDONESIA	-------------------------
THAILAND	-------------------------
SINGAPORE	-------------------------
HONG KONG	-------------------------

```
-2          -1          0          1          2
       DISAGREE                 AGREE
```

A/5/2 Supporting Data for "The Generic Societies" Hypothesis

In Chapter 4 (of this study) there are two tables in **EXHIBITS 4.4** and **4.5** (here labeled as **EXHIBIT A.10** and **A.11**) which list survey responses to questions (denoted by ■) about perceived quality of democracy and economy in four "transitional" societies. Following are the tables and questions with percentages of society's answers.

Appendix

EXHIBIT A10: Assessment of Democracy

Agreement in %	Czechs	Poles	Hungarians	Lithuanians
■ "satisfaction with the functioning of democracy"	36	30	27	23
■ "government acts in the interest of the whole society"	25	13	24	8
■ "we can influence the political environment better after 1989"	20	41	30	4

EXHIBIT A11: Assessment of Economy

Agreement in %	Czechs	Poles	Hungarians	Lithuanians
■ "living conditions are good"	27	22	8	8
■ "the economy of the country is sound"	4	12	6	1
■ "changes after 1989 have brought bigger profits (generally)"	23	24	15	7

Assume that we redefine the "percentages of agreement," in line with the statement we think such a fraction of society might wish to convey (given the question). Within the scope of the previously discussed **conversion tables** we postulate that interval <1% – 39%> would be rated "**bad**" and assigned artificial-scale value of 1; interval <40% - 59%> is branded as "**maybe good, maybe bad**" and assigned value 2 and interval <60% - 100%> would then be rated "**good**" and assigned value 3. These new *disutilities* are entered into the tables under the corresponding "percentage agreement."

For the **"generic society" test** we have used the four column sum of disutilities in each table and tested it on the **Paired Two-Sample t-test.**

For the **"failure of democracy leads to serious economic failure hypothesis"** we have used two full 12-element samples of corresponding disutilities from both tables and used the simple regression.

NOTE: Further discussion of Non-parametric and/or Rank Correlation Methods used in this study is provided e.g. by Maurice Kendall [153].

A/6 Conversion Table of the Indexes of Corruption in Individual Countries

Transparency International [117] publishes a ladder of "corruption index" in individual countries of the world. It is based on perception of professionals in the business sector, economic analysts and the societies at large. It converts those perceptions into the **scale of 0 to 10**, where 10 is absolutely "transparent" country whereas 0 is absolutely corrupt society and ranks the countries accordingly.

For the year 2001 several countries shape up as shown in **EXHIBIT A12**.

EXHIBIT A12: Conversion Table—Index of Corruption

Rank	Country	Value of Corruption Index
1	Finland	9.90
2	Denmark	9.50
3	New Zealand	9.40
4	Iceland	9.20
5	Singapore	9.20
6	Sweden	9.00
15	Austria	7.80
16	USA	7.60
17	Israel	7.60

20	Germany	7.40
31	Hungary	5.30
44	Poland	4.10
47	Bulgaria	3.90
48	Croatia	3.90
49	Czech Republic	3.90
52	Slovakia	3.70
69	Romania	2.80
81	Russia	2.30
91	Bangladesh	.040

A/7 Ranking Methods of Non-Parametric Statistics

Often in comparisons of two variables the actual values that they posses are either not very crucial, or, which in most cases is true, are not known with any degree of certainty. In any case (see e.g. [154; pp.223–225]), the importance of the order in which the values are placed becomes paramount.

For example, two judges, Mr. Fair and Mr. Wise, are judging exhibits A, B, C, ... F. They award the following scores:

	A	B	C	D	E	F
Mr. Fair	19	41	85	27	63	72
Mr. Wise	46	45	54	48	51	49

Is there evidence to show that the judges agree in their marking? It is clear that what matters here is not the actual scores awarded (for each marking system is probably peculiar to the judge using it) but rather the order in which each places the exhibit. So we code the scores for each judge giving 1 to the exhibit to which each gave the highest score, 2 to the second highest and so on. This is the process of *ranking* and we see the result below.

	A	B	C	D	E	F	
Mr. Fair	6	4	1	5	3	2	(x)
Mr. Wise	5	6	1	4	2	3	(y)

If the judges were in perfect agreement the ranks would be arranged in some order, such as:

1	2	3	4	5	6
1	2	3	4	5	6

If they had been in total disagreement, this would have been the result:

1	2	3	4	5	6
6	5	4	3	2	1

We would like a measure indicating how near to these two extremes our two judges are, and we therefore give a value of +1 for perfect agreement and -1 for total disagreement. We can present one measure which will do this: for perfect agreement the ranks are related by the straight-line equation **y = x** and for total disagreement by the straight line **y = 7 − x**, so we could use the correlation coefficient r. When applied to ranks **r** is known as *Spearman's coefficient* (of rank correlation). We will write it as **r_s**.

In our example we had:

$\sum x = \sum y = 21$ ...... $\bar{x} = \bar{y} = 7/2$

$\sum x^2 = \sum y^2 = 91$ ...... $\sum (x - \bar{x})^2 = \sum (y - \bar{y})^2 = 91 - 6 \cdot 7/2 \cdot 7/2 = 35/2$

$\sum xy = 87$ ...... $\sum (x - \bar{x})(y - \bar{y}) = 87 - 6 \cdot 7/2 \cdot 7/2 = 27/2$

.... $r_s = (27/2) / (35/2) = 27/35 \approx 0.77$.

Appendix

If, in general, n objects are ranked and there are no tied ranks,

$$\sum x = \sum y = \tfrac{1}{2} n (n+1) \qquad \bar{x} = \bar{y} = \tfrac{1}{2}(n+1),$$

$$\sum x^2 = \sum y^2 = 1/6 n (n+1)(2n+1)$$

$$\sum (x - \bar{x})^2 = \sum (y - \bar{y})^2 = 1/12\, n(n^2 - 1).$$

Hence $\quad r_s \;=\; \dfrac{\sum xy - 1/4 n(n+1)^2}{1/12 n(n^2 - 1)}$

When there are tied ranks this formula should not be used. In this case we can either use a modified form which is derived elsewhere [154; p.226] or calculate r_s from the original formula.

An alternative measure which is sometimes used instead of r_s is **Kendall's coefficient**, which we shall call r_k though it is often called τ. In this measure every possible pair of exhibits is considered; each pair is allotted a score of +1 if they are in the same order in both x- and y-rankings, and a score -1 if they are in the reverse order. The total of the scores is then obtained. The easiest way to calculate the coefficient is to arrange one of the variables so that the ranks are in the correct order as below:

	A	B	C	D	E	F	
Mr. Fair	1	2	3	4	5	6	(x)
Mr. Wise	1	3	2	6	4	5	(y)

Then the total is formed by starting at the left-hand y-number and counting +1 for each number greater than itself, and -1 for each number less than itself among the other y-ranks. This gives the score for the first y-rank. Similarly the score for the second y-rank is obtained by repeating the process but using only those y-ranks to the right of it in the table. We can verify that the total so formed is the same as the total in our original definition.

For our example Mr. Wise's **(y)** score:

(y)	1	3	2	6	4	5	
score	5 +	2 +	3 +	(-2) +	1 +	0	Total = 9

In order to convert this total to a coefficient taking value +1 for perfect agreement, we must divide it by the maximum possible total. It is not hard to see that if there are no tied ranks this must be just the number of pairs, 15 in our example and $1/2 n(n-1)$ in the general case, since if the agreement were perfect each pair would contribute a score of +1.

So in our example we have $r_k = 9/15 = 0.6$. Notice that this is not equal to r_s. The coefficient gives different numerical values, but, both indicate a reasonable measure of agreement between the judges.

In calculating r_k in cases where there are tied ranks, any pair which is tied in one or both of the rankings should contribute a score of 0 to the total score. The denominator should also strictly be changed from

$$\tfrac{1}{2} n(n-1) \text{ to } \sqrt{\{[\tfrac{1}{2} n(n-1) - U][\tfrac{1}{2} n(n-1) - V]\}}$$

where U is the number of tied pairs in the x-ranking and V the number of tied pairs in the y-ranking; but this latter correction is only important when the proportion of tied pairs is large, as otherwise the expression is approximately equal to $\tfrac{1}{2} n(n-1)$.

Of course we should like to be able to carry out a significance test before drawing any conclusion from ranked sample data. For large values of n, we can test r_s approximately by treating it as an ordinary correlation coefficient and using the method of goodness of fit and association, such as is discussed in [154; pp.190-221]. For small n, and in general for r_k, the tests are more complicated and by and large we shall simply regard rank correlation coefficients as giving a quickly-calculated approximate measure of the relationship between the two variables.

The significance tests for both r_s and r_k are non-parametric tests [154; pp.190–196].

A/8   The Gini Index

The Gini index of income or resource inequality **is a measure of the degree to which a population shares that resource unequally**. It is based on the statistical notion known in the literature as the "mean difference" of a population. The index is scaled to vary from a minimum of zero to a

Appendix

maximum of one, zero representing no inequality and one representing a maximum possible degree of inequality.

In order to begin a derivation of the Gini index, consider the lowest 20% of the population, ranked by per capita income, and ask what portion of the total income is attributable to this 20%? If the corresponding proportion of total income as a percentage is also 20% we will call this fair. If it is less than 20% we will say there is income inequality. It cannot be more than 20%. In general, to measure this, we define a function, $g(a)$, to be the fraction of the total value of a certain resource belonging to the lowest $(100a)\%$ of the population as ranked by per-capita ownership of that resource. This curve is defined on the interval $<0, 1>$ and is referred to as the Lorenz curve of the resource distribution. Here we convert the resource into money, usually dollars. Then the Gini index of inequality is a measure of the difference between $g(a)$ and the ideal which is assumed to be a, (i.e. same percentage of the resource as portion of the population).

EXAMPLES of the Gini Index:

Australia 35.2 (1944)
Austria 31 (1995)
Azerbaijan 36 (1995)
Bangladesh 33.6 (FY95)
Belarus 21.7 (1998)
Belgium 28.7 (1996)
Bolivia 58.9 (1997)
Brazil 60.7 (1998)
Bulgaria 26.4 (2001)
Burkina Faso 48.2 (1994)
Burundi 42.5 (1998)
Cambodia 40.4 (1997)
Cameroon 47.7 (1996)
Canada 31.5 (1994)
Central African Republic 61.3 (1993)
Chile 56.7 (1998)
China 40 (2001)
Colombia 57.1 (1996)

Costa Rica 45.9 (1997)
Cote d'Ivoire 36.7 (1995)
Croatia 29 (1999)
Czech Republic 25.4 (1996)
Denmark 24.7 (1992)
Dominican Republic 47.4 (1998)
East Timor 38 (2002 est.)
Ecuador 43.7 (1995)
Egypt 34.4 (2001)
El Salvador 52.2 (1998)
Estonia 37 (1999)
Ethiopia 40 (1995)
Finland 25.6 (1991)
France 32.7 (1995)
Georgia 37.1 (1996)
Germany 30 (1994)
Ghana 40.7 (1999)
Greece 32.7 (1993)

Guatemala 55.8 (1998)
Guinea 40.3 (1994)
Honduras 56.3 (1998)
Hungary 24.4 (1998)
India 37.8 (1997)
Indonesia 31.7 (1999)
Ireland 35.9 (1987)
Israel 35.5 (2001)
Italy 27.3 (1995)
Jamaica 37.9 (2000)
Japan 24.9 (1993)
Jordan 36.4 (1997)
Kazakhstan 35.4 (1996)
Kenya 44.9 (1997)
Korea, South 31.6 (1993)
Kyrgyzstan 34.6 (1999)
Laos 37 (1997)
Latvia 32 (1999)
Lesotho 56 (1986-87)
Madagascar 38.1 (1999)
Malaysia 49.2 (1997)
Mali 50.5 (1994)
Mauritania 37.3 (1995)
Mauritius 37 (1987 est.)
Mexico 53.1 (1998)
Moldova 40.6 (1997)
Mongolia 33.2 (1995)
Morocco 39.5 (1998-99)
Mozambique 39.6 (1996-97)
Nepal 36.7 (FY97)
Netherlands 32.6 (1994)
Nicaragua 60.3 (1998)
Niger 50.5 (1995)

Nigeria 50.6 (1996-97)
Norway 25.8 (1995)
Pakistan 41 (1999)
Paraguay 57.7 (1998)
Peru 46.2 (1966)
Philippines 46.2 (1977)
Romania 31.1 (1998)
Russia 39.9 (2001)
Rwanda 28.9 (1985)
Sierra Leone 62.9 (1989)
Slovenia 28.4 (1998)
Slovakia 26.3 (1996)
Sri Lanka 34.4 (1995)
Sweden 25 (1992)
Switzerland 33.1 (1992)
Tunisia 41.7 (1995)
Turkey 41.5 (1994)
Turkmenistan 40.8 (1998)
Taiwan 32.6 (2000)
Tajikistan 34.7 (1998)
Tanzania 38.2 (1993)
Uganda 37.4 (1966)
United Kingdom 36.8 (1995)
United States 40.8 (1887)
Uruguay 42.3 (1898)
Uzbekistan 44.7 (1998)
Venezuela 49.5 (1998)
Vietnam 36.1
Yemen 33.4 (1998)
Zambia 52.6 (1998
Zimbabwe 50.1 (1995)

Notes

[1] Havel, Vaclav (1997). One of Vaclav Havel's weekly talks to the nation from his summer residence in Castle Lany (March 1997). *Polygon*, 4 & 5, 1-22 (translation from Czech by M.K.)

[2] "Continental Divide" (1998). *Central European Econ. Rev.*, VI, 14-29.

[3] "Could it lead to Fascism?" (1998, Jul. 11). *The Economist*, 17-19.

[4] Nussbaum, B. (1997, Dec. 1). "Asia's Crisis: The Cold War's Final Legacy." *Business Week*, 30.

[5] Zakaria, F. (1997, Dec. 29/Jan. 5 1998). "Doubts about Democracy." *Newsweek*, 26.

[6] Karasek, M. (1985). "Criterion of Tolerable Error Limit in a Developing Country's Data-Base." In M. Hamza (Ed.), *Proc. IASTED Int. Sym.: Modelling & Simulation* (pp. 323-332). Zurich: Acta Press.

[7] Smith, A. (1976). *The Theory of Moral Sentiments*, (with an introduction by E. West). Liberty Classics. (Originally published 1759).

[8] Dallago, B. and L. Mintone (Eds.). (1996). *Economic Institutions, Markets and Competition*. Edward Elgar.

[9] Birner, J. (1996). "Decentralization as Ability to Adapt." In Dallago and Mintone (Eds.) *Economic Institutions, Markets and Competition*, 68.

[10] Pejovich, S. (1996). "The Markets for Institutions versus the Strong Hand of State: The Case of Eastern Europe." In Dallago and Mintone (Eds.) *Economic Institutions, Markets and Competition*, 116.

[11] Hayek, F.A. (1945). "Individualism, True and False." In Hayek, F.A., *Individualism and Economic Order*. Routledge and Kegan Paul, 10-11.

[12] Birner, J. (1996). "Decentralization as Ability to Adapt." In Dallago and Mintone (Eds.) *Economic Institutions, Markets and Competition*, 82.

[13] Alchian, A. and S. Woodward. (1988). "The Firm is Dead; Long Live the Firm." *Journal of Economic Literature*, 26, 65.

[14] Jensen, M. and W. Meckling. (1996). "Rights and Production Functions: An Application to Labour-Managed Firms and Codetermination." *Journal of Business*, 52(4), 470-472.

[15] Pejovich, S. (1996). "The Markets for Institutions versus the Strong Hand of State: The Case of Eastern Europe." In Dallago and Mintone (Eds.) *Economic Institutions, Markets and Competition*, 117.

[16] Nguyen, Tri Q. (1989). *Third-World Development*. Farleigh Dickinson University Press.

[17] Wright, B.D. and G.N. Masters. (1982). *Rating Scale Analysis*. Chicago: MESA Press.

[18] Emerson, T. and R. Moreau. (1997, Nov. 3). "Where is Everybody." Buruma, J., "Colonial Attitudes Never Die", *Newsweek*, 27, 33.

[19] Sugawara, S. (1997, Nov. 8-9). "Market Troubles Felt Far and Wide." *International Herald Tribune*, Paris, 1.

[20] "A person having a greater ability than another should have the greater probability of solving any item of the type in question, and similarly, one item being more difficult than another one means that for any person the probability of solving the second item correctly is the greater one." Rasch, G. (1960). Probabilistic Models for Some Intelligence and Attainment Tests, Danmarks Paedogogiske Institut, Copenhagen, 2.

[21] Kurian, G.T. (1991). *The New Book of World Rankings*. New York: Facts on File.

[22] Boland, V. (1997, Apr. 3). "Czechs find transition harder than they thought." *Financial Times*, 2.

[23] "Summary of the Czech Economy." (1997). *Polygon,* 8, 6.

[24] Karasek, M. and W. K. Alem. (1987). Socio-Economic Modelling and Forecasting in Developing Countries. The Book Guild Ltd. ISBN 0863322204

[25] Richardson, M. (1997, Nov. 15-16). "Crisis Tests 'Asian Values'." *International Herald Tribune*.

[26] Moreau, R. (1997, November 10). "Ready for the Worst." *Newsweek*, 26.

[27] Shaw, Sin-ming. (1997, Nov. 3). "Crashing Into the Real World." *Newsweek*, 32.

[28] Burton, S. (1997, Oct. 13). "Two-Way Street." *Time Magazine*, 34-37.

[29] Clifford, M.L. (1997, Nov. 24). "Korea's Crisis." *Business Week*, 28.

[30] "Asia's Economic Crisis: How far is down." (1997, Nov. 15). *The Economist*, 19.

[31] "Worries Deepen in Japan, Korea." (1997, Nov. 8-9). *International Herald Tribune*, 1.

[32] Samuelson, R.J. (1997, Dec. 15). "The Asian Connection." *Newsweek*, 4.

[33] Tedjasukmana, J. (1998, Jan. 8). "Crisis puts Indonesia's political system in spotlight." *Arab News*, 7.

[34] Wolf, M. (1997, Nov. 11). "Fast-track to nowhere." *Financial Times*, 15.

[35] Johnson, D.P. (1981). *Sociological Theory*. New York: John Wiley & Sons.

[36] Michels, R. (1915). *Political Parties*. Glencoe, Illinois: Free Press. 1915.

[37] Giddens, A. (1977). *Studies in Social and Political Theory*. Hutchinson of London.

[38] Johnson, D.P. (1981). *Sociological Theory*. New York: John Wiley & Sons, 466.

[39] *Financial Times*. (1998, Aug. 28), 1.

[40] Thornhill, J. (1998, Sep. 8). "Duma rejects Chernomyrdin for second time." *Financial Times*, 1.

[41] Greenwald, J. (1998, Sep. 28). "Sticky Currency." *Time Magazine*, 88.

[42] The author draws on firsthand knowledge and experience of Czech and Saudi societies and very thorough information about the Russian one.

[43] Munataka, T. (1979). *Matrices and Linear Programming*. San Francisco: Holden Day Inc.

[44] Samuelson, P. (1997). *Economics* (13th ed.). McGraw Hill.

[45] Goldberg, M. A. (1974). "Environmental Decision-Making: Social Indicators, Simulation and Public Choice." *Annals of Reg. Sci.*, 12-22.

[46] Samuelson, P. and W. Nordhaus. (1992). *Microeconomics*. New York: McGraw-Hill Inc.

[47] Willcocks, L. and C. Griffith. (1994). "Prediction Risk of Failure in Large-Scale Information Technology Projects." *Technology Forecasting & Soc. Change,* 47, 209.

[48] Layne W. A. (1986). *Cost Accounting, Analysis and Control*. Macmillan Co.

[49] Audretsch D.B. and T. Mahmood. (1995, Apr.). "New Firm Survival: New Results Using a Hazard Function." *The Rev. Econ & Statistics*, 98.

[50] Lassare P. and J. Probert. (1994). "Competing on the Pacific Rim: High Risks and High Returns." *Long Range Planning*, 27(2), 14-19.

[51] Modelski, G. and G. Perry. (1991). "Democratization In Long Perspective." *Tech. Forecasting & Soc. Change"* 39, 22-25.

[52] Karasek, M. (1985). *The Anatomy of Decision*. New York: Vantage Press.

[53] Highfield, R.(1999, Oct. 2). "Human error undermines rigid safety procedures." *The Daily Telegraph*, 12.

[54] Hulik, M. (1999). *Polygon*, 5-6, 44. "Just one day ...." (from Czech original "Jen jeden den..."). English translation of the excerpt : "with the utmost respect to the nowadays Czech democratic state ... it is my conviction that, according to my experience and notion, the communist justice ... was in 70's

and 80s on the higher professional, technical and judiciary level than the nowadays justice."

[55] Klitgaard, R. (1990). *Tropical Gangsters.* Basic Books.

[56] CATO Institute Report, (1997, Jun. 22). *The New York Times.*

[57] White, D.R.J. (1968, Dec.). "POED – A Method of Evaluating System Performance." *IEEE Trans. on Engineering. Management,* 117-182.

[58] Dopfer, K. (Ed.). (1976). *Economics in the Future.* London: The MacMillan Press Ltd.

[59] Melvin, M. (1992). *International Money and Finance* (3rd ed.). New York: Harper Collins Publishers, Inc.

[60] Krakowski, M. (1974). "PERT and Parkinson's Law." *Interfaces,* 5(1).

[61] "Bullets beat ballots every time." (1999, Oct. 23). *National Post,* B4.

[62] Epstein, L.I. (1958). *Nomography.* New York: Interscience Publications. Inc.

[63] Kahn, H. and A. Wiener. (1967). *The Year* 2000. New York: The Macmillan Co.

[64] Popper, K.R. (1979). *Objective Knowledge (An Evolutionary Approach).* Oxford University Press.

[65] Hammond, K.R. (1973). "The Cognitive Conflict Paradigm." In *Human Judgement and Social Interaction.* New York: Holt, Rinehard & Winston.

[66] Ackoff, R.L. (1983). "An Interactive View of Rationality." *J. Operational Res. Soc.,* 34(8),721-722.

[67] Shackle, G.L.S. (1968). *Uncertainty in Economics (and Other Reflections).* Cambridge University Press.

[68] Karasek, M. (1998). "With Adam Smith against the decay of societies." *Polygon,* 8, 60-64.

[70] Lindzey, G., and E. Aronson (Eds.). (1980). *The Handbook of Social Psychology,* second. ed. Addison-Wesley Publishing Company.

[71] Ignatius, D. (1999, May 25). "Look Out, 'the Older Social Structures Are Cracking'." *International Herald Tribune,* 8.

[72] Karasek, M. (1979). "A Forecasting Model of Ontario Tourism." *Contemp. Leisure Research,* Ontario Research Council on Leisure, 330-339.

[73] von Neuman, J. and D. Morgenstern. (1953). *Theory of Games and Economic Behavior.* Princeton University Press.

[74] International Herald Tribune. (2000, Feb. 17), 2.

Notes

[75] Bauerova, L. (2000, Feb. 19-20). "Head of Czech Bank Quits Amid Fraud Investigation." *International Herald Tribune.*

[76] Strom, S. (200, Feb. 15). "Hostile Effort To Buy Firm In Japan Fails," *International Herald Tribune*, 9.

[77] Keay, J. (2000, Feb. 15). "Amid Crisis, Ukraine Tries to Reschedule Some Debt." *International Herald Tribune,* "Europe."

[78] Crampton, T. (2000, February 14). "'Alarm Bell' From Departing IMF Chief." *International Herald Tribune*, 1.

[79] Ricupero, R. (2000, Feb. 12-13). "Seeking Lessons for Development in a Global Economy." *International Herald Tribune*, 5.

[80] Richardson, M. (2000, Feb. 4). "Dilemma in Jakarta: 'Money Politics'." *International Herald Tribune*, 1.

[81] Kirk, D. (2000, Feb. 5-6). "In South Korea, a Quiet Revolution." *International Herald Tribune.*

[82] "Building a Great Wall in Cyberspace" (2000, Feb. 7). *Newsweek,* 45.

[83] Erlanger, S. (2000, Feb. 7). "Croatia Is Moving Quickly on Reforms." *International Herald Tribune*, 5.

[84] Finn, P. (2000, Feb. 12). "Czech Communists Talk of a Comeback." *International Herald Tribune*, 8.

[85] Bergsten, F.C. (2000, Feb. 9). "Free Trade Is a Real Boon for the Developing World." *International Herald Tribune,* Op/Letters.

[86] "Goodnight, Vietnam." (2000, Jan. 8). *The Economist, 65.*

[87] Moore, R.E. (1979). *Methods and Applications of Interval Analysis.* Philadephia: SIAM, 10.

[88] Neild, R. (2000, Feb. 17). "Expose the Unsavory Business Behind Cruel Wars." *International Herald Tribune,* "Ed/Op."

[89] Cody, E. (2000, Feb. 9). "Serb Critics Say Murder Is Insights to Milosevic Era." *International Herald Tribune,* 1.

[90] French, H. (2000, Feb. 7). "Sex and Scoops in Land of a Very Cautious Press." *International Herald Tribune*, 1.

[91] Lindley, D. (2000). "Letter." *RSS News* 27(5), Royal Statistical Society, 8.

[92] Kuczmarski, J.G. and P. Rosenbaum. (2000). "Quantile Plots, Partial Orders,and Financial Risk." *The Amer. Statistician* 53(3), ASA

[93] Tofler, A. (1981). *The Third Wave.* London: Pan Books Ltd.

[94] Rose, A. (2000, Mar. 11). "All he is saying is give war a chance." *National Post*, Toronto, B5.

[95] Alexander, C. (2000, Mar.). "Alexander the Conqueror." *National Geographic*, 197(3).

[96] Minogue, K. (2000, Jan. 8). "What's the big idea." *National Post*, Toronto, B7.

[97] The Associated Press. (2000, Apr. 11). "Civil Unrest over Economy Spreads in Bolivia." *International Herald Tribune*, 6.

[98] Sims, C. (2000, Apr. 11). "An Old Slur Gives a Chill To Japan's Immigrants." *International Herald Tribune*, 1, 6.

[99] d'Estaing,V.G.and H. Schmidt. (2000, Apr. 11). "Time to Slow Down and Consolidate Around 'Euro-Europe'." *International Herald Tribune*, 8.

[100] Corcoran, T. (2000, Apr. 15). "Internet Markets Fall to Earth." *National Post*, Toronto, A1-A

[101] Friedman, T.L. (2000, April 19). "Russians Have a 'Very Depressing and Ugly State'." *International Herald Tribune*, 8.

[102] Karasek, M. (1997). "The End of Beginning or the Beginning of the End." *Polygon*, 3, 58-62.

[103] Spurny, J. (2000, Jun. 19-25). "The State Has Taken Over the IPB (Bank)." *Respekt*, XI(26).

[104] Mayer, L.S. (1973). "Estimating a Correlation Coefficient When One Variable is not Directly Observed." *JASA* (68), 420-421.

[105] Stewart, D. "We are mouse-clicking the Dark Age into retreat." *The Financial Post*.

[106] EU Survey of Candidate Countries (2000, October 23).Translation from *MF Dnes*, 4.

[107] Karasek, M. (2000). "Czech Question: Save the Society by Destroying the State or Vice Versa." *Polygon*, 2, 59-64 (in Czech).

[108] Shirer, W.L (1960). *The Rise and Fall of the Third Reich.* Greenwich, CT: Fawcet Pub. Inc., 94-95.

[109] Singpurwalla, N. (1988, Jun.). "Foundation Issues in Reliability and Risk Analysis." *SIAM Review*, 30 (2), 267.

[110] Lockhardt , Sir R. Bruce. (1937). *Retreat from Glory,* (7th Czech ed.). Prague: F. Borovy Pub., 112, 144.

[111] Pfaff, W. (2001, Feb. 17-18). "Culture Does Count – and in Africa Today It Counts for a Lot." *International Herald Tribune*, 6.

[112] Pfaff, W. (2001, Mar. 3-4). "Ethnic Nationalism Is Still Prevailing." *International Herald Tribune*, 10.

[113] Anders, G. (1972). Endzeit und Zeitende: Gedanken uber die atomare Situation, Munchen: Beck, 194.

[114] Ausubel, J.H. (1991). "Rat-Race Dynamics and Crazy Companies." *Tech. Forecasting & Soc. Dynamic*, 11-22.

[115] Kurtz, H. (2001, Feb. 23). "For New Media, the Late News Is Bad." *International Herald Tribune*, 17.

[116] Friedman.L. (2001, Feb. 26). "Now Watch the Internet Get Serious." *International Herald Tribune*, 10.

[117] Transparency International. (2001, Jun. 28). In *MF Dnes*, Prague (Czech original), A13.

[118] Campbell, A. and K. Sommers (1997). *Core Competency-Based Strategy*. London: International Thompson Business Press.

[119] Olive, D. (2001, Jul. 10). "Lessons from the U.S. cable wars." *The Financial Post*, C3.

[120] Watson, W. (2001, Sep. 8). "The paradox of inequality." *The Financial Post*, C11.

[121] Crane, D. (2001, Sep. 12). "U.S. tragedy shows peril of bad globalization." *The Toronto Star*, E2.

[122] O'Sullivan, J. (2001, Oct. 10). "Radical Islamism: 'bastard child' of Marxism." *The National Post*, A16.

[123] Friedman, A. (2002, Feb. 1). "'Biggest Risk to the Global Economy in 2002,' Financier Says." *International Herald Tribune*, 1.

[124] Bowring, P. (2002, Feb. 1). "Global Capital Crisis Is the Greater Peril." *International Herald Tribune*, 11.

[125] Rosenthal, E. (2002, Feb. 2-3). "A Cloud of Suspicion Covers Bank of China." *International Herald Tribune*, 9.

[126] Pfaff, W. (2002, Feb. 21). "A prospect of one war after the other." *International Herald Tribune*, 8.

[127] Gordon, M.R. (2002, Feb. 2). "Afghanistan risks new civil war, CIA warns." *International Herald Tribune*, 4.

[128] Editorial. (2002, Feb. 8). "How to Nation-Build." *The New York Times*. Reprinted in *International Herald Tribune*, 4.

[129] Mallaby, S. (2002, Feb. 15). "Making do with the United Nations we have." *International Herald Tribune*, 8.

[130] Crove, T. (2002, Feb. 16). "Black Hawk Down." *Daily Mail*, 44.

[131] Kristof, N.D. (2002, Feb. 6). "Helping to Fix Failed States Is Smarter Than Running Away." *International Herald Tribune*, 6.

[132] Friedman, A. (2002, Feb. 4). "UN Leader to Warn of Dangers in Wealth Gap." *International Herald Tribune*, 1.

[133] Leow, R. (2002, Feb. 1). "How can globalization become 'O.K.' for all?" *International Herald Tribune*, 9.

[134] Geldof, B. (2002, Feb. 7). "Debt Must be Cancelled." *The Daily Telegram*. Reprinted in *International Herald Tribune*, 6.

[135] News reports (2002, Feb. 23-24). "Savimbi, rebel leader, is reported killed in Angola." *International Herald Tribune*, 1.

[136] *The Washington Post*'s Op-Ed (2002, Feb. 9-10). Reprinted in *International Herald Tribune*, 4.

[137] Friedman, A. (2002, Feb. 5). "Forum Focuses On 'Wrath' Born of Poverty." *International Herald Tribune*, 11.

[138] Hoagland, J. (2002, Feb. 22). "Battling isn't the only show." *International Herald Tribune*, 6.

[139] Friedman, A (2002, Jan. 31). "World Bank Presses U.S. To Increase Foreign Aid." *International Herald Tribune*, 1.

[140] Kristof, N.D. (2002, Feb. 16-17). "Terrorism and Poverty: Guns are the wrong medicine for Philippine ills." *International Herald Tribune*.

[141] Schultz, G.P. (2002, Feb. 6). Speech in Washington reprinted under title "The State Is the Basis for Cooperation." In *International Herald Tribune*, 6.

[142] Uchitelle, L. (2002, Feb. 11). "Scholars suggest alternative routes to globalization." *International Herald Tribune*, 7.

[143] McFaul, M. (2002, Feb. 6). "Building Good States Is as Important as Destroying Bad Ones." *International Herald Tribune*, 6.

[144] Sokolsky, R., and J. McMillan. (2002, Feb. 13). "A robust foreign aid program." *International Herald Tribune*, 6.

[145] Greenspan, A. (2002, Feb. 28). "How the market is dealing with Enron," *Financial Post*, FP 15.

[146] Lewis, M. (2002, Feb. 24). "Bloomberg not a great fit, says Thomson." *Financial Post*, FP 4.

[147] "A Culture of Corruption." (2003, Feb. 28). Op-Ed in *The Washington Post*. Reprinted in *Fin. Post*, FP 1.

[148] Altman, D. (2002, Feb. 18). "How Enron 'hid' debts in the open." *International Herald Tribune*, 2.

[149] World Economic Forum. (2002, Nov. 29). Report.

[150] CIA *World Factbook*. Retrieved June 6, 2014 from https://www.cia.gov/library/publications/the-world-factbook/geos/tu.html

[151] Swerdlow, J.L. (1999, Aug.). "Global Culture." *National Geographic*, 16-33.

[152] Karasek, M. (2003). "O mandelince bramborove, kamikadze teroristech a konvergenci zajmu mladeze celeho sveta," (New) *Polygon 1*, 17-25.

[153] Kendall, M.G. (1948). *Rank Correlation Methods*. London: Charles Griffin & Company, 3-25; Chapter 4.

[154] Hodge, S.E., and M.L. Seed. (1972). *Statistics and Probability*. London: Blackie & Son Ltd.

[155] Lambert, C. (2003, Jul. 26). "At the crossroads." (Special Survey of Central Asia). *The Economist*, 6, Exh.1.

[156] Bouckhaert, P. (2003, Oct. 20). "A stolen election and oil stability." *International Herald Tribune*, 8.

[157] Wyman, Bill (2002). *Rolling With The Stone*. London: DK Publishing, 410.

[158] Cohen, M.D., March, J.D., and J.P. Olsen. (1972). "A garbage can model of organizational choice." *Admin. Science Quarterly*, 17.

[159] Levant, E. (2003, Nov. 4). "Putin's purge." *Financial Post*, FP 13.

[160] O'Brien, T.L., and E. Arvedlund. (2004, Jan. 3-4). "Putin and tycoon clash at Russia's economic edge." *International Herald Tribune*, 10-11.

[161] Hamilton, G. (2004, Jan. 27). "Quebecers urged to idolize own." *National Post*, 6.

[162] Friedman, T.L. (2004, Jan. 9). "The war of ideas." *International Herald Tribune*, 6.

[163] "Family Assets Mobilization Component." (2004, Jan.-Feb.). *ToR, Council of Ministers*, Uzbekistan.

[164] "The Basilwizi Project." (2004, Feb.). *ToR, The Bazilwizi Trust*.

[165] Maich, S. (2004, Feb. 21). "What language are they speaking ?" *Financial Post*, FP 1 & FP 6.

[166] Pratt, L. (2004, Mar. 15). "Management tip from the top." *Financial Post*, FE 2.

[167] Revel, Jean-Francois. (1977). *The Totalitarian Temptation*. Garden City, NY: Doubleday & Co., Inc.

[168] James and James. (1968). *Mathematics Dictionary* (3rd ed.). London: D. Van Nostrand Co. Inc.

[169] "Respect law in Chechen fight: Annan." (2004, Sep. 9). *Metro*, 12. Reprinted from *Reuters*.

[170] Cole, D. (2004, Nov. 10). "15 years later, unification disappoints." *National Post*, A18.

[171] Karasek, M. (2001). "Empty Heads" ("Dubove palice" in Czech original). *Polygon 4*, 55-58.

[172] Mejstrik, M. (2004, Jan. 29). "Speech of Sen. M. Mejstrik." The Czech Senate, November 30, 2004. *Novy domov*, 8-9.

[173] Samuelson, P.A., and W.D. Nordhaus. (1992). *Microeconomics* (14th ed.). McGraw Hill.

[174] "Rice allays Putin on Soviet bloc ties." (2005, Apr. 21). *The Associated Press* in "Toronto 24 hours," 11.

[175] Smith, Craig S. (2005, April 4). "Democratic uprising or coup." *International Herald Tribune*, 3.

[176] Beckenbach, E.F., andBellman, R. (1961). *Introduction to Inequalities*. New York: Random House, Chapters II – IV.

[177] Kay, J. (2005, Jul. 6). "Leave Africa to the experts." *National Post*, A14.

[178] Pflanz, M. (2005, Jul. 16). "All-Female Village Earns Wrath of Angry Elders." *Daily Telegraph,* in *National Post*, A 15.

[179] Solomon, L. (2005, Sep. 17). "A glimpse behind Third World China's smoke and mirrors." *National Post*, FP15.

[180] Nurse, P. (2007, May 1). "Remembering the Sepoy Rebellion." *National Post*, A 16.

[181] Corcoran, T. (2008, Oct. 25). "Quantum of Failures." *National Post*, FP 18.

[182] Johnson S., and J. Kwak. (2009, Mar. 21-22). "Off with the bankers." *International Herald Tribune*, 21.

[183] Janeway, Bill. (2009). "Six impossible things before breakfast: Lessons from the crisis." *Significance,* 6(1), 28-31.

[184] Pesaran, M.H. (1987). *The Limits to Rational Expectations*. Oxford: Basil Blackwell.

[185] Knight, F. (1921). *Risk, Uncertainty and Profit.* (Hart, Schaffner, and Marx prize Essays, No.31) New York: Houghton Mifflin.

[186] Dawidoff, N. (2008, Mar. 28-29). "Respected scientist takes on climate 'ideology'." *International Herald Tribune*, 2.

[187] Krugman, P. (2009, Mar. 28-29). "The Market Mystique." *International Herald Tribune*, 7.

[188] Krugman, P. (2009, Mar. 24). "Financial Policy Despair." *International Herald Tribune*, 6.

[189] Ferguson, Niall. (2010, May 1). *National Post*, FP3.

[190] International Monetary Fund. (2009, Mar.). *The Implications of the Global Financial Crisis for Low-Income Countries.* Retrieved June 6, 2014 from www.imf.org/external/pubs/ft/books/2009/globalfin/globalfin.pdf

[191] Burke, V. Nazim. (2010, Jan. 15). *2010 Budget Statement.* Presented to The House of Representatives, Government of Grenada. Retrieved June 6, 2014 from www.scribd.com/doc/36344208/Budget-2010

[192] Warner, J. (2011, Feb.). "If the Saudis revolt, the world's in trouble." *The Telegraph.*

[193] Draper, R. (2011, Feb.). "Opium Wars." *National Geographic* 219(2), 58-83.

[194] Table "*Compare the Ratings*" (2012, Jan. 28). Financial Post, *National Post*, FP 5.

[195] Jonas, G. (2012, Feb. 18). "Our One-night Stand with Freedom." *National Post*, A22.

[196] Povoledo, E. (2012, Mar. 31). "Lack of safeguards enables Italy corruption, report says." *International Herald Tribune*, 4.

[197] Suit, D. B. (1984). "Dummy Variables: Mechanics v. Interpretation." The Review of Economics and Statistics 66(1), 177-180.

[198] Fisher, F. M. (1965, Sep.). "The Choice of Instrumental Variables in the Estimation of Economy-Wide Econometric Models." *International Ec. Rev.* 6(3), 245-274.

[199] Mayer, L.S. (1973). "Estimation a Correlation Coefficient when One Variable is not Directly Observed," *JASA*, 68(342), 420-421.

[200] Morgenstern, O. (1963). *On the Accuracy of Economic Observations.* Princeton University Press.

[201] Greenwood, J. (2012, Jan. 28). "Safe havens difficult to find." *National Post*, FP 5.

[202] Bradley, John, R. (2011, Mar. 18). "Hatred." *Daily Mail*, 15.

[203] Karasek, M., and R. Singh. (2011). "An Analysis on the Vulnerability Flex and its Impact on Selected African, Caribbean and Pacific Basin Countries." *Project Report,* EC, EUROAID Brussels.

[204] Solomon, L. (2011, Aug. 2). "Science now settled." *National Post*, FP 17.

[205] Soliday S. (2010, Jun. 17). "Examples of Non-Renewable Resources." Retrieved June 6, 2014 from http://ezinearticles.com/?Examples-of-Non-Renewable-Resources&id=4496488

[206] *"Science On-line."* (2001).

[207] Transparency International (2011). "Corruption Perception Index." Retrieved June 6, 2014 from http://www.transparency.org/cpi2011/results

[208] Bradsher, K. (2011, Mar. 26-27). "China shows confidence in its nuclear future." *International Herald Tribune*, (Global Edition of *The New York Times*), 11.

[209] Povoledo, E. (2012, Mar. 31). "Lack of safeguards enables Italy corruption, report says." *International Herald Tribune*, 4.

[210] "Broken down and rusting,...." (2012, Mar. 19). *Daily Mail*, (life).

[211] Harrison, P. (2011, Mar. 15). "E.U. seeks tax cut on green fuels." *International Herald Tribune*, 20.

[212] Steyn M. (2006). *America Alone*. Washington, DC: Regnery Publishing, Inc., 88-90.

[213] Agarwal, N., M. Lim, and R.T. Wigand. (2014). Online Collective Action: Dynamics of the Crowd in Social Media. Springer.

[214] "Open Climate Letter (of 150 world scientists) to UN Secretary-General." (2012, Nov. 30). *National Post*, FP.

[215] Rubin, J. (2014, Feb. 5). "'Earned success' for the GOP." *The Washington Post*.

[216] "Conflict Management in Community Organizations." Ohio State University Fact Sheet. Retrieved June 6, 2014 from http://ohioline.osu.edu/cd-fact/l701.html

[217] Baker, D. (2013, Jan.). "The Fiscal Cliff Crisis and the Real Economic Crisis in the United States." *Intereconomics* 48(1), 67-68.

[218] Woods, Thomas E., Jr. (2009, Nov. 27). "The Forgotten Depression of 1920." *Mises Daily*. Retrieved June 6, 2014 from http://mises.org/daily/3788

[219] Huerta de Soto, Jesus. (2009). *Money, Bank Credit and Economic Cycles*. Auburn, AL: Ludwig von Mises Institute.

[220] Hunt, J., and G. O'Connor. (2011, Mar. 25). "A nuclear third way." *International Herald Tribune*, 8.

[221] Evans, D. (2008, Aug. 30). "Why I recanted." *National Post*, FP 15.

[222] Waterfield, B. (2013, Sep. 16). "The EU's climate policy right or wrong." *Telegraph Blog*. Retrieved June 6, 2014 from

http://blogs.telegraph.co.uk/bruno-in-brussels-eu-unplugged/brusselsbruno/480/480/

[223] Bradley, John R. (2011, Mar. 18). "Hatred!" *Daily Mail*, 15.

[224] "2012 Global Terrorism Index: Capturing the Impact of Terrorism from 2002 – 2011." (2012, Dec. 4). Institute for Economics and Peace.

[225] McNeil, C. (Sapper). (1959). *Bull-Dog Drummond: The Black Gang.* London: Hodder & Stoughton, Ltd., 502-503.

[226] Investopedia. "Definition of 'Usury Laws'." Retrieved May 20, 2014 from www.investopedia.com/terms/u/usury-laws.asp: "Regulations governing the amount of interest that can be charged on a loan. Usury laws specifically target the practice of charging excessively high rates on loans by setting caps on the maximum amount of interest that can be levied. These laws are designed to protect consumers."

[227] Jenkins, R. (2002). *Churchill,* Plume Books, New York, 174.

www.ingramcontent.com/pod-product-compliance
Lightning Source LLC
Chambersburg PA
CBHW031834170526
45157CB00001B/294